MUSLIM WOMEN
in POSTCOLONIAL KENYA

Women in Africa and the Diaspora

Stanlie James and Aili Mari Tripp
Series Editors

MUSLIM WOMEN
in POSTCOLONIAL KENYA

Leadership, Representation, and Social Change

Ousseina D. Alidou

THE UNIVERSITY OF WISCONSIN PRESS

Publication of this volume has been made possible, in part, through
support from the Ford Foundation Grant at Rutgers University.

The University of Wisconsin Press
1930 Monroe Street, 3rd Floor
Madison, Wisconsin 53711-2059
uwpress.wisc.edu

3 Henrietta Street
London WC2E 8LU, England
eurospanbookstore.com

Printed in the United States of America

Library of Congress Cataloging-in-Publication Data

Alidou, Ousseina, author.
Muslim women in postcolonial Kenya : leadership, representation, and
social change / Ousseina D. Alidou.
pages   cm — (Women in Africa and the diaspora)
Includes bibliographical references and index.
ISBN 978-0-299-29464-9 (pbk. : alk. paper)
ISBN 978-0-299-29463-2 (e-book)
1. Women civic leaders—Kenya. 2. Muslim women—Kenya—
Social conditions—21st century. I. Title. II. Series:
Women in Africa and the diaspora.
HQ1796.5.Z75A3   2013
305.48´6970967620905—dc23
2013015042

To all the women in this book for their stories of life and of activism for social change

To my husband, Alamin Mazrui, my sister, Silvia Federici, and my brother, George Caffentzis

To my daughters, Ummu Salma, Nafissa, Nuwayla, my son, Halirou, and

my twin sister, Dr. Hassana Alidou

With love and gratitude!

Contents

Illustrations

Acknowledgments

My deepest gratitude goes to all the Muslim women in Kenya in Mombasa and Nairobi (Jami'a Mosque, Pumwani, Pangani, Parklands) and other Kenyan women and men who welcomed me and contributed to the research that led to the writing of this book. The research for this book began as a humble question as to whether there was a Muslim women's rights movement in Kenya, a predominantly non-Muslim country, and, if there was, what types of rights these advocates were claiming and what mechanisms they were using to achieve their goals. My fieldwork in Kenya was conducted between 2006 and 2008, thanks to a grant from the Ford Foundation, through the Nairobi office, under its program for Human Rights and Social Justice, which I am grateful for and delighted to acknowledge. At that time the program was directed by Willy Mutunga, the current chief justice of Kenya. I am most thankful for his encouragement, wonderful support of my research proposal, and for providing me with (Muslim) women contacts and pointing me to networks in the field. My great appreciation to Anna Mnogolia for her effective administration of my grant from the Ford Foundation and to Alva Walker, from Rutgers University's grant office.

I owe a debt of gratitude to the then executive dean of arts and sciences Holly Smith and dean of social sciences Edward Rhodes at Rutgers University for their support of my research. Kim Butler, then chair of my Department of Africana Studies, was very helpful in supporting this research and I express my thanks to her. I am also deeply grateful to Barry Qualls, vice president for undergraduate education, for his support of my work, Douglass Greenberg, executive dean of arts and sciences, Robin Davis, associate executive dean of arts and sciences, Fran Mascia-Lees, dean of social and behavior

sciences, and Jimmy Swenson, dean of humanities, for granting me a semester of sabbatical leave in fall 2012 to complete the revisions to this book. I owe
a special debt of gratitude to Abena Busia, then associate director of the Center for African Studies, and Renee Larrier, current associate director, for their
formidable and unconditional support in all my work while directing the Center for African Studies. Their mentorship as senior colleagues, founding members of the Center for African Studies and then directors, and their friendship
and generosity of heart and mind have continued to have a great impact on my
life. I am grateful to Renee DeLancey, my assistant at the Center for African
Studies, for the energy and enthusiasm she brings to working together, which
has been important in helping me find balance between time devoted to
directing a very dynamic center, teaching, and writing this book. Thank you,
Renee! My deepest gratitude goes also to Jane Grimshaw, who agreed to fill
in for me as director of the Center for African Studies for one semester to
allow me to focus on the revisions to this book. My utmost thanks to the
wonderful members of the center's executive committee—Carolyn Brown,
Barbara Cooper, Rick Schroeder, David Hughes, Renée Larrier, and Julie
Livingston—and other esteemed colleagues and friends such as Meredith
Turshen and Allen Howard for their unfailing support of me and my work.

During fieldwork I encountered many people in Kenya who directly or
indirectly served as crucial sources of information and data and who helped
me network with various people and communities. Foremost among these
are the Muslim women whose biographical narratives informed the writing of this book, namely, Bi Swafiya Muhashamy-Said, Mwalim Azara
Mudira, Justice Abida Ali-Aroni, Honorable Naomi Ummi Shaban, Honorable Amina Abdallah, Amina Abubakar, and Nazlin Umar Rajput. I am
sincerely indebted to them all for receiving me with open arms and entrust-
ing me with their oral narratives of their personal lives and their accounts
of their roles in and their contributions to the social changes that have
been wrought in their communities and in the nation. I was also welcomed
by the many other Muslim women I interviewed and greatly enlightened
by their oral narratives, including Fatma Khalfan, Maryam Sheikh Abdi,
Yasmin Jeneby (aka Yvonne Oerlemans), Maryam Sheikh at Little Bird,
Wambui Wahida, Muslim women in Pumwani, Pangani, Parklands, the
Nairobi Embakasi Young Muslim Women's Self-Help Association, vendors
at Mombasa Market, young Muslim women I met at the Mombasa Blue
Room using computer facilities, shopkeepers and shop owners and young
Muslim women teachers. I discuss some in the introduction, while others I

do not discuss in the book at all, but their contributions provided useful data and were essential to the analysis that is presented in this book. My sincerest gratitude to all of them. Of course, I am fully responsible for the analysis I present here, and I hope they will forgive me where my analyses diverge from their views and perspectives.

I was blessed to have Shamsiya Ramadhan as my primary field research assistant. Her professionalism, her connections with networks of (Muslim) women across communities, her personal involvement with Muslim women's organizations, and her activities at Jami'a Mosque (Nairobi), as well as her dedication for and enthusiasm about my research topic were invaluable assets as I conducted my fieldwork in Nairobi. I owe her a debt of gratitude. I am deeply thankful to several people who contributed to the initial transcription of the data while I was still in the field, including Shamsiya, along with Susan Bantu (then an employee of Green Belt Foundation of Nobel Laureate for Peace Dr. Wangari Maathai), and Kingwa Kingwa (then a graduate student at the University of Nairobi). Elizabeth Muranga, a young typist at Ambalal House, Mombasa, performed the tremendously helpful task of typing most of my fieldwork notes. I am thankful to Dr. Beverly Lax for the friendship and hospitality to me and to Alamin and Salma and for helping me find research assistants to transcribe my data.

I am also sincerely grateful to Sheikh Hamid Slatch, director of the Young Muslim Association of Kenya whose office is based at Jami'a Mosque in Nairobi, for welcoming me and for making himself available to discuss aspects of my fieldwork. His input regarding the work of the Young Muslim Association in promoting Muslim girls' education in the Northeastern Province and in assisting elderly Muslim women in Pumwani has been invaluable to my research.

There are many other family members, colleagues, and friends who have helped me in my research. In Nairobi, I would like to mention the sisterly embrace by Salma Khalfan Mazrui-Watts and Fatma Khalfan Mazrui of me and my daughter Umma Salma Alamin Mazrui. Their enthusiasm about my research was invaluable, and their introducing my project to their family members and women friends from all backgrounds helped enormously in expanding my resource network. *Nashukuru sana Dr. Fatma na soeur Salma!* Both Umma Salma and I still rejoice in the cherished memories of your family's wonderful hospitality in Nairobi and unfailing support even in a moment of trial. Simply, thank you! My gratitude, too, to Saade Abdallah for your family kindness and hospitality in Nairobi!

In Mombasa, in addition, I am deeply grateful for the hospitality from my husband Alamin Mazrui's extended family and friends. *Nashukuru sana!* My fieldwork benefited from the tremendous support of his relatives, who introduced me to some of the Muslim women of Old Town Mombasa. I was privileged to meet and interview Bi Swafiya Muhashamy-Said, featured in chapter 1, and her deputy, then Najma Rashid, to who I am sincerely thankful. Sincerest gratitude to Huda Mazrui and Hafida Mazrui for making contact for me. I am also grateful to Alamin's siblings, to Sheikh Munir Mazrui for inviting me to a workshop on an Islamic-inspired trilingual (Arabic, Kiswahili, and English) HIV/AIDS curriculum that Muslim clerics participated in, to Muslim medical doctors, to Muslim teachers and social workers at the Mombasa Nyali Beach Hotel, and to Chief Kadhi Sheikh Hammad Muhammad Kassim for inviting me to assist in the launching of the HIV/AIDS curriculum in Nairobi with the support of the Kenya Institute of Education. I am thankful to Radio Rahma in Mombasa for granting me permission to use the transcript of Amina Abubakar's interview with Nazlin Umar Rajput under its *Ukumbi Wa Mamama* program. My gratitude also goes to many Muslim women shop owners and/or shopkeepers who welcomed me for long hours of conversation during my fieldwork in Mombasa's Biashara Street (Mwembe Kuku), at Jami'a Mosque Business Center, and among street vendors of Pumwani Nairobi.

I presented versions or sections of the chapters that constitute this book at a seminar on the culture of rights/rights of culture, a seminar on Islam and gender in Africa, and a seminar on gender and justice in Africa all held by the Rutgers Institute of Research on Women; at a seminar on narratives of power hosted by the Rutgers Center for Historical Analysis and at the Department of African, Middle Eastern, and South Asian Languages and Literatures faculty colloquium; at the African Studies Association annual conferences; at Boston University's Department of Women, Gender, and Sexuality Studies; at the Harvard School of Divinity; at Howard University; at Kent University's West African Research Association as part of its sponsored lectures on Islam in West Africa series; at the University of Iceland Nordic Africa 2012 conference; and at Barnard College. I wish to express my sincerest gratitude to all participants in these forums for their helpful and constructive comments, especially Dorothy Hodgson, Beth Hutchison, Catherine Sameh, Salma Maoulidi, Abena Busia, Barbara Cooper, Susan Hirsch, Carolyn Brown, Al Howard, Deborah Gray-White, Dona Murch, Belinda Edmondson, Pamela Morgan, Erin Augis, Fallou

Ngom, Wendy Wilson, Jennifer Yanco, Shahla Haeri, Ann Braude, Hauwa Ibrahim, Abosede George, Tayo "Zindzi" Jolaosho and the late Roberta Ann Dunbar.

The editors of the University of Wisconsin Press's series Women in Africa and the Diaspora gave me another opportunity to expose my work on African Muslim women to the wider scholarly community. In this regard, I am deeply indebted to Aili Tripp and Stanlie James as well as to the two anonymous reviewers whose invaluable critical comments helped me produce what I believe is a stronger and more coherent text. And of course, thanks to Gwen Walker, who was always there with her encouragement and guidance throughout the review process. My sincerest gratitude to her!

This book would not have been completed without the diligent editorial work of Ruthmarie Mitsch. She was devoted and meticulous in helping me bring the final manuscript into conformity with the editorial guidelines of the University of Wisconsin Press. My deepest appreciation!

I am deeply indebted to my dearest friend and sister Silvia Federici, who has so much confidence in my ability to overcome the challenges before me and has kept me focused on the writing of this book. Your voice that says "Ousseina, you must let the stories of the strong women be known" still resonates! I love you and brother George for your love, nourishment, and support to me, Salma, and Alamin. I am forever grateful to both of you for keeping me focused on the struggles that matter. I dedicate this book to you.

Throughout the research and writing of this book, my husband, Alamin Mazrui, provided the utmost support as my caring partner at home and work and as a reader, making invaluable comments (which I agreed or disagreed with) to various drafts of the chapters of this book. He bore witness to traumatic moments of aggression I experienced in the field— partly as a result of an electronic vendor who pirated a section of my data and tried to use it for extortion and partly as a result of both me and our daughter Umma Salma as well as other relatives being under the gun of armed robbers for a long hour—and he offered the best possible support he could and encouraged me to stick to my goal of finishing writing this book. My utmost gratitude and love to you, Alamin, and to our daughter chérie Umma Salma, who has been a joyful, peaceful, and supportive child. Here is Mama's humble zawadi (gift) from sleepless nights dedicated to you, your beloved Daddy Alamin, sisters Nuwayla and Nafissa, your brother Halirou, and your Mama Hassana!

My love and deepest gratitude to my relatives in different places: my sister Fatouma (Gado) Alidou and her children Hannatou, Abdrahmane, and Toumani, my brother Mamane (Alpha) Alidou, my cousin Moctar Hima, his wife, Beth Hima, and their daughter Mounira, cousin Zeid Mazrui, his wife, Maryam, and their daughter Zamzam, my sister Salma Edarus and her children Abu and Ghazi Alawy, *ma soeur* Nora Chalfont, Cory, and Sean in Yellow Spring. Our extended Sidibé family in Niger provided reassurance to Umma Salma and me. In Somerset, New Jersey, where we live, I owe a debt of gratitude to Elaine Greenburg for her availability, love, and tender care to Salma when both Alamin and I are too busy with our demanding work schedule. I am also thankful to Salma's Auntie Debie Ackerman for her sweetness, humor, and love. Sincerest appreciation to Mary Liberti, Sujata Ravindra, and Helene Hu for letting their children, Adreana, Mickey, and Anant and Andie, form a sweet community of children bound with Salma. Their neighborly solidarity has contributed to helping me handle the solitude that writing often requires. I got inspired every day when Adreana, Mickey, Anant, Andie, Christian, and their other friends rang our doorbell to come in to play with Salma and make us laugh with their candid humor! I am grateful to them all. A heartfelt thank you to sister Abena Odukoya for inviting Salma to play with her African sisters Fisayo, Anjola, and Motunrayo Odukoya at your home and to all her other wonderful Cedar Hill Prep friends and parents.

This book is dedicated to all the Kenya Muslim women who have shared with me their stories of life and of activism for empowering social change. My deepest gratitude!

Abbreviations

FGC	female genital cutting
FGM	female genital mutilation/modification
IPK	Islamic Party of Kenya
KANU	Kenya African National Union
MCCK	Muslim Consultative Council of Kenya
ODM	Orange Democratic Movement
ODM-K	Orange Democratic Movement—Kenya
NMCK	National Muslim Council of Kenya
SUPKEM	Supreme Council of Kenya Muslims

MUSLIM WOMEN
in POSTCOLONIAL KENYA

Introduction

I want to pour water into hell and set paradise on fire, so that these two veils disappear and nobody shall any longer worship God out of fear of hell or a hope of heaven, but solely for the sake of [their] eternal beauty.

—Rabi'a al-'Adawiyya of Basra

PRELIMINARY REMARKS

Muslim Women in Postcolonial Kenya: Leadership, Representation, and Social Change examines the ways in which Kenya Muslim women leaders have been using the space opened up by the democratization momentum that began in the 1990s to bring about important transformations in critical domains of society while also reclaiming their citizenship rights within their communities of faith, within regional and national women's organizations and movements, and within the secular postcolonial nation-state as members of a minority constituency. The analysis explores the tools, strategies, and resources that these agents of social and political change use in their activism to inscribe Muslim women's rights issues into cultural and political spaces and to make their contributions to democratic processes in local, national, and international arenas. In addition, I examine the ways that Kenya Muslim women leaders critically read the forces against them within society and how they are depicted in hegemonic discourses. We see in the analysis how their readings are significant in their construction of alternative visions of a just, multicultural, multiethnic, and multireligious democratic citizenship. Their intervention is informed by a women-centered framework that is sensitive to gender ideologies, drawing on a range of both secular and religious perspectives to transform their "work places" and other spaces available to them—the family home, the school, the legislature, the mosque, the media—in order to create new avenues of opportunities for (Muslim) women, their communities, and the nation.

A close examination of the discursive practices of the Muslim women discussed here as they pursue their rights as gendered citizen-subjects within their communities of faith and the nation-state and in their struggles against marginalization within dominant women's organizations sheds light not only on the development of their critical consciousness but also on their determination as actors to challenge that oppressive impact of these forces on their lives. At the same time that they transform the discourses and practices of Islam at the local and national level by offering a modern women-centered interpretation of the religion, they also draw on competing understandings of Islam as articulated in plural global Islamisms as well as on other non-Muslim (religious) and secular sources to redefine the question of (Muslim) women's citizenship within their own community of faith and within the nation. And as some of the case studies reveal, the success of their initiatives has assumed a transnational dimension.

The seemingly sudden and forceful emergence of Muslim women leaders in Kenya beginning in the 1990s can be accounted for by reference to the conjuncture of three interrelated developments in the nation. The first is, of course, the post–Cold War upsurge in national demands to end authoritarian rule and embrace political pluralism. Naturally, pluralistic representation included voices of women, ethnic minorities, religious minorities, the youth, the disabled, and so forth. National women's organizations like the International Federation of Women Lawyers became extremely active in their efforts to ensure that women would be equally represented in all facets of the movement for political change in the nation. This development inspired the emergence of women leaders across ethnic, religious, and regional boundaries, including those of Muslim background studied here.

Secondly, new forms of information communication technologies and expanded opportunities in education, travel, trade, and education that accompanied post–Cold War globalization quickly multiplied the networks of contact and relations between Kenya Muslim communities and Muslim communities in other parts of the world. Whether through the coverage of Al Jazeera programs or Western electronic media giants, through information available on Muslim websites or bilateral scholarships to Muslim institutions of higher education in the Sudan, Saudi Arabia, Malaysia, Pakistan, and Western countries, or through new transnational trade partnerships in a variety of commodities relevant to Muslim cultures, Kenya Muslim men and women were exposed to and influenced by new ideas and politics that challenged their insularity within the nation-state. These influences galvanized them to new forms of activism that required new kinds of social, cultural, and political engagement within their own diverse local communities and with other non-Muslim communities in the nation. In their gendered effects, these influences, which included the rereading of Islam, became yet another force inspiring creative agency on the part of Muslim women.

The winds of political change locally and the expanding networks of relationships globally were bound to have an effect on local Muslim attitudes toward women. Patriarchal views and practices that have long stood in the way of the advancement of women educationally, culturally, economically, and politically, of course, are still common in Muslim Kenya as elsewhere in much of the world. There are still readings of Islamic doctrinal texts that seek to justify the exclusion of women from a leadership role even in an institution like the kadhi courts where over 90 percent of the applicants are themselves women ("Enhancing Access" 2011; Mwinyihaji 2007, 53–57). And because the call for increasing Muslim women's representation in public leadership positions is frequently supported by non-Muslim women's rights activists, its Muslim advocates are often accused by their detractors of coming under the sway of "foreign" ideologies. It is equally true, however, that more and more, Muslims are being challenged by the powerful winds of change to reflect afresh on some long received, albeit selectively chosen, interpretations of Islamic doctrines and to adopt other, equally defensible readings that are more compatible with the current state of societal being. Under pressure to overcome the historical marginalization of Muslims in Kenya, the patriarchy has had on occasion to accommodate the urgent need that resulted from the opening up of the political space to have many capable members of the community, men and women, rise to positions of greater visibility as representatives of the Muslim polity.

I use the term "patriarchy" to refer to the system in which social life and societal institutions in a given society are structured in such a way as to give men relative control over critical aspects of women's lives. The notion of patriarchy, however, is one that is hotly contested in the African context (Amadiume 1998; Bakare-Yusuf and Signe 2004; Imam, Mama, and Sow 1997; McFadden 1997, 2003; Mikell 1997; Ogundipe-Leslie 1994). According to Bibi Bakare-Yusuf (2003), there are at least two competing schools of thought on the question of patriarchy in Africa. The first, represented by such scholars as Nkiru Nzegwu (2001), Oyeronke Oyewumi (1997), and Niara Sudarkasa (1987), holds that because men and women in Africa have different and complementary functions, and therefore equal and complementary power relations, in society, the concept of patriarchy has little if any relevance to the African condition. In the view of these scholars, then, the fact of sexual difference in Africa does not amount to sexual inequality, and the patriarchal framework in the study of African societies is itself seen as yet another epistemological imposition from the West.

The second school is one that recognizes systemic hierarchical structures between men and women. Espoused by scholars like Simi Afonja (1990), April Gordon (1996), Patricia McFadden (2003), Molara Ogundipe-Leslie (1985, 1994), and others, this view does not entirely disregard the fact that in some African societies women do hold positions of power and authority in a culturally inscribed way. Even in the best of circumstances, however, such "female power" has always been subject to male authority and highly circumscribed in terms of what it could accomplish in critical areas of social and cultural life of the community. Wifehood, motherhood, reproduction, the sexual division of labor, and so forth are all seen as sites that are used to validate patriarchal dominance in economic and political spheres of society.

As I have indicated elsewhere (Alidou 2005), however, there are indeed societies in Africa that had been strongly defined by unequal distribution of power and authority between men and women long before the inception of European colonial rule. Invariably, women became an important part of a cultural machinery that both justified and transmitted this ideology, beginning at the family level and extending to wider networks of relationships. In this sense, patriarchy as a system and ideology was homegrown, and there are numerous traditional folktales, proverbs, and sayings that demonstrate this inequality in power relations between men and women (Kolawole 1997; Mwihia 2011; Schipper 1992). What European colonialism did was to lend extra validation to preexisting patriarchal structures and practices, sometimes aggravating their negative effects on the lives of women. When European colonial administrators in Northern Nigeria, for example, complied with local male authorities in denying girls educational opportunities in the newly established secular schools, they were strengthening the arm of patriarchy to the great detriment of women.

What is sometimes distinctive about patriarchy in Muslim societies like the one in Kenya (Dekha Abdi 2010; Kariuki 2006; Sesay 2010)—as in other religious communities the world over—is the extent to which it is given doctrinal validation (Mwinihajii 2010). As a result, rereading the canonical texts becomes an important part of the struggle to challenge patriarchy. For example, a central concern in the Muslim debate about patriarchy is the matter of women serving in offices of public leadership, as inscribed in verse 34 of chapter 4, *Al-Nisa'* ("The Women"). The interpretation of the verse varies from one translation of the Qur'an to another, perhaps reflecting the ideology of the translator on the matter. In most conservative translations, for example, the two most widely referenced translations, those by Muhammad M. Pickthall (2001) and Abdallah Yusuf Ali (2002), the preferred sense is that men are in charge of women because God has privileged men over women, either physically (Yusuf Ali) or in other accomplishments (Pickthall). On the other side is a more liberal reading by Edip Yuksel and his colleagues in their *Qur'an: A Reformist Translation* (2006), where the preferred translation of the verse is given as "Men are to support the women by what God has gifted them over one another," implying that men who have had the opportunity to acquire material advantage have the responsibility of providing for women in their household who do not have the means and have not had the opportunity to acquire such means. In her translation titled *Sublime Qur'an*, Laleh Bakhtiar (2007) concurs with Edip Yuksel when she renders the verse as "Men are supporters of wives because God has given some of them an advantage over others." It is significant that Bakhtiar's translation has been fully certified by Al-Azhar University in Cairo.

Over the centuries, influential male Muslim scholars have repeatedly validated the more conservative reading of this verse as well as other verses and hadiths, and many have argued that as much as some of the scriptural texts refer to the domestic arrangement, they apply with equal force to the public arena.[1] In their interpretation, if the woman cannot be the head of the household, she cannot be the head of anything! As Rabiatu Ammah-Koney demonstrates, the issue of gender relations in Muslim doctrinal texts is ultimately "deeply rooted in the power and practice of interpretive texts" (2009, 160). It is this male interpretative hegemony that both male and female scholars such as Abdullahi an-Na'im (1990, 1991), Margot Badran (2011), Asma Barlas (2002), Khaled El Fadl (2001), Riffat Hassan (2000), Fatima Mernissi (1991a, 1991b), Fatima Sadiqi (2006), Omid Safid (2003a, 2003b), and Amina Wadud (2000, 2006) have set out unambiguously to challenge.

A Muslim scholar—a woman—who has come out strongly in favor of limiting the interpretation of verse 34 of *Al-Nisa* to a very narrow area, that of inheritance and its use, is Amina Wadud. She defines the advantage that men have over women as exclusively a matter of inherited wealth, for it is only inheritance that the Qur'an explicitly gives more of to men than to women. Wadud's interpretation of the verse, then, is that men must draw from their inheritance to provide for women's needs in view of their roles in childbearing, mothering, and the "continuation of the human race." In her words:

> The childbearing responsibility is of grave importance: human existence depends on it. This responsibility requires a great deal of physical strength, stamina, intelligence, and deep personal commitment. Yet, while this responsibility is so obvious and important, what is the responsibility of the male in this family and society at large? For simple balance and justice in creation, and to avoid oppression, his responsibility must be equally significant to the continuation of the human race. The Qur'an establishes his responsibility as *qiwamah*, seeing to it that the woman is not burdened with additional responsibilities which jeopardize that primary demanding responsibility that only she can fulfill. (Wadud 1999, 73)

Far from claiming that women are inferior to men and that only men can be leaders of women (and therefore of society), the verse, in Wadud's view, requires men to play their part in the "continuation of the human race" by providing for childbearing women who cannot be expected to work to support the family at the same time. Whatever the "correct" interpretation of this verse or other verses from the Qur'an and texts of hadiths that have been used by many male scholars over the centuries to justify the exclusion of women from positions of public leadership might be, the profiles of the women in this book tell a different story. In a climate of political transition, Muslim women have emerged who have taken advantage of the opening up of the politico-cultural space to reread both religious and secular discourses and devise strategies of reshaping them in a way that would better serve the interests of women in particular and their communities at large. The six Muslim women whose stories I present—Bi Swafiya Muhashamy-Said (chapter 1), Azara Mudira (chapter 2), Amina Abdallah and Ummi Naomi Shaban (chapter 3), Abida Ali-Aroni (chapter 4), and Nazlin Omar Rajput (chapter 5)— have undertaken initiatives in the context of dynamic sociopolitical transformations that have fostered new modes of interaction between Muslims and Muslims, on the one hand, and Muslims and non-Muslims, on the other.[2] They suggest that the Muslim community in Kenya, as elsewhere, is increasingly being affected by and caught in the crosscurrents of sociocultural and politico-economic change emanating from global sources as well as local bases in the direction of greater openness of mind toward Muslim women's leadership in the public arena.

It is true, of course, that some of these currents, like the influence of Saudi-inspired Wahhabism and Salafism, are generating more conservative patriarchal tendencies even among younger Muslim men. But one cannot overlook the fact that the Kenya Muslim society as a whole is under increasing pressure to come to terms with the new politico-economic dynamics in the nation through a new understanding of Islam. It is not an accident of history, then, that male-dominated Muslim organizations like the Supreme Council of Kenya Muslims (SUPKEM) and the Muslim Consultative Council of Kenya (MCCK) sought the leadership of someone like Ali-Aroni, that women educators like Muhashamy-Said and Mudira received the support of Muslim male leaders even if sometimes they had to negotiate their way around Muslim male sensibilities, that at one point Rajput received the backing of Sheikh Hammad Mohamed Kassim, the chief kadhi of Kenya at the time, in her efforts to ensure the Muslim voice and Muslim perspective were taken into account in the process of revising Kenya's constitution, or that some local Muslim male leaders of the Orange Democratic Movement (ODM) would endorse the nomination of Abdallah to the parliament. This Muslim male support, conditional and divided as it may be at times, is partly a product of the new cultural-material conditions in Kenya.

The 1990s politics of pluralism have forced Kenya Muslim men and women to share politico-economic and social platforms on a wide range of issues of local, national, and global relevance. Similarly, under the impetus of the new global forces, Kenyan Muslims now have to respond to global Islamism with its multilateral implications—for example, in new religious and secular education and trade networks, with respect to labor migration to oil-producing Islamic Gulf countries, or as a target of the new war on terrorism (Hirsch 2006a; Lynch 2011; Mwinyihaji and Wanyama 2011; Seesemann 2007, 156–76). As part of a global phenomenon, therefore, the experiences of Kenya Muslim women are similar to the realities of Muslim women in several other parts of the world (Alidou 2005; Ask and Tjomsland 1998; Augis 2005, 2009; Badran 2004; Buggenhagen 2012; Diouf and Leichtman 2009; Lebanc 1999; Ong 2006; Rosander 1997; Schulz 2012; Sharify-Funk 2008; Yuval-Davis 2000; Yuval-Davis and Anthias 1989) as well as to those of women from other religious traditions (Badran 2011; Sabbagh 2003).

Of course, all six women studied here can be described as predominantly educated elite members of the middle class. That it is members of the more educated privileged classes that have assumed the reigns of national leadership in Muslim Kenya, however, is quite in conformity with the general trend

in Kenya at this moment of transitional politics (Kabira 2012).[3] There is no
doubt that citizens at the grassroots level were fully involved in the struggle
for change and that in many instances they bore the brunt of the police bru-
tality and killings. Likewise, as my fieldwork in the Nairobi slum area of Pumwani reveals, there are many local initiatives that are led by Muslim women.
At the national level, however, the reform movement in the country, especially
in its political, constitutional, and social articulations, was and continues to
be primarily a project of the middle and upper classes, with the national
leadership drawn heavily from those classes. It is perhaps for this reason that
Willy Mutunga, the current chief justice of the High Court of Kenya, titled
his monumental study of the politics of transition in Kenya *Constitution-
Making from the Middle* (1999), essentially locating the core of this historical
landmark in the evolution and expansion of the middle class in Kenya. Of
course, modern secular education has often been an important force in class
(re)structuring in Kenya as elsewhere in Africa, as Benedicta Egbo amply
demonstrates in her *Gender, Literacy and Life Chances in Sub-Saharan Africa*
(2000).

The six women this book explores share the privilege of having had access
to Western education—ranging from high school to university level—which
provided them the resources and skills to shape their modes of engagement
with diverse communities and frame their advocacy on behalf of the majority of disenfranchised Muslim women on issues ranging from education to
access to public welfare. Though there has been a steady increase in educational opportunities for girls, especially at the level of elementary and secondary education, since the days of Muhashamy-Said's childhood during
the colonial period, Muslim girls in Kenya, whether from impoverished backgrounds or aristocratic families, have continued to experience the weight of
(patriarchal) cultural restrictions. So women like Muhashamy-Said, whose
father was highly educated for his time, or Ali-Aroni, whose father had no
formal Western educational training at all, considered themselves particularly fortunate to have had the kind of parental support that allowed them
to pursue their educational dream, enabling them to exceed cultural expectations, and that opened for them the door of professional success and,
eventually, public leadership. In the case of Rajput, it is precisely the cultural
restriction against Muslim girls' pursuit of education beyond the high school
level that underlined her determination to educate herself and step in as
activist for Muslim girls and women's rights in connection with the fight against

HIV/AIDS in Muslim communities, sexuality and reproductive health, and Muslim women's rights to participate in public political life.

Although the leadership experiences and orientations of the six Muslim women leaders whose lives are presented here converge in certain respects, there is no doubt that these women represent diverse social histories. The majority, in fact, have "mixed" heritage. Some are linked to traditional Swahili aristocracy, while others are products of British colonial history of labor importation from South Asia. Some can trace their lineage through the long history of Africa-Arab Peninsula and Indian Ocean interactions, while others belong to minority indigenous African Muslim communities including the Taita in the coastal region of Kenya, the pastoralist Borana or Oromo in Kenya's Northeastern Province, and the Somali in the Horn of Africa. For a long time these different trajectories fostered different gendered subjectivities within the wider Muslim community.

As several other scholars have observed, race, ethnicity, gender, class, and religion intersect in Kenyan history through both the history of Arab-Muslim plantation slavery on the East African coast of Kenya (Allen 1974, 1; F. Cooper 1997; Curtin 1983; Mwinyihaji 2007; Pouwels 1987, 72) and the British colonial legacy that added South Asian features to Kenyan Islam. The privileges afforded by slavery and colonialism still have implications for gendered intra-Muslim dynamics, as reflected in the social and political network formations among contemporary Muslim women (Eastman 1988; Glassman 1995; McIntosh 2002, 2005; Strobel 1979; White 1990) and in their consciousness of belonging to the same political community—umma—within their Muslim societies and the nation (Fuglesang 1994, 48–50; Mirza and Strobel 1989).

In the postcolonial period, the manipulation of ethnic and racial identities for politico-economic ends—sometimes with tragic consequences—frequently had the effects of heightening intra-Muslim tensions. In the 1990s, for example, under pressure for multipartism, President Daniel arap Moi effectively played the race card to divide the Muslims along so-called African-Arab lines at a time of growing Muslim militancy against his regime.[4] In this divisive strategy, Moi explicitly linked the intra-Muslim ethnoracial dynamics of the region to the precolonial history of Arab enslavement.

The Muslim women presented here, however, inspire hope that intra-Muslim divisiveness resulting from old historical and new political forces can be overcome. They all bring an orientation to their leadership and activism that focuses on the good that could result from a collective spirit that is unencumbered by the fact of difference of any kind. In the process, they have forged alliances across religious, ethnic, and even gender lines at both the local and national levels in an attempt to promote a Muslim women's agenda. In this respect, the women here reflect a new sensibility among Muslim women in various organizations like the International Federation of Women Lawyers, the Kenyan Muslim Women's Alliance, Muslims for Human Rights, the League of Muslim Women, the Center for Advocacy and Development of Muslim Women, and Muslim Women for Equality in the Family that seek to create a new social and political culture that looks at difference as a resource and an opportunity rather than an impediment to political and cultural action.

MUSLIM WOMEN IN KENYA: A SKETCH

According to the 2009 Kenya national census figures, Muslims represent a little over 11 percent of the country's population. Needless to say, these results are highly contested by Muslims. Indeed, other aspects of the census figures have been questioned by other constituencies (O'Brien 2003, 8; Oded 2000, 11; Seesemann 2006, 3). Such grievances explain why census reports may not become public information for a long time.

Whatever the exact number, this population of Muslims represents a multiethnic and multiracial entity that is socioculturally and politically complex. Ethnic groups like the Somali, the Digo, and the Swahili are predominantly Muslim. Among other eastern and coastal groups such as the Borana, Pokomo, and Duruma, Muslims constitute a high, if not majority, percentage. Kenyans of Muslim faith are also found in varying proportions among several other ethnic groups, including the Luo, Kikuyu, Kamba, Taita, and Luhya. Some of these would identify themselves as "Swahili Muslims" as opposed to ethnic Swahili. While they still maintain some roots in their respective ethnic groups, many have been deeply Swahilized in linguistic and cultural terms.

Within the small but economically influential Kenyan communities of South Asian origin, there are also subgroups that are entirely Muslim—either of Sunni or Shi'a denomination—including the Isma'ili, Bohra, Ithnasheri, Bhadala, Kokni, and others (Ghai and Ghai 1970; Herzig 2006; Nagar 1998; C. Salvatori 1989). Pascale Herzig (2006) offers an exciting study of gendered and cross-generational interactions among these multireligious and multilingual South Asian communities and identifies their transformations in the Kenyan contexts. Herzig also highlights female life histories written by women of those communities such as Zarina Patel (1997), Parveen Walji (1980), Shirin Walji (1974), and Rasna Warah (1998). Rashida Keshavjee's dissertation, titled "The Redefined Role of the Ismaili Woman through Education and the Professions" (2010), is an insightful (post)colonial account of educated Isma'ili women in Kenya. In addition, there is also a substantial proportion of "Muslim reverts." The concept of reversion is becoming popular in some parts of the Muslim world. The belief is that all people are born into Islam, even though few end up growing in it. Those who do not grow in Islam but decide to adopt it at a later stage in their lives are seen as "going back" to the "original" religion of their birth—Islam. Some have embraced Islam as the result of the influence of current global Islamic movements and their successful proselytization networks, others by virtue of marriage with Muslim spouses, and still others for other reasons. Reverts include Kenya women from diverse ethnic backgrounds as well as non-Kenyan citizens married to Kenya Muslim men. A case in point is Wambui Wahida, a lawyer born into an educated Christian Kikuyu family who explains that she embraced Islam as a result of her interactions at school with devout young Somali Muslim women friends. As she points out, Islam is important to her for the protection it provides her from male harassment in the public space. As she told me in an interview, "Once I put on the hijab in the public space I am spared the humiliating gaze of males and their harassment at the workplace." Another example is Yasmin Jeneby (formerly known as Yvonne Oerlemans), a Dutch-born journalist married to a Muslim man. Jeneby "reverted" to Islam and wears the hijab. She is currently writing a book that provides her own analysis of the tragic killing of the Dutch filmmaker Theo van Gogh in relation to religion and global politics. Many revert women tend to adopt the modern Muslim women's dress fashion, complete with the hijab.

The average percentage of women in these Kenya Muslim communities is likely to concur with the overall male/female ratio contained in the national census figures, which is about 49.7/50.3 (Kenya National Census Report 2009). Again in line with the census figures, the majority of these Muslim women are likely to be between the ages of fifteen and thirty-five years. Here the influences of the Arabian Peninsula and of Persian and South Asian cultures are immediately visible in the ways Islam presents itself through the people, both male and female, that I have interacted with in various domains—home, markets, mosques, and offices. Kenya Muslim women's Islamic experiences are shaped by the ideas, trends, and cultures of Muslims of the Arabian Peninsula and South Asia (India, Pakistan, Indonesia, and Malaysia) (Beckerleg 1995; Lodhi 1994, 88; Pouwels 2000, 251–66; Salim 1979).

There is also an immense variation in the ways Islam is lived by Muslim women, from one place to another, across class, ethno-racial background, generation, and professional life. Arabism, for example, is most prominent among the more urban sections of the Swahili populations commonly referred to as "wamiji" ("town dwellers").[5] It is far less visible among rural Swahili and other African Muslim groups such as the Digo, Taita, Kikuyu, and Borana. The traditional *buibui* (long black overdress) with an attached black headpiece is much more common among the Swahili of urban sections of the coast than among rural Swahili women. Many rural Swahili women wear a pair of identical wrappers called *kanga* or *leso* that provide similar *sitara* (modesty). Because Islamization among Kenya Africans is often associated with Swahilization, one encounters familiar Swahili attire among noncoastal Muslim women.

Among the younger generation, and across ethnicities of the Swahili, Nubi, Somali, Kikuyu, and others, the trend of the Saudi Arabia abaya style is becoming increasingly predominant, showing the continued influence of the new transnational Islam drawn from the Gulf countries, particularly Oman and the Arab Emirates. The abaya is a loose black dress covering the whole body except for the head, worn over other clothes and accompanied by a separate hijab (head covering) when women venture into the public sphere. A section of these younger Muslim women, again across ethnicity, also wear partial or total face covering that has come to be commonly referred to as the ninja style. Regardless of their Islamic ideology, the ninja style is often associated with a new Wahhabism or Salafism, the order of Islam most prominently in practice in Saudi Arabia. Whether one visits shops of Muslim women entrepreneurs in the center of town in Nairobi or in Mombasa or visits schools, one sees the unfolding of the competition between "traditional" Swahili *buibui* and *kanga* and the new fashion commodities for Kenya Muslim women tied to new transnational Islamisms (Eastman 1988; Fuglesang 1994, 205–9; Porter 1998, 636–40). Among groups like the Somali and the Borana, on the other hand, one notices the continued influence of a pastoral worldview in the way Muslim identity is experienced by women members of them. The vibrant and conspicuous presence of Somali businesswomen across the age range, competing shoulder to shoulder with men, is demonstrative of the resilience of the pastoral worldview that posits that women have a productive life to lead in the public space. With their own distinctive dress styles, these dynamic Muslim women entrepreneurs are contributing immensely to the economic well-being of their communities in Kenya. Among the prominent though numerically small community of Asian Muslims in Kenya of both Sunni and Shi'a denominations, both the Bohra and the Ithnasheri Muslim women wear attire that distinctively marks their religious communities. A great exception are Isma'ili men and women, whose mode of dressing is usually Western, as encouraged by the late Aga Khan III (Keshavjee 2010, 111). Among Sunni Asian communities, on the other hand, one notices a range of Muslim women's attire, from those close in style to the Bohra and Ithnasheri's to the Swahili *buibui*.

Through my discussions with Somali women, I have learned about the challenge of citizenship that Kenyan Somali are confronting and its gendered implications. Their "physical" profiling and their dress fashion (Akou 2011) are used by functionaries of the state to demand that they prove their "Kenyanness," a pattern of Somali marginalization that predates the recent wave of Somali immigrants precipitated by the collapse of Somalia and Kenya's November 2011 invasion of Somalia. I have come to realize, furthermore, that the fragmentation of neighboring Somalia and the rise of a political Islam associated with Saudi Arabia and the Gulf countries are redefining Somali women's identity as Muslims. How this Muslim woman's identity is perceived is, of course, a continuing subject of contestation. One topic of debate is the question of the extent to which the increasing forces of political Islam are slowly encroaching on the freedoms that the pastoralist worldview traditionally afforded Somali women. Cawo Abdi (2007, 2006), Lidwiens Kapteijns (1995), and Lidwiens Kapteijns and Maryan Ali (1999) have argued with regard to women in Somalia itself that political Islam has been detrimental in this respect. Kenya's military invasion of Somalia in 2011, ostensibly to curtail the activities of Al-Shabaab and the rise of the Mombasa Republican Council in the coast of Kenya, a political party with a Muslim base, secessionist objectives, and alleged links with Al-Shabaab, are likely to exacerbate the plight of Kenyan and non-Kenya Somali women on both sides of the Kenya-Somalia border.[6]

Another topic of debate is the practice of female genital cutting/mutilation (FGC/FGM) among the Somali in Kenya and the extent to which re-reading Islam can serve as a new tool for challenging it.[7] Maryam Sheikh Abdi, for example, a graduate of Kenyatta University, program officer at the Kenya Population Council handling issues of female genital cutting or mutilation among the Somali community, and author of the powerful poem "The Cut" (2006), argues that FGM could be successfully eradicated in Somali society by engaging the ulama (religious scholars) and by providing Somali women and men with access to both Islamic and secular education.[8] Sophia

Abdi Noor, a Muslim woman member of Parliament (MP), pushed for the passage of the 2010 Prohibition of Female Genital Mutilation Bill in the Kenyan Parliament by offering her personal testimony on how her life was negatively affected by the rite. On September 14, 2011, President Kibaki signed the FGM Act of 2011, legislation that Noor had fought for eighteen years to see passed into law.[9]

It is not uncommon to find a stereotypical depiction of this wide range of Muslim women as uneducated in the secular Western sense. It is true, of course, that Muslims in Kenya have repeatedly made the claim that they have been educationally disadvantaged by successive postcolonial regimes. With regard to women in particular, there has been an additional constraint of patriarchal Muslim cultural restrictions that has contributed to the lower ratio of Muslim women with significant Western educational credentials (Chege and Sifuna 2006, 22–26; Ngome 2006; Strobel 1979). In spite of these constraints, however, there is a long record of Muslim women receiving Western schooling, and their number has been steadily increasing (Strobel 1979, 106, 112–16). The recent establishment of a Kenyatta University campus in Mombasa and Pwani University at Kilifi provides a solution for parents who fear sending their daughters to distant lands for higher education.

In all these Kenya Muslim communities, women have played leadership roles even when those roles have not been officially recognized. Whether Western educated or not, whether vying for political office or not, Muslim women have been central in political mobilization at the community level as well as national level. The phenomenon of Muslim women seeking political office may be recent. But Muslim women as political activists are not a recent postcolonial phenomenon. For example, Margaret Strobel (1979, 173–81) offers an insightful account of how a Muslim women's dance association led to the *leso* boycott of the Asian textile industry in response to the extreme inflation of food and clothing prices during World War II.[10] This was truly significant given the centrality of *leso* in Muslim women's fashion and dance associations and how it was (and still is) an important imported commodity from Asia. In this case, their protest paralleled Gandhi's 1920 boycott in India of the Lancashire textile industry (Gandhi 2008).

In addition to entering into business ventures of various kinds, Muslim women of Somali Kenya background have also been playing important leadership roles in peace education, conflict resolution, and the struggle for women's rights in reproductive health. A prominent example of a Kenya Somali woman with an impressive record of human rights activism is Abdi Noor, cofounder in 1989 with Hubbie Hussein Haji of the nongovernmental organization Womankind Kenya in Garissa, the mission of which is to eradicate the practice of female genital cutting, promote girls education, and improve the livelihood of pastoralist women in the Northeastern Province. In 2007, Abdi Noor won two human rights awards, the Father John Kaiser Human Rights award and the Law Society of Kenya's Human Rights Person of the Year award. According to the Women's Islamic Spirituality and Equality website, Abdi Noor was "the first woman from the [Northeastern] province to seek political office; however, her nomination was cancelled due to the cultural and religious argument used against her as justification that a woman cannot lead a Muslim community."[11] Part of the opposition to her political leadership arose directly from her courageous and open advocacy work against cultural practices detrimental to (Muslim) women, like FGM, early child marriage, and levirate (wife inheritance).[12] Previously, she was a 1996 recipient of an international democracy fellowship from the Les Aspin Center for Governance in Washington, D.C., for her work on Muslim women's empowerment and democratization.

In 2008, Noor became a member of the Tenth Kenyan Parliament, having been one of the nominees to the House. She became one of four Muslim women MPs. The other Muslim women members are Naomi Ummi Shaban and Amina Abdallah, also subjects of this book, and Shakila Abdallah, who is a strong advocate of education for Muslim girls. Abdallah, a nominee of the ODM from Lamu East, had formerly been a chairperson of the Lamu East branch of Labor Democratic Party.

An equally significant Muslim woman leader of social change of Somali origin is the late Wajir-born Dekha Ibrahim Abdi (1964–2011), who was especially renowned for her transformative leadership in conflict resolution and peace building through the mobilization of women at the grassroots. Joining Wajir women for peace initiatives, she raised national and international awareness of the unaccounted clan-based war that ravaged the marginalized Northeastern Province of Kenya. In her activism for peace she effectively drew on faith-based and (pastoralist) local cultural approaches of conflict mediation and principles of restorative justice. Like some of the Muslim women featured in this book, Abdi encouraged and capitalized on inclusiveness and interfaith dialogues and linkages in search of common peaceful solutions (Ibrahim 2004; Reinhardt 2010). Her exemplary work earned her national and international recognition, including the 1999 Kenya Government Distinguished Medal for Service, the 2005 Kenya Peace Builder of the Year, the nomination in 2005 for the Nobel Peace Prize, becoming a member of the prestigious 1,000 women for peace across the world, the winner of 2007 Right Livelihood Award known as the "Alternative Nobel Prize," and the 2009 Hessian Peace Prize (Germany). As a legacy to her work as a woman peacemaker Abdi left behind the highly active Oasis of Peace Center located in Mombasa, which did not escape the notice of Kenya Nobel Peace laureate Wangari Maathai (2009, 284). In addition, her views about and commitment to the peace mission are articulated in interviews, some of her own insightful publications on the subject, including articles such as "Women's Role in Peace-Making in the Somali Community in North-Eastern Kenya," which appeared in *Somalia: The Untold Story: War through the Eyes of Women* (2004), in her coauthored book titled *Working with Conflicts, Skills and Strategies for Action* (2000), and in her lectures, which are featured on the Internet, such as on the websites of the World Peace Foundation and Responding To Conflict, at Mediate.com and OpenDemocracy.net, and on YouTube. Moreover, she served on numerous boards of international organizations focusing on conflict mediation and sustainable peace across the world.

Muslim women from the Kenya South Asian community have been particularly prominent in philanthropic work of one kind or another. Their record is visible not only in local organizations formed by the respective members of the Kenya South Asian communities, but also in local chapters of international organizations like the Lions Club. A good example is Dilshad Mohamed, a social worker of Isma'ili origin who was awarded an honorary degree by Kenyatta University and the Lions International President's Special Leadership Medal for her humanitarian work in, among other activities, providing access to technical vocational training to students from marginalized communities who are unable to afford secondary school education in Nairobi. She also mobilizes women regionally in East Africa to develop strategies for greater involvement in nation-building projects through volunteerism.

A recent important gain for Muslim women in Kenya in general resulting from the politics of representation in national democratization is the recent appointment of Salma Ahmed of the Old Town (Mkanyageni) Mombasa as the Kenyan ambassador to France. She is the first Muslim woman ever to be appointed an ambassador in Kenya. As a "veiled" coastal Muslim, it is ironic that she has been appointed to France, a European country that in 2004 enacted a law banning the wearing of hijab in public space to its Muslim female citizens on the grounds that the hijab is an attack on France's liberal secularism (Scott 2007; Keaton 2006).[13]

The significance for Muslim women in Kenya of Ahmed's appointment to one of the highest international diplomatic posts is described in the following words by Amina Zuberi, the district convener of the Mombasa Women's Regional Assembly and founder of Tangana Women Development Group: "The Coast women, in general, particularly the 'Hijab' ones are proud of Ambassador Salma Ahmed as she has remarkably built a distinctly good image of the Coast women in high public institutions. . . . She is an inspiring personality—remarkably dignified, humane, and easily accessible with a strong sense of integrity and an imposing personality. We are proud of her" ("Salma Ahmed" 2011).[14] The same article provides information on Ambassador Ahmed's background, describing her as a "vastly experienced diplomat who has passed through various desks, at the Ministry of Tourism and International Co-operation. . . . Salma has her A-level studies at Alidina Visram High School where her linguistic talents and diplomacy acumen sprouted. . . . She is a graduate of Nairobi University with a B.A., majoring in linguistics with political science as her subsidiary and with postgraduate in diplomacy. . . . She has high command of French, impeccably articulate with its euphemisms, nuances and cultural subtleties" ("Salma Ahmed" 2011). Clearly then, her solid and stellar credentials in the diplomatic area of Kenya's relationship with the rest of the world played a large part in her appointment to this international civil service-cum-political position.

An even greater gain for Muslim women's leadership came soon after the March 2013 election. The newly elected president of the country, Uhuru Kenyatta, set an unprecedented record by appointing four Muslims to his eighteen-member cabinet. One of these appointees is Ambassador Amina Mohamed, the first Muslim woman to ever hold a cabinet office in Kenya. It is equally important that Amina Mohamed's appointment is to head one of the most powerful ministries in the government, the Ministry of Foreign Affairs. A Kakamega-born Kenyan of Somali background, Secretary of State Amina Mohamed is a polyglot in Kiswahili, English, Russian, and French and has a distinguished record as a career diplomat. With a degree in law from the University of Kiev (Ukraine) and Kenya Law School and a graduate diploma in international relations from Oxford University (England), she has been an important player in Kenya's multilateral negotiations in bodies like the Commonwealth and the World Trade Organization. From 2006 to 2007 she served as the Permanent Secretary of the Ministry of Justice, National Cohesion and Constitutional Affairs, during which period she played a crucial supervisory role in drafting and promulgating the new constitution. During this same period she provided leadership in drafting Kenya's foreign trade policy, a role that gave her a great opportunity to demonstrate her skills in economic and commercial diplomacy. Prior to that, from 2000 to 2006, she was Permanent Representative of Kenya to the United Nations Office at Geneva. In 2011 she became United Nations Assistant Secretary General and the Deputy Executive Director of the United Nations Environment Program in Nairobi. Mohamed's story then leaves no room for doubt that her appointment as Cabinet Secretary of Foreign Affairs was based entirely on the merit of her own career credentials and experience over the years (*Daily Nation* [Nairobi], April 23, 2013).

Intensive interactions with Muslim women in Pumwani and other poorer communities reveal that their experience of Islam sharply diverges from upper-class and middle-class Muslim women's experiences. A clear and typical example of this difference in the experiences of many of the Muslim women I interviewed in Pumwani was tied to the question of availability of basic resources such as clean water and sanitary infrastructures, which are fundamental to human survival and certainly crucial to Muslim rituals of cleansing. Furthermore, in a place harshly affected by poverty, unemployment, drug abuse, and the HIV/AIDS pandemic, the moral economy associated with Muslim women's dress code was never raised as a burning issue for Pumwani Muslim women. Many dressed modestly in a variety of ways, with *leso* or *kanga* being more dominant than *buibui*, which they regarded as an imported dress feature of "ethnic" Swahili rather than of Swahili Muslims, which is what they self-identified as.[15] But noticeably, Pumwani Muslim women dress differently in most cases from non-Muslim women, who do not wear the headscarf or wear Western attire.

Other Pumwani Muslim women I interacted with are engaged in small-scale trading of cooked food, selling of *leso/kanga* or religious literature, and in selling their labor as domestic workers and sex workers. Some of the younger women from Pumwani are paid workers or volunteers in NGOs focusing on HIV/AIDS and other public health issues in the communities. Others, seeing the limitations of private HIV/AIDS NGOs targeting women of the slums, have taken it upon themselves to form self-help support groups for Muslim women affected by the HIV/AIDS pandemic that provide what they see as more realistic options given slum culture and resources. The leadership of Saumu Saidi, a native of Pumwani of Kikuyu Muslim background who also identified herself as Swahili Muslim, has been crucial in the activities of the group in Pumwani, where there is a scarcity of public health resources and employment or income-generating opportunities, inspired by a vision for self-empowerment in fighting HIV/AIDS and poverty.

Another leader, Bi Halima, one of the senior Muslim women community leaders I interviewed in Pumwani, opened a Muslim women's shelter for widowed women and senior women with no relatives and to raise awareness among Muslim religious bodies and communities of the importance of securing a proper Muslim burial for the residents of the shelter, including herself, rather than continuing to let their bodies be buried by well-meaning non-Muslims. This undertaking was motivated by the fact that in spite of their efforts to fend for themselves, Pumwani Muslim women rely a great deal on support from both Muslim and non-Muslim charity organizations, such as the Young Muslim Association and the St. John Catholic Relief Center—Caritas, which provide free access to public health resources to people living with HIV/AIDS, orphans, and widows. Bi Halima constantly reminds Muslim religious leaders and the community of their duty to restore to her and Muslim women widow residents in her shelter their right to their Muslim identity even at death.

Women from these diverse Muslim communities at times respond with a common voice as Muslims with regard to certain national issues, such as the Equality Bill and the Sexual Offences Bill. When there are differences of opinion among Muslim women of these communities on such national issues, they are seldom based on intra-Muslim divisions. Of course, the Equality Bill and the Sexual Offences Bill were national questions that were of greater concern to Muslim women of some communities than others. A good case in point was the debate about whether the kadhi courts should be maintained under the new constitutional order (Athena Mutua 2003, 2007; Hashim 2010; Hirsch 2010).[16] Here it was mainly Sunni women of non–South Asian origin who were most vocal on the question and who agitated in favor of retaining the institution. Kenyan Muslims of South Asian origin, on the other hand, were virtually silent about the matter. Part of the reason may lie in the fact that the kadhi court is an institution that so far has primarily served non-Asian Muslims of Kenya. In fact, as Susan Hirsch (1998) demonstrates, these Kenyan non-Asian Muslim women have been particularly effective in using the spaces of the kadhi courts to their advantage even in the absence of a strong women's movement.[17] Kenyan Muslims of South Asian origin, on the other hand, normally have their own community structures designed to address grievances related to issues of personal law, including marriage, divorce, inheritance, and child custody.

One can gain a rich understanding of the profile of Muslim women in Kenya through a number of important and pioneering studies covering a wide range of topics. Margaret Strobel's insightful work *Muslim Women in Mombasa, 1800–1975* (1979) and Margaret Strobel and Sarah Mirza's *Three Swahili Women* (1989) provide exciting historical insights into how *makungwi*, women who conduct rituals related to the female life cycle, transgress dividing class, ethnic, and racial boundaries among womenfolk established by slavery and colonialism, in their attempt to reconfigure a new sense of Muslim womanhood. Mary A. Porter's dissertation, "Swahili Identity in Post-colonial Kenya: The Reproduction of Gender in Educational Discourses" (1992), and her article "Resisting Uniformity at Mwana Kupona Girls School: Cultural Production in an Educational Setting" (1998) are insightful ethnographic accounts of the impact of secular education on the lives of Swahili adolescent girls at the intersection of competing hegemonic ideologies of belonging and differentiation within their community of faith and the nation-state. She demonstrates, for example, how the transformation of a school that during the colonial period only catered to Muslim girls into a secular state-run girls school open to non-Muslims from up-country settler communities such as the Luo and Kikuyu at the coast has led to an increase in moral policing of Muslim girls as manifested through the dress code (1998, 631). New Islamic dress, *suruali* (loose-fitting pants) and hijab different from the traditional Swahili *buibui*, have been adopted as the school uniform for Muslim girls to mark their Islamic identity within the secular state school and to enable them to exhibit their *heshima* (respectability and virtue), which is expected of "good" Muslim girls (Porter 1998, 635). However, Porter also contends that the moral policing does not prevent Swahili Muslim female adolescents from using their agency to subvert normative gender representations in their pursuit of advanced educational goals, which hitherto had been the privilege of Swahili males.

Minou Fuglesang's *Veils and Videos: Female Youth Culture on the Kenyan Coast* (1994) is another fascinating analysis of how young Lamu Muslim women consume modern knowledge about sexuality transmitted through romantic melodramas from the West (Hollywood), India (Bollywood), and the Middle East, and how modern Muslim women's subjectivities compete against the normative images of pious virgin Muslim women within circumscribed cultural boundaries, where discussions of sexuality and desire remain taboo. Moreover, Fuglesang's work is significant for its examination of how a constructive usage of youth media culture can be an effective educational tool in transforming young Muslim women's vulnerability to infectious diseases such as HIV/AIDS that might result from the uninformed risky behavior young Muslim female youth engage in in an effort to subvert Islamic sexual morality. Susan F. Hirsch's *Pronouncing and Persevering: Gender and the Discourses of Disputing in an African Islamic Court* (1998) offers a powerful postcolonial account of Swahili women's subjectivities in their matrimonial trial performances in the Mombasa kadhi courts during which they have sought to challenge the Swahili normative concept of *heshima*, which prevents women from airing problems arising within marital homes.[18] Equally important in the literature on Islam and gender in Kenya are Mwanakombo Mohamed Noordin's "Ufasiri wa Ufeministi wa Kiislamu katika Utamaduni wa Mwanamke Mswahili: Mkabala au Ushirikiano?" (2009) ("An Interpretation of Islamic Feminism in the Tradition of Swahili Woman: Conflict or Complementarity?"), and Esha Faki Mwinyihaji's "Contribution of Islam towards Women Emancipation: A Case Study of the Swahili Women in Mombasa District" (2001). An important study that focuses primarily on FGM among Muslims in northeastern Kenya is Esther K. Hicks's *Infibulation: Female Mutilation in Islamic Northeastern Kenya* (1996), which shows the pervasiveness of the practice among Muslims and its embeddedness in a long history of fusion between cultural traditions and religious beliefs. Hicks argues, therefore, that developing adequate educational resources for an anti-FGM campaign requires taking into account the wider context within which the practice itself is situated.

There are other important texts with substantial sections devoted to colonial or modern experiences of young Muslim women of the Kenyan coast. These include, among others, Janet Bujra's *Anthropological Study of Political Action in a Bajuni Village in Kenya* (1968), which touches on coastal Muslim women's involvement with the tourism and prostitution industry, and Luise White's *The Comforts of Home: Prostitution in Colonial Nairobi* (1990), which relates the processes of conversion into "Muslimness" by which up-country rural-urban migrant women in Pumwani (Nairobi) retained their domestic Muslim male partners who were laborers in the colonial workforce. More recently, Susan Beckerleg has made significant contributions to the study of young Muslim women's use of both injection drugs and heroin, which challenges the cultural normative Islamic representation of what "Muslim women ought to be." She shows how the intersection of gender ideology, neoliberal development programs in Muslim society, and the structural disadvantage of Muslim youth, especially young women, exposes them to drug culture, prostitution, and increased vulnerability to HIV/AIDS infection. This dimension of young Muslim women in coastal Kenya is analyzed in Beckerleg's "Brown Sugar or Friday Prayers: Youth Choices and Community Building in Coastal Kenya" (1990) and "Women Heroin Users: Exploring the Limitations of the Structural Violence Approach" (2005).

Each of these studies offers a fascinating examination of the ways in which the cultural contexts of the moment—slavery, British colonialism, the development of postcolonial conflicts and the tourist industry, associations between modernist Islamism(s) and Pentecostal Christianity, drugs and the HIV/AIDS pandemic—contribute to the reshaping of young Muslim women's identity in Kenya. Together with other studies they have been important in providing part of the background against which I try to understand the leadership histories of the six Muslim women covered in this book.

METHODOLOGY

My research in Kenya was conducted for several months at a time, with special intensity between 2004 and 2006. From a methodological point of view, it is important to note that Kenya is where my husband, Alamin Mohamed Mazrui, was born and bred and where he continues to maintain strong family ties. It was almost natural, then, that my initial entry into my research space would be through the networks that Alamin's family shared. Fully conscious, however, of the Mazruis' historical and contemporary prominence in the leadership of the Shafi'i school of thought within East African Sunni Islam, which is hostile to other Islamic traditions, and of the institution of the chief kadhi that Alamin's brother, Sheikh Hammad Mohamed Kassim, was heading during the time of my research, I quickly realized that I had to navigate the social space in ways that would allow me to form independent networks and explore other Islamic thoughts and practices and other Muslim identities, especially as they related to women.

The fact that already I had made some Kenyan contacts and friends, both Muslims and non-Muslims, in the United States and had met some during my very first visit to Kenya helped me in broadening my networks, especially outside Mombasa. In addition, I attended Muslim workshops and symposia on Islamic perspectives on HIV/AIDs that were held while I was in Kenya as well as public lectures by Muslim medical doctors and public health practitioners and social workers. These forums were a wonderful opportunity for me to meet a large number of new people, many of whom were very keen and willing to work with me on the subject of my research. In fact, it was at one of these forums related to the launching of the HIV/AIDS curriculum from an Islamic perspective, presided over by the officials of Kenya Institute of Education and Chief Kadhi Hammad Mohamed Kassim, that I met Shamsiya Ramadhan, who became my most resourceful research assistant. A discussion between the two of us over a very powerful documentary film dignifying the humanity of HIV/AIDS-affected Muslims sparked a closeness between us that led her to introduce me to a prominent Muslim photojournalist and filmmaker, Khamis Ramadhan, her older brother.

Shamsiya Wanjiru Ramadhan, a native of Kibera and a native speaker of Kiswahili, is extremely involved in and well respected by various Muslim women networks across class and communities in Nairobi. Her Nubi-Kikuyu background makes her particularly sensitive to the ethnoracial complexities of intra-Muslim relationships as well as to the different historical trajectories of different Muslim communities in Kenya and of the power relations between them. After all, the Kikuyu constitute the largest single ethnic group and wield tremendous political and economic muscle. The Nubi, descendants of Sudanese conscripts who settled in Kibera after World War I, are among the smallest minority group; their Kenyan citizenship is yet to be fully recognized by the state (de Smedt 2011; Hussein 2006; Kokole 1985; Parsons 1997). In addition, her training in religious studies from the Catholic University of East Africa, her previous experience as a research assistant to other social scientists, and her nongovernmental organization work within disadvantaged Muslim communities and women's associations were a great asset that she brought to my research in Pumwani and in other communities.

Of course, my subject of research at any particular time also opened up new networking opportunities. For instance, while exploring the life of Muhashamy-Said, I had the opportunity to travel to a number of the schools that her center was working with, both in urban and rural areas. In this way I was able to connect with some of the teachers and, in a few cases, with the families of the students and other community members. In time I also got into the habit of spending several hours visiting public spaces like the Mombasa market in Mwembe Kuku, the Jami'a Mosque in Nairobi, and the adjacent Jami'a shopping center with its vibrant multiethnic Muslim women business owners and customers, where I had the opportunity to interact with women from all walks of life engaged in a variety of activities. The section of the Mwembe Kuku street market that specializes in clothing is essentially dominated by Muslim store owners, both male and female. The Jami'a Mosque in Nairobi is arguably the most prominent Muslim structure in Kenya. Run by the Jami'a Mosque Committee as well as some Muslim groups like the Young Muslim Association, the mosque and its accompanying buildings used as offices and businesses is a hub of diverse religious and secular activities for both men and women. The Jami'a Mosque Committee is also in charge of the production of a weekly periodical, the *Friday Bulletin*, devoted to Muslim affairs. Conversations with these new contacts were never limited to my immediate subjects of investigation. They always covered a wide range of topics, from religious to political, from youth culture to poverty alleviation, from women's contributions to the economy to the HIV/AIDS pandemic in the Muslim communities, that provided me with a multiplicity of perspectives on how different people viewed different leaders, especially from the ranks of women.

As my network grew, I found myself in the home of one person or another for dinner, lunch, or tea. I was seldom alone with my host at these meals. My presence would often be an opportunity for a get-together between family members and their friends to whom the host wanted to introduce me. These "family" gatherings were full of animated discussions—often triggered directly by my general questions about Muslim women in Kenya—revealing underlying hopes and fears, passions and prejudices, challenges and accomplishments in many social and professional domains. The challenge for me was always one of trying to resolve the tensions between my own position in these interactions as an insider—a woman (in most cases), a person of Muslim background, a community member (even if by association through marriage)—and as an outsider—a linguist working in the U.S. academy and originally from the West African Sahel, more specifically, Niger Republic, which is predominantly of the Tijaniyya Sufi order.

Even though I have a Muslim background, my professional location in the United States proved to be particularly challenging in some of my early encounters as a result of Muslim experiences in Kenya in the aftermath of the 9/11 tragedy. In time, however, even the skeptics began to appreciate my research on Muslim women's contributions in Kenya and began to take me into their confidence. In fact, whether in Nairobi neighborhoods like Pumwani, Pangani, Eastleigh, or South C, at Jami'a Mosque, at the Kenyan Parliament, professional offices, schools in Mombasa, Kwale, and Nairobi, or in other communities, I was very fortunate and pleasantly surprised by the tremendous enthusiasm and support I received from so many Muslim women in all the communities I visited. As the word got around about my research through either my research assistant or relatives and friends, I was surprised by the number of Muslim women who were calling me, seeking to be interviewed, or to provide information about groups of Muslim women I should interview. Some came to my house to make themselves available for interviews or provide useful documents such as newspaper clips, documentary videos, or video clips of events they thought important for my research. They wanted their stories to be told.

In this wide range of spaces of social encounter, the question of Muslim women's leadership kept recurring. More important, I began hearing more or less the same names being mentioned over and over again of women that my interlocutors clearly regarded as leaders in their own right, whether or not they agreed with their orientation and style of leadership. It was partly through this process that I began exploring the lives of specific Muslim women leaders in Kenya, some of whom are the subject of this book. I could have chosen to write about Muslim women leaders in a single profession like politics or law, but as my network of prominent Muslim women leaders in education, parliamentary politics, medicine and public health, legal practice, and other professions continued to grow, I decided to attempt a cross-section by focusing on a range of women who were active and influential in several different arenas of society. My analysis reveals the dynamism of social, economic, and political class mobility of each Muslim woman discussed and the conditions that foster class, regional, and ethnic solidarity among Muslim women, despite the diversity of Muslim communities and their historical and contemporary positioning within postcolonial Kenya. Furthermore, I demonstrate the strength of the intra-Muslim women's solidarity, a solidarity that extends beyond boundaries of class and ethnoregional difference and that fosters another point of strength in Muslim women's coalition with other Kenyan women of all faith and ethno-regional and class backgrounds in their struggle to advocate for women's rights within their communities of faith and the Kenyan nation (Dekha Abdi 2010; Gordon 2010).

My contacts thus were established primarily through snowball sampling, one person leading to another, one network connecting with another. In addition, much of my primary data was collected mainly through open-ended interviews, complemented by a process of participant observation. My research, then, was essentially based on a qualitative, interpretive approach with all its strengths—in providing an open space within which we might be able to discover the meanings the subjects attach to their own "readings"—and with the limitations that accompany intersubjectivity.

The stories and interviews were collected in Swahili, then transcribed and translated into English by Shamsiya Ramadhan when they involved subjects who did not speak English, as was the case for most elder women in Pumwani. Complementing Shamsiya's transcription and translation work was that of two other university graduates, Kingwa Kingwa, who graduated from the Department of Literature of the University of Nairobi, and Susan Bantu, then a Swahili teacher and communications specialist in Nairobi. The Muslim women interviewees were very patient and welcoming throughout the months and the days of long interviews and/or follow-ups on parts that were not clear to me or that needed further elaboration. Although I always had a set of questions based on the issues I wanted to focus on at the beginning of the interview, my approach was also to permit the interviewees the freedom to ask me questions or to bring up topics that they saw as very crucial to them. My interviews with the majority of Muslim women across different levels of (religious or secular) education, especially the six who are the subject of this book, however, were conducted entirely in the English language, in which they were very competent. In fact, I was struck by the level of proficiency in English of the young Muslim women in places like Pumwani, which is a low-income neighborhood in Nairobi. The schooling of many young Muslim women was cut off after eighth grade because their poor parents were unable to pay the required school fees that the Kenyan government abolished only in 2000. Yet I had no problem communicating with this target population in English.

Although my research was about Muslim women, it was important for me to engage with and interview several male Muslim scholars and leaders and non-Muslim men of authority. After all, the institutions that Muslim women leaders are seeking to reform are precisely those that have been shaped by normative gender ideologies and other hegemonic ideologies embedded in the realms of culture, religion, and politics at the local, national, and global levels. I was interested in finding out how various individuals or groups of male leaders were receiving Muslim women's social and political reform activism. It was in this process that I learned about the male leaders who are opponents and those who are strong allies of Muslim women's rights activists. In fact, some of the Muslim women reform leaders covered in this book make overt references to both male authorities in the religious and/or secular realms of power who oppose women's rights and those who support them.

Outline of the Book

Though the concern with education is shared by all, it is a focus of special attention in the work of Muhashamy-Said (chapter 1) and Mudira (chapter 2). Muhashamy-Said, a retired teacher in her midseventies, initiated a program to modernize the traditional Qur'anic school in order to respond to the structural inequalities created by the expensive private nursery schools. Her work takes a novel approach that presents an alternative to both the traditional Qur'anic school, which does not respond to the competitive demands of modernity, and the secular nursery school system, which is unaffordable to the majority and which culturally alienates Muslim children from their faith. The "modernized integrated madrasa curriculum" intends to make learning about Islam an integral part of learning about other "secular" subjects.

Mudira, on the other hand, set a new precedent by opening a formal boarding school in Pangani, Nairobi, for advanced Islamic theological training for Muslim women, amid the opposition of conservative Muslim ulama and the skepticism of the Muslim community. She named her school "ma'had" (a word meaning "school"), and its mission is to challenge the exclusionary male-centered tradition of higher education in Islamic studies. Chapter 2 thus shows how Mudira seeks to challenge patriarchal control of religion in Kenya Muslim societies through this educational project. The idea of a boarding school is partly a response to the continued denial in Muslim societies of girls' and women's rights to public space and access to Islamic or secular knowledge beyond the basics. The chapter discusses the *ma'had*'s strategies for recruiting young female high school graduates and examines the transnational roots and impacts of Mudira's vision.

Chapter 3, "Muslim Women Legislators in Minority Status: Contributions to Representative Politics," examines the leadership roles of Muslim women members of the Kenyan Parliament. One of the greatest impacts of the 1990s democratization process in Africa has been the emphasis on the question of national political representation of marginalized groups in legislative bodies and in other public and private institutions. This has led, in many countries, to concerted efforts to appoint members of marginalized groups to executive positions in government, parliament, and local municipal councils. This embrace of greater pluralistic representation is perceived as necessary to sustainable peaceful national governance. However, while it has been possible to address (and at times even accommodate) ethnic, religious, and regional differences, this has not been the case with gender.

As in many African and other countries of the world, in Kenya there has been great resistance to the idea of women occupying executive, legislative, and other civic leadership positions (Seager 2009, 92; Tripp 2000). Women are marginalized in this respect not only at the national level but also at the local level, as patriarchal assumptions are deeply embedded in a variety of structures within their own communities of faith, ethnicity, region, and professions, to list a few. The chapter examines the ways in which the only two Muslim women MPs in Kenya at the time of my research exploit a terrain opened up by the democratization process to contest negative forces both within their own communities and within the nation that exclude women from ascending to national political leadership positions. Furthermore, the chapter analyzes how once in executive seats, these Muslim women MPs use their power to advance (Muslim) girls' and (Muslim) women's agenda through, for example, their focus on education and literacy programs targeting disadvantaged girls and women in predominantly poor (Muslim) areas. It discusses how Muslim women MPs use the tropes of wifehood and motherhood as subversive tools for achieving gains in critical areas of interest on behalf of women, girls, and themselves as political leaders. Finally, the chapter provides an analysis of the arguments advanced by the two Muslim women MPs to justify their embrace of a secular rather than faith-based politics in their struggle to achieve equal rights and socioeconomic and political opportunities for Muslims in general and Muslim girls and women more specifically within their community of faith and the nation at large.

Chapter 4 focuses on the social biography of Abida Ali-Aroni, the first ever Muslim woman trained in secular law to be appointed judge of the High Court in Kenya. Prior to this most recent national appointment in June 2009, she had risen to public prominence in 2005 as the second chairperson of the Constitution of Kenya Review Commission, one of the most significant national undertakings since the mid-1990s, when the state began its experimentation with democratic governance. The chapter offers a (con)textual analysis of Ali-Aroni's personal account of her family background and educational and professional journey into spaces culturally reserved for men. It reveals the development of her political consciousness through her involvement with Muslim politics during the constitutional review process and her contribution to reform movements involving (Muslim) women's rights through coalition with non-Muslim activist women's organizations such as the Federation of Kenya Women Lawyers. A subject of critical importance that also emerges in this chapter is that of the status of the kadhi courts in Kenya's judicial system. Finally, Ali-Aroni offers an important critique of the culture of political activism of Muslim women in Kenya. She sees it as too sporadic and narrow in its focus and generally operating under the patronage of Muslim male organizations.

The proliferation of private media broadcasting stations and private newspapers and magazines resulting from democratization processes in most African countries has created an outlet for the emergence not only of pluralistic voices within various national constituencies but also of ideologically divergent perspectives within the Muslim polities. This development in old and new information and communication technologies—radio, audiocassettes, television and satellite, Internet, and magazines—plays a key role in shaping sociopolitical discursive practices within Muslim societies (Abu-Lughod 2005; Alloo 1999; Eickelman and Anderson 1999; Haenni 2002; Hirschkind 2006; Salvatore 1999; Schulz 2005, 2012). This interplay between democratization and media is especially significant as educated Muslim women become active agents as media producers, hosts, and consumers (Alidou 2005; Fuglesang 1994; Mernissi 2005; Nouraie-Simone 2005; Skalli 2006) and offers them a platform for advocating for their rights within the nation. Chapter 5 illustrates this interplay between information and communication technologies and Muslim women's activism by focusing on two case studies in Kenya: a Muslim women's magazine—*The Nur* (*The Light*), produced in Nairobi— and a women's radio program—*Ukumbi Wa Mamama* (*Women's Forum*), hosted by the Islamic-oriented Radio Rahma (Voice of Mercy) in Mombasa. I apply critical textual analysis to show how secular learning and skills have been mobilized by the Muslim women discussed here to religious and sociopolitical ends on behalf of Muslim women in particular and the Kenya Muslim community at large within the political context of the nation in transition. These are examples of Islamist women's voices that challenge prevailing and deeply entrenched orthodoxies that have defined relations not only between men and women within the Muslim communities but also between Muslim women and non-Muslims, including their non-Muslim "sisters.""Islamist women" in the Kenyan context refers to Muslim women whose activism is shaped by an Islamic framework rather than by secular reasoning, which they reject as constituent of Western colonialism. Partly as a result of this understanding, they are strong supporters of the continued existence of the kadhi courts, but within a reformed framework sensitive to women's rights.

From the totality of the experiences of the six Muslim women leaders covered in these chapters, then, we see—as summed up in the conclusion—

that Muslim women in Kenya, whether secularist or Islamist, are religious agents and/or sociopolitical agents. As agents, they use a critical reading of Islam and cultural, state, and international institutions and policies in their quest to democratically transform their societies and the nation and thereby reclaim their citizenship rights.

1

Bi Swafiya Muhashamy-Said

A Pioneer in Reforming *Chuo* (Madrasa) Nursery Curriculum in Kenya and Beyond

INTRODUCTION

Having been subject to British colonialism for decades, the East African countries, including Kenya, all inherited the educational system that maintains a distinction between schools designed for religious training and those for the material world. But under the impact of globalization, Muslim women educationists in this region are rethinking the question of modernity and designing creative alternative educational setups. One of these novel approaches to Muslim education is the "modernized integrated madrasa curriculum" intended to make learning about Islam an integral part of learning about other, secular subjects. The integrated madrasa now endeavors to prepare students for both religious and secular life. And it is this alternative educational paradigm that this chapter explores by focusing on the pioneering works of its main architect, Bi Swafiya Muhashamy-Said from Mombasa. This social biography of Muhashamy-Said makes an important contribution to history of knowledge production by African Muslim women educationists who have attempted to incorporate religious epistemology into a secular framework.

One of the most comprehensive studies on East African Islamic leaders, for example, is a book by renowned Muslim scholar and jurist Sheikh Abdallah Saleh Farsy titled *The Shafi'i ulama of East Africa, 1820–1970: A Hagiographic Account* (1972). The book does not provide an account of a single woman *mu'alima* (female scholar) from the region in spite of the fact that his mother was his first Qur'anic teacher and indeed was a renowned Qur'anic teacher in the community. Among the Qadiriyya Sufi order, Mwana Alama, the wife of the Sufi Sheikh Shauri bin Hajj Mshirazi, was known for her leadership in popularizing the Sufi ritual of *dhikr*—a gathering of Muslim women (in Northern Zanzibar and among the Sufi of the Kenyan coast) who chant collectively the various attributions of God (Pouwels 1981, 159). Likewise, all existing studies of Islamic reformers from Kenya, Tanzania, and Uganda recognize only male figures. Muslim women leaders and reformers have continued to be erased from historical memory over and over again.

In addition to this marginalization of Muslim women as knowledge producers and critics, they have been objectified as the oppressed subjects of study of the "other." Within this construction of colonial modernity in the West, the Muslim woman is seen as the ultimate cultural "other" of her liberated Western counterpart.[1] Both Western and Muslim scholars are party to this scholarly trend. These two factors—the marginalization of Muslim women's agency and colonial modernity's assault on the Muslim woman—have motivated predominantly women scholars of both Muslim and non-Muslim background to pay special attention to the study of Muslim women as producers of knowledge and cultural (active or passive) agents of modernity (Abu-Lughod 1993, 1998; Ahmed 1993; Alidou 2005; Badran 2008a; Badran and Cooke 2004; B. Cooper 2001; Gole 1996; Hill 2010; Kandiyoti 1996, 1998; Mack 2004; Mahmood 2004; Masquelier 2009; Mbow 2009; Mernissi 1991a, 1991b, 2005; Sadiqi 2003; Sharawi 1987; Schulz 2012, to cite a few). My work is in line with this trend in scholarship, as I explore Muslim women's modern agency and their contributions as (Islamic) knowledge producers. In the remainder of this chapter I focus on the pioneering work of Bi Swafiya Muhashamy-Said from Mombasa, the main architect of the integrated madrasa curriculum, and on the teachers who benefited from her training in East Africa.[2] I interviewed her in her home and at her office over several sessions in 2005 and 2006 and visited the schools where her curriculum is implemented.

A native of Mombasa born in 1935, Muhashamy-Said is unique among many Swahili women of her age for having attained two university degrees—the BA and MA—in her sixties. After retirement as a primary school teacher in Kenya in the early eighties, she became the founder of the Mombasa Madrasa Resource Center, a pioneering institution devoted to the promotion of an integrated (Islamic-secular) curriculum for preschool children. Given the success of her work, Muhashamy-Said was appointed the regional director of East African madrasa resource centers, covering countries such as Kenya, Tanzania, and Uganda, a position she held until her retirement in 2006.

THE COLONIAL BEGINNING:
A HISTORICAL BACKGROUND TO MUSLIM EDUCATION

During the late nineteenth century, British colonialists used both mission-ary education and Christianity as tools for consolidating their domination in Kenya. However, as Charles Ngome (2006, 3) rightly observes, the cultural production of African colonial agents through this educational and religious process was not uniform throughout Kenya, partly due to the way the dif-ferent regions were incorporated into the colonial economy and partly because of the specific responses of local cultural communities to British colonial subjugation. Here I focus mainly on Muslim responses to the legacy of British colonial education in postcolonial Kenya, paying particular attention to com-munity leadership.

Although hope of economic returns was one reason colonialists wanted to educate Africans in their colonies, British missionaries introduced a West-ern style of schooling mainly to facilitate the spread of Christianity in Kenya (Brown, Brown, and Sumura 1999; Eshiwani 1993, 15–18; Mukudi 1993, 84). This process, however, was a gendered one that denied women educational opportunities and transformed traditional gender identities, again at the expense of women (Chege and Sifuna 2006, 24, 26–28; Mukudi 1993, 84).

The coastal strip of Kenya, though under the British colonial power, was still considered part of the East African coastal territory of the sultan of Zan-zibar during the colonial period. The region was populated mainly by ethnic groups from the Mijikenda- and Swahili-speaking people (some of Arab-African origin) and a range of South Asian settler communities (Hindu, Muslims, Sikh, and others) (Asani 1994; Ghai and Ghai 1970; Herzig 2006; Patel 1997, 2006). But because of its links with the Zanzibar sultanate, the British government privileged the Arab-Swahili constituency in the local power hierarchy (Salim 1984).

The Arab-Swahili constituency was suspicious of colonial education to an extent, especially with regard to women, partly because of the centrality of the Christian missionary establishment in colonial education (Pouwels 1981, 186–87). The Arab-Swahili constituency in the more cosmopolitan Mombasa was the least suspicious, while Lamu, which hosts one of the main Islamic centers of learning in East Africa, known as the Riyadha Mosque, was the most suspicious.

For centuries, the only form of education with a formal school structure that existed in the space that would become Kenya (Ngome 2006) was the

Qur'anic school, or *chuo* (pl. *vyuo*) in Swahili. These focused mainly on the reading of the Qur'an and some preliminary introduction to the hadith. The structures themselves were often spaces within the residences of the teachers (especially if the teachers were women) and mosques. Pupils were expected to *hitimu* (that is, be able to recite the entire Qur'an) by approximately age twelve and aim to be *hafidh* (that is, to have fully mastered the memorization of the Qur'an) as soon as possible after that. The *chuo* phenomenon was initially an urban one at the coast, centered in places like Lamu and Mombasa. It was not until much later in the early twentieth century (Sperling 1998) that it spread to the rural areas. Male students who completed the *chuo* stage with distinction then had the opportunity to delve into higher and deeper study of other Islamic disciplines, conducted by leading *shaykhs* either in their own homes or in community mosques. This is how the Riyadha Mosque in Lamu came to acquire its reputation as the "Al-Azhar" of the Swahili coast, comparing itself in local terms to Al-Azhar University in Cairo, which is one of the oldest and most prestigious Muslim institutions of higher learning.

In most cases, the *chuo* educational system aimed at developing the capacity to read but not the capacity to write. As a result, those who did not get an opportunity to pursue further education in Islamic studies—and, until recently, this was invariably true of women—often developed only a rudimentary ability to write by reproducing the letters of the Arabic alphabet as they read them in texts of the Qur'an. Thus, the printed rather than the cursive style one would find among those trained in both reading and writing of Arabic was common in the writing of many Kenyan Muslims, but especially of women. Nonetheless, even this indirect method of acquiring writing skills made Swahili writing using the Arabic script a thriving tradition for several centuries (Loimeier 2003).

Because of the nature of the relationship between the sultan and the British, however, the colonial authorities in Kenya tried to accommodate Swahili interests by making provisions for Islamic education and the teaching of the Arabic language as a subject within the colonial school curriculum, as well as provisions for the exclusion of Christian religious education in those schools. For example, in the Mombasa colonial schools known as the Arab Boys School (which later became Serani Primary School), the Arab Girls School (which became Mbaraki Primary School), and the Sir bin Ali Salim Primary School (later Malindi Primary School), Christianity was never taught as a subject.

Kenyans of non-Arab Swahili origin like the Kamba, Kisii, Kikuyu, and Luo, who became Muslims and eventually became linguistically and culturally assimilated into Swahili society, underwent a different experience from the Arab-Swahili of the coast. Because they were subjects of a settler colony and lacked the kind of leverage that the Arab-Swahili had by virtue of being subjects of the sultan of Zanzibar, they were mostly educated in integrated schools, many of which were controlled by Christians. As a result, there were many cases of nominal conversion by black Kenyan Muslims to Christianity in colonial missionary schools. These differences between the Arab-Swahili Muslims and non-Arab Swahili Muslims notwithstanding, it is true that Muslims in Kenyan were educationally disadvantaged during the colonial era due partly to their own suspicions of the Christian control of colonial education. After all, education is not a neutral process. As Peter McLaren rightly observes, "Schooling is a form of cultural politics, a legitimation of particular forms of social life. In acting to maintain the dominant culture, schools exert hegemony (the moral and intellectual leadership of a dominant class over a subordinate class). This hegemony is evident in 'the hidden curriculum' and in the legitimacy of certain forms of 'cultural capital'" (2003).

Schooling consolidated foreign rule by socializing a particular ideology of socioeconomic and political hegemony (Kelly and Altbach 1984, 1). That colonial schools had this function partly explains why Kenyan Muslims were particularly averse to colonial education. After all, unlike the non-Muslim Kenyans who traditionally did not have institutionalized schooling, the Kenyan Muslims did. Their Qur'anic schools conflicted fundamentally with the British colonial schooling paradigm in terms of the ideologies and aims they sought to impart. As a result, the number of Muslims enrolled in schools during the colonial period was disproportionately lower than that of their non-Muslim counterparts, and thus when Kenya finally acquired its independence in 1963, Muslims lagged far behind non-Muslim citizens in secular educational accomplishment.

Furthermore, there was an ironic convergence of gender ideology between the colonial administration and Muslims and non-Muslim Kenyan cultures. The patriarchal orientation of local cultures and Muslim societies meant that women were regarded as custodians of "traditions" and therefore should not be exposed to "foreign" cultural influences. As a result, most Kenyan indigenous peoples preferred not to send their daughters to school. On the other hand, the reigning Victorian conception of female domesticity led colonial authorities to become complicit in excluding African girls from schooling.

And when colonial administration did offer schooling to girls—the Native Girls Homes in central Kenya is one example—it was in an attempt to "save" them from the barbaric cultural assault on their sexuality through the ritual of excision rather than part of an effort to genuinely promote female education. As Fatuma Chege and Daniel Sifuna observe, "Christian missionaries, particularly in Central Kenya, are on the record as having been among the first groups of Europeans to support female education through the practice of sheltering runaway girls who entered the mission and sought refuge based on a host of cultural reasons. . . . The missionaries provided these girls with minimal education while at the same time converting them to Christianity" (2006, 26).

African girls were thus incorporated into the framework of Victorian domesticity of good Christian wives for their subaltern African male workers (Chege and Sifuna 2006, 22; Hansen 1992, 214). The Christian hegemony that suffused the missionary schools reinforced the notion of the submissive, dutiful housewife and mother according to colonial Christian traditions. Conversion to Christianity was the tool through which the construction of this new African female identity as the "African man's wife" was cemented, and the supplementary curricular content further consolidated the process. As Chege and Sifuna further point out, "Such women were . . . trained in the social grace of Victorian fashion and etiquette, cake making, needlecraft and other domestic occupations that narrowed down to nothing beyond housewifery" (2006, 23).

In spite of the state of quasi-indirect rule at the coast of Kenya, Muslim students did not completely escape the Euro-Christian indoctrination of colonial schooling. Before the establishment of the schools that catered to the Arab-Swahili Muslim community, Muslim students had to attend government or private schools with a Christian orientation. And for those who later attended "Arab boys" and "Arab girls" schools, Euro-Christian content and/or worldview was systematically transmitted through textbooks used in subjects like history, social studies, and literature. For example, Muslim students learned regularly about influential Christian heroes inspired by Christianity, like Joan of Arc, rather than (local) Muslim historical figures. Thus, the more the colonial schooling transformed the identity of African girls along European and quasi-Christian parameters, the more the Muslim communities in Kenya recoiled from sending their daughters to school. It is against this background that we should understand the following statement by Muhashamy-Said:

They started their work a long time ago to try to get to our minds through the teaching of the scripture: Muslims resent that. The year was . . . I was very big because I was to do my Qur'an first and then go to school. It was in 1946. When my father said I should go to school in 1946, the whole community was against it except his own mother, who said, "Why not?" So when my grandmother agreed, then I was taken to a Catholic school because there were no Muslim schools. So I was taken to a private girls community school run by Asian Goans. Even in my own family, my grandaunt did not like the idea of sending me to school because of the Muslim community's fear of the possibility of converting the children, and also the fear of girls mixing with boys. But all the time, my mother would counsel me not to talk to boys. Because it is very dangerous, just talking could lead to many other things. So every night, she would ask me, "Who were you with? What happened today?" You know.

Muhashamy-Said's remarks underscore several significant points. First, they reveal the concern of Muslim communities about European influence in the wake of World War II. This is another historical moment when Africans were absorbed into European internal conflicts. Second, it highlights the circulation of the colonized who were engendered by colonialism. Here we have the Goans, a Catholic community of Indian origin once colonized by the Portuguese, now serving the British civilizing mission through education on the East African side of the Indian Ocean.[3] Third, the mixing of the genders was itself considered one of the European cultural vices wrought by colonial education. Even those parents who saw some value in sending their children (especially girls) to colonial schools were still worried about its alienating effects. And some, like Muhashamy-Said's father, had to devise domestic strategies to limit the Euro-Christian impact of the school:

My father was liberal, but still he had his own attitude. I am really lucky, I always thank him and pray for him that he took me to school. So he suggested that I become a teacher; and I said, "All right." So I joined a teacher training here in Mombasa, Coast Teachers Training [College]. I became a P1 [primary 1] teacher; in fact it was a mixed school. But when I had to take Christian Scripture in form 4 [the last year of secondary school], he was very concerned. He said, "OK! If you are not going to be converted, you are just taking it as a subject, [then] all right!!" But at the same time when I took the Scripture he came and asked me, "How many times in a week do you have Scripture?" And I told him. So he marked the days I took Scripture. The day I have Scripture he made time to sit with me, asked me what I learnt in the Scripture, and then he would refer me to Yusuf Ali's translation of the Qur'an. He would say, "Let us open this chapter and see what Islam tells us on this issue." So I learnt my Islam with my [Christian] Scriptures. Every time I read [Christian] Scripture in school, I read the Qur'an with my father. He would sit with me and discuss with me what our culture is saying, what is our gain? This is how I finished my school there.

Important here is the active agency of Muhashamy-Said's father as an intercultural mediator between Islam and Christianity and as her supporter against the objection of the Muslim community. In an attempt to ground his daughter in both Islamic values and the "modern" secular world of knowledge, he employed a dialogic method of processing the Christian Bible through Islamic lenses. The ultimate aim of this conversation facilitated by her father was primarily to define how this new knowledge was useful to shaping a modern educated Muslim girl. Going against the grain of the Muslim community of his time, Muhashamy-Said's father was able to dispel the fears of his community.

It did not seem to matter that the then leading and influential East African Muslim scholar Sheikh Al-Amin bin Ali Mazrui had come out in support of sending Muslim girls to secular colonial schools.[4] Of course, Sheikh Al-Amin himself had a limited vision of the value of such an education for Muslim girls. At best it would provide them with skills—some literacy and home economics—to enhance their domestic roles as wives and mothers. In a sense, then, Sheikh Al-Amin's position was in perfect harmony with the British Victorian agenda. Rather than following the statements of their clergy, however, many Muslims followed their own instincts as to what the results would be of the kind of education introduced by colonialism: "Up to now there are people who fear education for girls, and the other reason they fear is because education came with the missionaries, with their cross. The aim was to convert people. And they won. Some of us became Christians. And I have observed also that all of us who have gone to secular schools, our thinking is Western thinking; however religious you are, you pray five times [in a day], your way of thinking is not Islamic thinking. So there is a reason why our people fear secular education." For Muhashamy-Said, then, different epistemologies engender different worldviews. Being a Muslim by fulfilling ritual obligations does not amount to thinking Islamically. She provides a philosophical articulation of the fears of her community with regard to the culturally alienating dimension of (post)colonial education. This concern is not unique to Muslims but expressed throughout colonized worlds.

Muhashamy-Said was among a handful of coastal Muslim girls to attend secondary school in the immediate aftermath of World War II. As a pioneering Muslim woman student, she had to overcome several cultural barriers. Pursuing her training as a young Muslim woman coming of age in a society in a period of transition between colonialism and national liberation, she found herself having to negotiate between her yearning for a modern education and a career and the expectation of her society that as a woman, she was a custodian of tradition and identity.

Muhashamy-Said comes from a very prominent family in coastal Kenya. Her father, Sheikh Salim Muhashamy, served as a *liwali* (governor) in districts like Mombasa and Malindi for several years before becoming *liwali* of the coast, the paramount colonial officer of the region of Kenya that was still nominally under the suzerainty of the sultan of Zanzibar. Under his leadership the British colonial government's indirect rule over the area was legitimized. For a brief period he also served, on a temporary basis, as one of the coast representatives in the colonial legislative council. Muhashamy-Said's aunt, Bi Shamsa Muhamad Muhashamy, popularly known as Mwana Kutani, was a formidable leader and political mobilizer whose record included the *leso* revolt (Mirza and Strobel 1989, 91–116). Along with her mother, Muhashamy-Said's father and aunt had a lasting influence in her life, preparing her to seize the moment when her leadership becomes necessary.

Soon after Muhashamy-Said was born, a certain Bi Fatma came to see her mother, Ma Shifu, bringing with her a little *furushi*—some clothes tied into a bundle with a *kanga*. At that time, this was a declaration of intention that Bi Fatma would like her son, Mohamed, to be the husband of the newly born once she reached a marriageable age. As fate would have it, Mohamed Jirafu—from the English "giraffe," due to his impressive height—officially became engaged to her soon after she completed high school and ended up marrying her while she was in the second year of her teacher training certificate course at the Coast Teacher Training College, on the condition that she would be able to continue with her studies. She was then nineteen. A prominent news anchor for the Swahili service of what was then the Voice of Kenya, Mohamed Jirafu was a liberal-minded, forward-looking man who supported Muhashamy-Said's academic and professional ambitions.

Muhashamy-Said then became pregnant while still in college. This development disoriented her a great deal. For a while, she was even a little upset with her husband: "And when I got pregnant, I told my husband, 'You did not want me to have a career. Now I am going to be a housewife and bring babies for you?'" Even though her husband insisted that she could still continue with her studies while pregnant, this option appeared inconceivable to Muhashamy-Said. After all, she came from a community that even today prefers to keep pregnancies a secret until there is no way of hiding them. Pregnancies conjure up facts of sex and sexuality, which Muslims prefer not to dwell on, though they are part of a very natural and expected act of union between husband and wife in the privacy of their bedroom. Familiar with her community's traditions and mindset, then, Muhashamy-Said was too embarrassed to go back to college. "I feel ashamed to go to training with a womb coming up and all that. I don't want to go through that," she complained to her husband.

Unable to persuade her to continue with her studies, her husband solicited the support of the principal of the college, a certain Mr. Bradley, who convinced Muhashamy-Said to be proud of her pregnancy and not ashamed of it. He assured her that her fellow students would be very understanding and supportive of her in her condition. He refused to accept her withdrawal from the college and tried to inspire her with a story from his own country of Britain. In her recollection of Bradley's words: "You see, there was a lady in Britain who trained as a teacher. But she did not start teaching because she did not need teaching. Her husband was well off and she started getting children. And then suddenly her husband died and she had to find work. And this certificate became very useful. It is the same with you, Swafiya. You don't have to work. But you take the certificate. Remember, in Mombasa here, there isn't a single [Swahili] girl who has reached this stage."

Bradley also reminded Muhashamy-Said that her husband too had wanted to train as a teacher. But because of cultural sensitivities about engaged couples studying or working at the same institution, he decided to pursue a different career altogether. With Bradley's advice and the support of her husband, she finally decided to continue with her training, which she completed in 1958. With Bradley's intervention, Muhashamy-Said was received extremely well by her fellow students, who displayed a degree of understanding and support that she had not expected.

Soon after completing the teacher training certificate course, Muhashamy-Said joined her husband in Britain, hoping that she would get an opportunity to pursue further studies in education. Her husband had gone there for advanced training in broadcasting. Because she took one of the children with her, however, she didn't have enough spare time to enroll in a degree program in Britain. Some years later, her husband won the Eisenhower Fellowship and went to study in the United States. Though she was primarily a house-wife during these periods, she had the opportunity to travel widely both in Europe and the United States. This experience was very enriching for her, opening up her mind to new possibilities and new ways of doing things.

In his narrative of the woman in Britain who trained as a teacher but married to a man of means, Bradley was almost prophetic. Not long after they returned from the United States, Mohamed died in a tragic car accident on the Mombasa-Nairobi Road. The housewife now had to put her certificate to use and begin to pursue a career in teaching. This is a profession she stayed with and enjoyed until her retirement.

In this self-portrait, we see a modern love story emerging out of a very traditional institution of arranged marriage and child betrothal. That bond of love provided space for the remaking of the cultural value attached to each gender, thereby permitting a Muslim girl to evolve into an educated cosmopolitan woman leader. We also see that those who came to the "rescue" of Muhashamy-Said then were not only people from her own community—her husband and fellow Kenyan students—but also, and more important, the representative of colonial educational administration, Mr. Bradley. In this regard, it is possible that Mr. Bradley was just a very good human being bent on fulfilling his responsibility as an educator-mentor to the best of his ability. On the other hand, his position, reflected in his encouragement and support of Muhashamy-Said, might also have been the expression of the more general reorientation of British colonial education in the aftermath of World War II and even more so with the rising tide of African nationalism. The British colonial government, like the French colonial government, was now under pressure to produce a class of educated elite who would take over the bureaucratic and managerial functions of the country once they departed (Eshiwani 1993, 25). Muhashamy-Said may thus have been among the first Kenyan women—and certainly Muslim women—beneficiaries of this new colonial educational policy.

In spite of the problematics of colonial education and its continuing legacy in the postcolonial period, however, it was educational developments in independent Kenya that played the more critical role in Muhashamy-Said's decision to initiate an alternative educational paradigm. And it is to this postcolonial background that we now turn.

POSTCOLONIAL DEVELOPMENTS: MUSLIM EDUCATION

Like most African countries, the newly independent Kenyan state saw formal mass education as a fundamental pillar of development. To disengage from the discriminatory approach to colonial education, the new Kenyan government endorsed a politics of compulsory mass education for all children starting at age seven, regardless of gender and ethnicity. Owing to the success of this postindependence colonial policy, Kenya is one of the African countries with a high literacy rate, estimated at about 83 percent of the population (UN Human Development Report 2004). Yet, in spite of these figures, Kenya is also one of the places in Africa where the problem of Muslim children's education is most acute (Chege and Sifuna 2006; Ngome 2006; and others).

In the early days of independence, under the banner of de-ethnicitizing government schools and rendering them multicultural, multiethnic, and secular, the few predominantly Muslim schools of the Arab-Swahili became de-Islamized—in population and in curriculum—terminating the teaching of Islam and the Arabic language. Schooling in this period became the site of struggle for resolving the nation's historical contradictions vis-à-vis race, ethnicity, and religion. Toward the end of colonialism, settler nations like Kenya sought to deconstruct the racial pyramid of privilege erected by various colonial powers and confronted a struggle between uniracialism and multiculturalism in nation building (JanMohammed 1976, 195; Strobel 1979, 208–9). The Kenyan coastal communities had to resolve the issue of Arab hegemony even among Muslims (Oded 2000, 123). Islam and Muslimness became almost indistinguishable from Arabism and Arab historical hegemony, especially in the minds of a great majority of non-Muslim coastal Kenyans. This frame of reference resulted in the adoption of "Africanization" policies that in turn led to the disenfranchisement of Muslims educationally. Africanization amounted to African "secular Christianity," a worldview that continues to associate cultural Westernization with the project of modernity. Consequently, because the British ruled indirectly through the sultan of Zanzibar, Kenyan coastal Muslims felt more accommodated educationally by the colonial government than by postcolonial Kenyan leaders. It is even arguable that the postcolonial schools on the coast became more alienating for Muslims than the colonial schools had been.

In the Northeastern Province of the country, the independence era brought new trouble for its Muslim natives who were predominantly Somali. The rise of irredentism in Somalia and the quest by Kenyan Somali to be reunited with their kin in Somalia led to a prolonged confrontation between the Kenyan state and the Somali natives of Kenya in what was then called the Northern Frontier District. Since that period, the Somalis of Kenya have come to be regarded as third-class citizens at best, and their region has been completely marginalized in terms of the developmental projects of any kind. To this day, the rate of schooling of the population of the northeastern region remains the lowest in Kenya (Chege and Sifuna 2006; Ngome 2006).

The popular Muslim belief was that the increasing alienation that Muslim children were experiencing in the postcolonial schools explained their declining academic performance even in such subjects as the Kiswahili language, which is the native tongue to most. As a result, Muslim parents and children increasingly disengaged from the postcolonial schools. It is within the context of this history of education that we must understand the formation of Muhashamy-Said as a pioneer of a new, decolonized, modern educational paradigm that sought to address the schooling needs of Muslim children.

THE NEW VISION:
MODERN INTEGRATED MADRASA NURSERY CURRICULUM

The early stages of Islamic education that in the past had been carried out at the Qur'anic school, most commonly referred to as *chuo* in Kiswahili, introduce the child to practices central to the process of shaping the Muslim child's identity: the verbal artistry of Qur'anic recitation and memorization, reading of the Arabic alphabet, and the ritual of *salat* (prayers). Most Kenya Muslim children, like Muslim children in Muslim societies throughout the world, undergo this faith-based early childhood schooling before entering secular primary schools in both rural and urban centers.

By the 1970s, this *chuo* tradition rooted in Islam gradually began to lose students as the newly introduced private secular nursery schools started to spread nationally, especially in urban centers. The new nursery school posed a challenge to the Muslim children's education on a number of grounds. First, it further reduced, if not eliminated, the little room left to Muslim parents to instill the early seeds of their faith-based identity, since its curriculum was molded by a secular vision. Because Kenyans of South Asian communities of both Muslim and non-Muslim faith controlled their own educational institutions, they were less concerned about cultural alienation than the Muslims of Arab or African descent. Secondly, because its aim was to provide a curricular head start to primary education, it gave an unfair advantage to children of parents who could afford the fees. Finally, in the postcolonial period

English began to be introduced earlier and earlier in the educational structure, as early as the nursery level in many urban private schools. Children of
the better-to-do families ended up better prepared not only academically
but also in terms of English linguistic skills, giving them better opportunities
in the competitive primary schools. Here again, the effect of English-based
instruction at such an early stage resulted in a degree of cultural alienation
from the child's own society and milieu. From the very formative stages of their
lives, the epistemological world of these children was being reconstructed
through a language that distanced them from their cultural and religious
universe.

Aware of the ways that educational institutions (re)produce socioeconomic
classes and of how educational structures were being used to achieve hegemonic goals, Muhashamy-Said began to explore creative approaches to coun-
tering the alienating threats to Islamic identity posed by the newly embraced
secular nursery schools as well as the class disparities it was producing. As
she puts it:

> When I saw that the girls we teach in our Muslim Women's Institute do not
> know the Qur'an, I told my fellow women that there is a big problem here, and
> we must all be concerned about this since our children don't know our religion
> because they attend the nursery schools. . . . So they asked me, now what are we
> going to do? I said, now in Kenya, because people are all interested in sending
> children to [formal] school, the Qur'an has been pushed into the corner. When
> we went to school, we had to finish our Qur'an before we joined school. . . .
> But now, children are sent to nursery before even going to Qur'an [school].
> Madrasa will take children when they are six to seven years old. But we are
> sending children at three years to the nursery.[5]

Part of the blame, of course, can be laid squarely on the teaching approach
in the *vyuo*, as many of the teachers there rely more on the "stick" than on the
" carrot." Muslim parents themselves now prefer the pleasant environment
of the nursery school to the disciplinarian environment of the *vyuo*:

> The *mu'alims* in the madrasas are using the stick to teach. So no parents will
> send their children of three or four years old to the madrasa. But in nursery
> schools they are very happy children. They are playing; it is secular learning.
> Thus, most parents are sending their children to the secular system till they
> start primary 1; then they go to the madrasa in the afternoons. . . . And because

the learning system or the teaching system in the Qur'an is not systematic, they do not acquire the reading skills in those three years when they are very young.

These observations led Muhashamy-Said to the conclusion that under the new circumstances, the only way the community could fully reclaim the *vyuo* tradition was to change both the content focus and the instructional approach of the institution:

> So I explained this [problem] to my ladies and let them understand that here in our institution, our club, we must start nursery schools that will teach both [the Qur'an and secular subjects]. We can prepare children to be ready for secular [education] and at the same time to be ready for Qur'an [school]. Then the women started to complain, "Oh Swafiya, we have our hands full already. Who is going to do that?" But in my mind I kept saying, I am going to start a madrasa that is going to prepare children for Qur'an and secular content.

It is within this context that, although not an expert of early childhood education, Muhashamy-Said pioneered an Islamically inspired secular nursery curriculum that integrates an Islamic perspective. This is an innovative approach, now widely known in East Africa as the integrated Islamic nursery school curriculum, and it aims not to teach Islam as one of the subjects but to use Islam as a framework of understanding whatever subject matter is being taught, be it in the social sciences, the sciences, or humanities.

By the early 1980s, Muhashamy-Said had retired from her teaching career as a primary educationist and had taken over the responsibility of looking after her toddler grandson in the afternoons after he returned from the nursery school. This extended contact with her grandson gave her an additional opportunity to reflect on the impact of the nursery school on Muslim children. It also gave her access to the curriculum content of the nursery school, which she later transformed using an Islamic framework:

> When I got my grandson, and when he started school, I began [to take care of him] because I had retired and I was teaching a half day. So what I did is that I started preparing Islamic songs. For instance, the same songs that they learn in the nursery, I changed the wording, not the tune. I give you an example: There is a song well known all over the world, which says:

> Twinkle, twinkle little star

Bi Swafiya Muhashamy-Said showing math posters and a demonstration kit

So what I did, I said:

You are a shining little star
Who has made you as you are
Allah Almighty *subhana-l* Allah
Twinkle, twinkle Masha Allah

So you see, this is what I had started with. So I had my grandchild. I started composing nursery rhymes, and at the same time, in the afternoon, I sat with the boy and started teaching him "alif" [is for] "Allah." I started making simple words and associating the alphabet letters with an Islamic word or event or I started telling stories with Islamic roots. So I started this initiative with my grandson. I said when I get some cash, I will start and open a small school madrasa with my new approach. But this was not possible without the means.

Henceforth Muhashamy-Said appropriated a number of nursery songs and Islamized them and sometimes even Swahilized them. There is a nursery rhyme, for example, that begins with the words "two little birds sitting on a wall, one named Peter, one named Paul." Peter and Paul are central figures in the early history of Christianity. In Muhashamy-Said's version, in addition to other changes, these names—Peter and Paul—were changed to Ali and Hassan, two influential figures in the early history of Islam:

Secular nursery rhyme	Islamic nursery rhyme, from Bi Swafiya Muhashamy-Said
"Two Little Dicky Birds"	"Two Little Dicky Birds"
("Fly Away, Peter, Fly Away, Paul")	("Fly Away, Hassan, Fly Away, Ali")
Two little dicky birds sitting on a wall,	Two little dickie birds resting on a tree,
One named Peter, one named Paul.	One named Hassan, the other one Ali
Fly away, Peter, fly away, Paul,	Fly away, Hassan, fly away, Ali,
Come back, Peter, come back, Paul!	Come back, Hassan, come back, Ali

Another example of Muhashamy-Said's creative attempts to "Islamicize" nursery school rhymes is "One, Two, Buckle My Shoe," often used in early counting activities:

"One, Two, Buckle My Shoe"	"Number Du'a"
One, two, buckle my shoe	One, two—may I be true
Three, four, shut the door	Three, four—wherever I go
Five, six, pick up sticks	Five, six—*Ya Qudus* [O! Jerusalem]
Seven, eight, lay them straight	Seven, eight—guide me straight
Nine, ten, a big fat hen	Nine, ten—*Allahuma Amin, Allahuma Amin* [O God, the trustworthy]
Eleven, twelve, dig and delve	Eleven, twelve—*Ya Latwif* [O! Sensitive one]
Thirteen, fourteen, maids a'courting	Thirteen, fourteen—*I am Mu-Umin* [I am a believer]
Fifteen, sixteen, maids in the kitchen	Fifteen, sixteen—take me in
Seventeen, eighteen, maids a'waiting	Seventeen, eighteen—*Janatu Naim* [Exalted Paradise]

"The Humpty Dumpty" song is again appropriated and re-presented as a Swahili riddle (Aga Khan Foundation 2008, 47).

"Hammadi Maridadi"	"Hamadi the Smart-Looking"
Hamadi maridadi kapanda ukutani	Hamadi the smart-looking climbed on the wall
Hamadi maridadi kaketi ukutani	Hamadi the smart-looking sat on the wall
Hamadi maridadi ka-anguka chini	Hamadi the smart-looking fell from the wall
Masikini masikini hamadi yuchini	Poor, poor Hamadi is on the ground
Watu wote majumbani	All the people from the homes
Watu wote mtaani	All the people of the neighborhood
Watu wote mjini	All the people of the town
Hawakuweza kumkusanya Hamadi maridadi masikini.	Could not reconstitute poor Hamadi the well dressed.
Ni Nani Hamadi?	Who is Hamadi?
Yai.	Egg.

Appropriating the British-inherited texts used in the Kenyan national curriculum was crucial for exposing Muslim children to the material that shapes the scholastic development of their non-Muslim Kenyan contemporaries.

However, in addition to appropriating texts and activities from the British-inherited secular nursery school curriculum, Muhashamy-Said drew extensively from local lore and wisdom in the crafting of her own integrated curriculum. Moreover, her curriculum also introduced the students to other subjects, including mathematics, environmental studies, health education, and even the more controversial subject of sex education (attempts to introduce sex education in Kenyan schools failed because of the opposition of the clergy; see chapter 3).

Since education is not a neutral process but rather serves an ideological aim with socioeconomic consequences, it follows that the implementation of any educational curriculum will require the right combination of institutional legitimacy and funding support. Very often, curriculum content and framework are provided by the powerful, for adoption by "the masses." But fortunately, Muhashamy-Said's grassroots vision and approach coincided with the Aga Khan Foundation's mission of making early childhood education accessible and affordable to Muslims. However, because of the intra-Muslim denominational divide, Muhashamy-Said, as a Muslim belonging to the Sunni majority community in Kenya, was careful to crosscheck the implications of accepting funding from the Aga Khan Foundation, as a Shi'a Isma'ili organization. She was concerned not only about the religious implications of receiving funding from the Aga Khan Foundation but also about whether there would be pressure on her to convert to Shi'ism at a time of growing Iranian Shi'a activism in the region (Oded 2000, 68). After consultation with her community members, she agreed to accept the offer.

With the offer, I consulted the womenfolk with whom we do the *da'wa* [preaching of Islam]. My female *da'wa* colleagues warned me against taking the offer, fearing that they will force me to embrace their Shi'a ideas and make me do this and that. When I consulted my mother, she told me that this is a great opportunity . . . in order to implement what I had long envisioned to do. I moved on and consulted another principal of Sheikh Khalifa School, [Muhammad] Sabir. He was a colleague I was working with. He was working with the boys school and I was dealing with the girls school. He said, "Well, Swafiya, I think you'd better take it because it will get into the wrong hands and you will be answerable because the offer went to you. But I have known you throughout

Reading English books and a math book with Arabic numbers

these years, nobody can change you. And if anything goes wrong you are able to stop it." So he gave me the courage. Then I went back and took the offer.

The Aga Khan Foundation was particularly keen to see that the project would cater specifically to the poor. This objective could not have found a better advocate than Muhashamy-Said. In consultation with her, the Aga Khan Foundation established an executive board to which Muhashamy-Said was answerable. However, she was given a free hand in designing a curriculum. In addition to enlightening herself about early childhood education, for which her training in elementary education did not prepare her, Muhashamy-Said had to begin putting together the infrastructure for the project. And so her integrated madrasa project finally came to full fruition in 1986 with a small grant from the Aga Khan Foundation to her as the newly appointed director charged with the responsibility of designing a curriculum.

It is noteworthy, of course, that Muhashamy-Said's initiative received initial funding from the Aga Khan Foundation, a body linked to the Isma'ili community. Isma'ilis, and especially Ismai'ili women, have long played an important role in educational investment and development. The Aga Khan Nursery School (founded in 1939) as well as the Aga Khan Academy, established in August 2003, have been successful models of early childhood education, all under the leadership of Isma'ili women. Through the Aga Khan Foundation, then, the important educational legacy of Isma'ili women was transmitted to the school communities.

The Aga Khan offer was to start madrasa schools for the very poor people who cannot afford the nursery school. When I asked them who is going to give me a curriculum for this, I was told, "One of your tasks is to conceive the curriculum." So Allah is with me *Alhamdulillah*! So I got to implement my curriculum initiative. Of course, I received their support and worked with a board to which I was answerable. I was to report every month. I started from nothing and I had not been trained in early childhood education. I was trained as a primary school educator. So I started learning. And since my grandson was in nursery school in the morning, I was getting all the songs from him and in the process, like I told you, I started changing many of the songs into Islamic. The board was very supportive. We started the first school in October 1986. My duties were to train the teachers, establish the school, and form a committee. Since the Aga Khan Foundation was not going to pay the teachers, it was the community that was supposed to pay. It is a community school. So I was to mobilize the community around the madrasa and form a committee to run the school.

Her commitment to bringing an Islamic perspective to early childhood education as well as her determination to modernize the traditional approach to teaching Islam to young Muslims led Muhashamy-Said, at age sixty, to embark on the path of further education in this new field, first through self-instruction. She studied the national authoritative documents issued by the Kenya Institute of Education in order to better shape her own innovative integrated methodology. In particular, she was able to secure a copy of the government-sponsored syllabus for Islamic religious education for grade 1 students and use it in devising her curriculum. As a matter of strategy, she also involved some of the more prominent *walimu* (teachers) from the *chuo* to participate in the preparation of the religious section of the curriculum:

> Since I was told that I was to develop the curriculum, I suggested to my [consulting] board that we should invite *mu'alims* and sell the idea to them, give each person in the group a topic like, for example, asking him about how to design the tawhid curricular content for nursery. What should nursery level pupils know? Another person is assigned a topic on *akhlaq* [Islamic character], another is assigned the article of faith or the Qur'an to three- to four-year-old kids. Of course, the *mu'alims* were very pleased that we included them in this initiative. So within the committee, we had one school advisor who was advisor to the secular school. Mr. Omar Basharahil brought the national Islamic curriculum. So we took the content of standard 1 [of the elementary school] and moved it to the level suitable to nursery pupils. So that it connects with the rest. Actually, they gave me purely the hadith, the *akhlaq* in the hadith, what hadith should these little children be taught, which sign rituals should the nursery children learn. Then I sat and started reviewing and reforming the curriculum and brought the developed material to the board, and three members of the board examined what was given to us, and the three of us should come up with what content that three- to six-year-olds should learn.[6]

Muhashamy-Said's methodology consists of bringing an Islamic perspective to everyday life activities taught in the secular curriculum while also respecting the functional distribution between Qur'anic language, the child's mother tongue, and English in the process. As she notes, because she had control over her own curriculum, she was able to develop a sex education component. And by introducing the subject from an Islamic perspective, she was able to neutralize objections from her own community. In the process, by constructing a curriculum in all these subjects, she developed a trilingual education program based on Swahili, Qur'anic Arabic, and English. Swahili provided the foundation for local identity, Arabic opened the door to Islamic learning and contributed to the consolidation of an Islamic identity, and English was the key to the material world of professional success and trans-ethnic national integration. At the initial stages, however, Muhashamy-Said's project involved a two-tiered educational arrangement. She recruited young women from marginalized Muslim communities who had dropped out of school prematurely and provided them with training in content pedagogy and English-language skills. For the young women, their participation in this innovative project was also a source of income and professional development. This cadre of trainees was then mobilized to implement the Islamic-oriented trilingual program in early childhood education:

> We had targeted at least secondary school graduates as teachers. But it was very difficult to recruit from the secondary level, because most young people don't want to become teachers. So I had to be satisfied with [graduates of] primary school education and very few failures of secondary schools. So the caliber of the teachers was very low and [the level of education] varied. So we had to adjust our teacher training accordingly and use Kiswahili and English to train. I used to give them English classes whenever I had time. So I wanted them also to acquire some literacy in English. In the third year English is intro-duced. . . . We had planned that the first year the child comes to school, we use Kiswahili. . . . *Qir'a* [reading] operates like we are teaching the alphabet. We teach the alphabet in Arabic. Like: *alif, ba, ta*. But we don't teach them letters. You take a picture, with the name of Allah, *alif*, ainabu, *be*, batatun, *te*, tetajun. So Arabic words [are introduced] like that in a song form, in a picture with a story, with a few Arabic words as you are telling the story. . . . The Qur'anic alphabet will be in Arabic. The words will be in English. Like all English words will be all in English, Kiswahili words all in Kiswahili. And Arabic words all in Arabic. So we are working with three languages.

Muhashamy-Said's educational approach has earned the appreciation of many Muslim parents, who feel that what their children are getting is of direct rel-evance to their own lives:

In fact, the feedback I got when I established the third school, from the parents and many people, is that some are saying, "We are learning Islam from our children." When it is snack time, besides saying "Bissmillahi," there is a *du'a* [invocations used in Muslim rituals], we teach them the *du'a*. So they go home and they tell their parents, "Don't eat, we have the *du'a* to say." So the parents also come to me and say, "We are also learning along with our children," and that gave me a lot of enthusiasm and support.

In my earlier work on Niger Republic, I discuss new women-run madrasa initiatives in which mothers and daughters sometimes come together to share the experience of learning together. Azara Mudira's *ma'had* (chapter 3) too developed a parallel program that made it possible for mothers and daughters to be students together. Even when mothers do not attend the new schools, however, as in the case of Muhashamy-Said's initiative, they become a part of their children's learning experience in one way or another, fully appreciating the knowledge that their children are acquiring.

This experience provided an opportunity for Muhashamy-Said to return to school to obtain a university degree in her sixties, which is very unusual for African women regardless of their religious background: "As far as my own academic qualifications, I remained a P1 teacher until I joined this organization [Aga Khan Foundation]. Then, I did my two degrees, BA and MA in education, in my sixties. I did that with other colleagues through the Ezeta University in Britain. But I did it very late when I was old, and I am still studying . . . [laughs]. I am one who believes learning never ceases from the cradle to the grave." Her academic advancement in the secular field came to complement her pursuit of Islamic learning and Arabic language skills. She was now standing with one foot solidly in Islamic knowledge and the other in secular education:

So before this BA and MA training, I was involved with the mosque doing my religious training with a woman teacher, a graduate of Al Azhar University. She was teaching us how to do *da'wa*. She taught us many things in religion. She lived in Egypt and she was a lecturer there. Her name was Su'ad. She was originally from Zanzibar. She took a group of ten of us and said that we must learn Arabic, otherwise we would not understand the religion. So she gave us lessons in Arabic. We went through the *nahau* [grammar]. And of course, we did a lot of Qur'anic translation. She gave us the skills, so [we] were preaching at the mosque. Up to now it is going on, every Thursday the ladies meet and one of us presents a lecture.

Although the desire to instill Islamic teaching along with secular knowledge in the preschool years was the inspiration for Muhashamy-Said's new integrated curriculum, her creative methodology became an inspiration for both her secularist as well as Christian educationist colleagues: "In fact, the people from Kenya Institute of Education, we caught them by surprise because they are the people who developed the [Islamic] curriculum. So when they came to our school, they were so impressed in the sense that we are rewriting education in totality. It means we are developing the children mentally, physically, socially, emotionally, and spiritually, which none of the schools do." Programs like these thus offer the same opportunity to the Muslim child to develop that a Christian child receives: "KIE, after they came to visit us and saw the day in madrasa, they started inviting Christians to tell them what is happening. We had a consultation meeting in Nairobi and they invited me in order to know what we are doing. And the sister there came out to compliment us and told us, 'We have not been able to do what you are doing.' Although they are teaching in the church, that method of interrelating everything is not there. They teach religion as a subject. They have not integrated [it] in the whole system." Through her modernist vision, Muhashamy-Said thus opened up a space for a constructive interfaith dialogue on holistic ways of injecting a religious perspective into a secular curriculum in both a modern and nonhegemonic manner.

In spite of her pioneering role at making the secular nursery curriculum culturally relevant for Muslim children, Muhashamy-Said still had to deal with the sensibilities and vested interests of the teachers in the traditional Qur'anic schools, who are predominantly male. If secular education has opened its door to women's leadership, especially in early childhood education, traditional Islamic schools, which are still controlled by the male *mu'alims*, have not. Because her goal is primarily to make the Muslim educational environment respond to the demands of a competitive modern world while resisting cultural alienation, Muhashamy-Said was ready to adopt a stay-behind-the-scenes strategy if that would help transmit the new idea to conservative teachers and its testing in the communities. Muhashamy-Said took a diplomatic approach with respect to *mu'alims* she met when the members of the board at the madrasa resource center invited them to come see her school:

Yes, I was very sensitive and I took care of that. . . . That is, I was in the background. In the meetings, I did not appear because I knew if this has to work, I have to go by the Islamic cultural way as they understand it. Every time I had the meeting with the people, I was behind. Until the *mu'alims* themselves accepted me, and they themselves say, "Please, Mama, we want to see you. You are just like our Mama" . . . [*laughs*] . . . You see . . . [*laughs*].

There is a sense in which the vision of an integrated curriculum was inspired partly by her own understanding of the educational requirements that Islam imposes on its believers.

So in my mobilization, I tell the people around, especially the women, to be aware of the strategy for success. These will be women and men. Then, I will quote the prophet (PBH) Salallah Alayhi Wassalam, who says, "Seek knowledge, even in China." You see, if it is religious knowledge, he had it in Medina. But he said, "Seek knowledge in China!" China!! It is this other *ilimu* [knowledge] which is preferred. This *fard'ain* is with him, but *fard kifayah*, you have to seek to be a doctor, to be a nurse, to be all these things. So the Prophet Muhammad had no margin in between the *ilm*. *Ilm* was holistic for him.

In Islam, *fard'ain* refers to what is obligatory to individual Muslims (like observing the five pillars of Islam). *Fard kifayah*, on the other hand, is what is obligatory in every Muslim community—like ensuring that there are enough doctors, teachers, and engineers to meet the developmental needs of the society. By foregrounding this distinction between the two types of Islamic obligations, Muhashamy-Said is emphasizing once again that the acquisition of secular knowledge from the vantage point of Islam—the concept around which her nursery curriculum and approach are designed—is itself an act of Islamic faith. In fact, she sees Islam as a faith that shatters the boundary between the religious and the secular, giving further credence to her integrated Islamic-secular approach.

After about twenty years of her leadership, the madrasa resource center project had grown into a vibrant educational program, spreading throughout East Africa and bringing over two hundred schools under its direct supervision. In the words of it sponsors, "From the seed that was planted here in the Coastal Region some 25 years ago—when Bi Swafiya Said received her grant from the Aga Khan Foundation—the East African Madrasa Programme has grown to include 203 preschools, with nearly 800 teachers,

reaching some 30,000 households and serving more than 54,000 children"
(Aga Khan Foundation 2008, 4).

Conclusion

I started this chapter with the observation that modernity has often been a
catalyst for secularity. This has been true as much in national governance as
in educational socialization. Many educational institutions in the West, in
fact, started as church-based religious academies and later shifted to secular
paradigms under the impetus of the momentum for modernization.

In the Islamic world, on the other hand, modernity is still caught up in a
contestation between religiosity and secularity. This tension is, of course,
rooted in the history of European conquest and colonialism of the Muslim
world. Muslim educational institutions seeking to modernize have often had
to respond to this challenge precipitated by its encounter with the European
other. Al Azhar University in Cairo, a leading Islamic institution, responded
by introducing an almost independent secular leg in its curriculum, transforming it from a one-tier institution that was wholly Islamic into a two-tier
institution that is part Islamic and part secular. During my fieldwork in
Kenya in winter 2005 and spring/summer 2006, I found out that there is a
growing number of Islamicist schools that have adopted the Al Azhar model
to one degree or another, teaching secular subjects and religious subjects as
independent units.

Muhashamy-Said's contribution is the integration of the secular and the
religious into a unified curriculum. This is unique in East African Islamic
experience. Of course, her experiment started where it should have started,
at the nursery stage of socialization. The challenge that confronts this model
now is whether it can be extended to the upper levels of the educational structures. Will her creative curriculum synthesis now be appropriated for the
benefit of Muslim children in more advanced educational stages?

Equally significant, however, is Muhashamy-Said's own personal accomplishment. Hers is a social biography that provides an understanding of the
challenges and the hurdles confronting Muslim women born during colonialism at the onset of a major struggle between an indigenous worldview and a
domineering alien one. It is a story of reshaping Islamic education, of protecting Muslim communities and local institutions against the hegemonic
legacy of colonialism as well as local traditionalism. And by incorporating
the poor both as teachers and as students and making their parents participate in her educational design, Muhashamy-Said manages to challenge class

boundaries rooted in local socioeconomic inequalities and exacerbated by colonial and postcolonial structures. In the final analysis, then, Muhashamy-Said is that personal embodiment of the very curriculum to which she gave birth. Like her curriculum, she is the convergence of the old and the new and of Afro-Islam and secular modernity.

2

The *Ma'had* Tradition of
Mwalim Azara Mudira

Creating a Woman's Space for Islamic
Education in Kenya

We tell them our needs as women to know our *din* [religion] because
that is when the men also will understand our *din*. We are the
mothers, we are the daughters. We are the very important backbones
of the society. And with your education, you can have your *din*.

—Mwalim Azara Mudira

INTRODUCTION

This chapter looks at the pioneering work of Mwalim Azara Mudira, who
set a precedent by opening a modern boarding school for advanced Islamic
theological training of young Muslim women in Pangani, Nairobi, in the face
of opposition from conservative Muslim *walimu* and the skepticism of many
members of the wider Kenya Muslim community. She named her institute
"ma'had." Its mission is twofold: to challenge the exclusionary male-centered
tradition of advanced education in Islamic studies and to create an alternative space for authoritative intervention by Muslim women Islamic scholars
in the religious realm.

In his book titled *The Ulama in Contemporary Islam: Custodians of Change*
(2002), Muhammad Qasim Zaman made an insightful observation regarding how the modernist revivalist Islamist movements throughout the Muslim world and beyond clearly demonstrate the hold of the ulama on modern
Muslims' private and public religio-political lives. Furthermore, Zaman points
out how very often studies on the ulama do not take into account the evolution of their thought and how they respond to the forces confronting Muslim societies. The "tradition" of the ulama in sub-Saharan Africa is similar to

that of those in South Asia and the Middle East, which are the main focus of Zaman's study, and the ulama continue to play a key role in Islamic societies amid the internal contestation of their authority, a contestation that has been exacerbated by democratization movements since the 1990s (Alidou 2005; Bakari 1995; Glover 2007; Kane 2003; LeBlanc and Soares 2008; Oded 2000).

In spite of their hold, however, postcolonial mass secular education, which opened its doors to women—including Muslim women—has led to the rise of educated Muslim women in secular as well as religious schools who are using the platform of (higher) education (Alidou 2005; Augis 2005; Badran 2011; Mack 2004; Masquelier 2009; Schulz 2012; Soares 2011; Umar 2004) and civic rights activism to seek the gendering of the space of authority in religious knowledge (Alidou 2005; Badran 2008a, 2011; Hill 2010; Manjoo 2011; Robinson 2009). These Muslim women religious reformist activists are seeking the inclusion of Muslim women graduates in Islamic theology in the ranks of ulama (Alidou 2005; Badran 2008a, 2011; Robinson 2009; Umar 2004). They draw their arguments from the historical legacy of earlier Muslim women religious leaders who had played major roles in educating Muslim women and even at times men (Abu-Zayd 2006; Arkoun 2006; Badran 2011; Berkey 1992, 145–51; Mernissi 1991a, 1991b; Nadwi 2007; Rhouni 2011; Shaheed and Shaheed 2004; Shaikh 2011), and from the modern demands of contemporary lives of Muslims. Mudira is yet another example of a Muslim woman activist shaped by the conjuncture of historical precedents and new demands of the present.

Muslim Women Educators: A Background

There have long been women educators in the various Muslim communities of Kenya. Invariably they would be married, widowed, or divorced women. Until recently, however, their instructional role was almost exclusively limited to the *chuo*, usually a space within the home used to train young boys and girls of premenstrual age to read and memorize the Muslim holy book, the Qur'an. For some of these women educators, the *chuo* also became a source of an independent income, as parents were expected to pay a minimal fee for the Qur'anic education of their children. This highly restricted space for Muslim women educators was a direct reflection of the extent to which Muslim women were denied the opportunities to pursue higher Islamic learning beyond the "necessary" basics. Like the children that some of them ended up teaching, they would learn to read the Qur'an and would memorize many of the shorter chapters often used in Muslim prayers as well as a variety of short Arabic *du'a*.

Leading early Muslim scholars in Kenya, like Shaykh Al Amin Bin Ali Mazrui (d. 1947) of Mombasa and Sayyid Ali Badawi (d. 1963) of Lamu, fell short of incorporating women in their authorial hierarchy.[1] The Mazrui Shafi'i reformists saw themselves as anti-*bid'a*. The literal meaning of *bid'a* is "innovation," referring to practices that were introduced into Islam above and beyond the *sunnah* (tradition) of the Prophet Muhammad himself and what he supported in his pronouncements. Of course, what constitutes *bid'a* is often a matter of contestation, many times boiling down to which religious authorities are considered credible and/or to the power struggle of religious leadership within a given society as characterized by the rivalry between the Mazrui anti-*bid'a* followers and the Shariif—a designation referring to Muslims who claim blood lineage with the Prophet Muhammad and who, as a result, are often revered by many members of their communities—and their followers. In their anti-*bid'a* campaign, the Mazrui male scholars made no effort to enhance opportunities for women to secure higher Islamic learning even as they emphasized the prophetic injunction that "the pursuit of knowledge is mandatory for all Muslims, male and female."

The Badawi Shariifs of Lamu, on the other hand, did produce women religious scholars, such as the contemporary Nafissa Khitami Badawi, within the ranks of their kith and kin (Noordin 2004). It is even ironic today that some Mazrui womenfolk from a long tradition of Mazrui Muslim male scholars have come to rely significantly on the Islamic teachings of Badawi. However, the knowledge of Islam that the women display is reflective of the patriarchal interpretation of the ulama who instructed them. Though, for example, Badawi has built a reputation as a female Islamic authority among Kenyan coastal Muslim women, especially in Old Town Mombasa, a close listening of her sermons reveals a strong internalization of patriarchal Islam. This clearly suggests that not all female acquired knowledge is emancipatory.

What Badawi has been doing—offering instruction to other women in a quasi-formal setting at home or a neutral space outside the home, like the Mombasa-based Muslim Women's Institute—is part of a more recent and relatively limited practice. In places like Lamu, Mombasa, and Nairobi, there have emerged a few women committed to teaching other women about Islam above and beyond the Qur'an. Some even offer lessons in hadith, *fiqh*, tawhid, and *tafsir*. Some women offer instruction throughout the year; others hold sessions weekly; still others limit them to the month of Ramadhan. Yet it is

fair to say that neither the women educators nor their women students conceive of this process as one leading to the production of a professional cadre
of Muslim women teachers or scholars. For all intents and purposes, the
ultimate objective of most of these recent, women-to-women educational
initiatives is simply to give women the opportunity to learn more about their
religion than preexisting structures had allowed them to do.

It is the aim of training women to be Islamic scholars that makes Mudira's
ma'had project unique and pioneering in the tradition of Muslim women
educators in Kenya. Institutionally it is more formalized that any other Kenyan
Sunni Muslim woman "school" so far, with a clear, structured curriculum
pegged to specific learning goals. And graduates from the *ma'had* are expected to be ready to enter the professional world in the relevant areas that
require a deeper and more comprehensive knowledge of Islam to which women
in the past seldom had access.

THE MAKING OF MWALIM AZARA MUDIRA AND THE FOUNDING OF THE *MA'HAD*

The origin of Mudira's *ma'had* is directly related to her background. Her own
family is a product of the history of interracial marriages between Africans,
South Asians, and Arabs on the African side of the Indian Ocean. She meta-
phorically refers to her kinship as one "brought about by monsoon winds." Her
great-grandfather, himself already of mixed Arab-Indian parentage and seemingly connected to the Indian Ocean trade network, moved from India with
his Indian wife and settled in Lamu, Kenya. Like the majority of Lamu residents of Indian descent, his family quickly became Swahilized linguistically.

In Lamu, her great-grandfather married a local African woman, popularly
known as Maa, with Zanzibar heritage. In protest against her husband's polygamous union, the Indian wife left and returned to India, leaving her only
child, a son, to be brought up by her great-grandfather's African wife, who,
in time, had several children of her own. Once an adult, this son of maternal Indian descent decided to marry an Indian woman. These were Mudira's
grandparents. And in her words:

> My grandmother and my grandfather were called the first sellers of herbal
> medicine in the coast. They were called the Surat because they come from the
> area of Surat [in the Indian state of Gujarat]. . . . But we still have at the coast
> a lineage of our local African family, and we have a very close relation. I still
> call them my aunties and uncles. And whatever I need, I still go back to them.

So we have kept a close relation with that side of the African lady who gave birth [to many children]. They gave birth, and they intermarry with us, the Indians. They know us as family and we know them as family. We still meet and we are very, very close. *Alhamdudillah* [Thank God]!

One of the sons of these grandparents became Mudira's father and, though less certain about her maternal lineage, her recollection was that her mother too was a product of Indian and Arab (Yemeni) intermarriage.

This kinship history partly accounts for her multilingual competency in Kiswahili, Urdu, Arabic, and English, made possible by Kenya's and India's shared British colonial pasts. In her narrative we see also how she makes Islam mediate the remnants of racial and ethnic hierarchies and ethnic tensions emanating from the history of Arab-Islamic slavery and British colonialism in East Africa. Although referring to herself as Indian, she makes a distinction between her "Kenyan Indianness" that has been Swahilized and her husband's subcontinental Indianness, as a "real Indian" with Urdu mother-tongue competency, which she had to acquire in order to communicate with his extended family based in India.

Mudira grew up and studied in secular schools in Kenya, receiving an Islamic religious education as a secondary area of training outside the school structure. After high school she became increasingly interested in Islamic studies. This quest finally got her admitted into the Islamic University in Mbale, Uganda, and later into Umm al-Qura University in Makkah, Saudi Arabia. Umm al-Qura University is internationally known in the Muslim world for its rigorous two-year training program in the Arabic language catering especially to students from non-Arabic-speaking areas. The university also places great emphasis on education and the training of teachers of Islamic knowledge, though its overall curriculum is multidisciplinary.

It is not the content of the education she received at Umm al-Qura, nor the large population of Saudi students she met at the university, however, that triggered her interest in establishing the *ma'had*. Rather, the inspiration came from an Indonesian woman who was also studying at the university and with whom she developed a certain closeness. The Indonesian friend informed her of the Islamic reforms introduced by Indonesian Muslim women's ulama and the strategies they used to accomplish their reform mission. In Mudira's words:

The good thing is that, you know, in Saudia I got exposed. I really didn't get exposed to Saudis, I got exposed to foreigners who were coming there [to study].

And this idea [of the *ma'had*] was an Indonesian idea. There was a student from Indonesia and we used to talk a lot. And she told me that "we have these types of *ma'hads*, institutions of Islamic learning, and they teach a lot." And it struck me that that is exactly what we should have if I am here [in Kenya]. She really encouraged me that "if you don't want to give your services to an institution or an organization, then you have to come up with your own institution."

Mudira knew that in Kenya, at best she would be appointed as a high school teacher of Islamic studies. She now wanted to be of greater service both to her community and to the future of Islamic education in Kenya.

A close reading of Mudira's discussion of the mission of feminizing Islamic education in Kenya reveals characteristics that are, in fact, similar to the Indonesian Muhammadiyah 'Aisyiyah's mission to reshape Islam through education (van Doorn-Harder 2006, 87–164). 'Aisyiyah is the women's wing of the Indonesian reformist organization Muhammadiyyah, whose main activities are religious and educational. The Muhammadiyyah organization is known to have built many modern Islamic schools. When Mudira finally returned to Kenya after graduating from Umm al-Qura with a bachelor of arts degree in Islamic education at the age of twenty-seven, she had made up her mind to establish the *ma'had*.

Given that she had such a loving and tightly knit extended family, it was natural that relatives would rise to the occasion and give her the support she needed when she launched the *ma'had* in 1987. Most dedicated among these were her parents. And her Swahili ties continued to be an important source of "local legitimacy." Her parents left their home to stay with Mudira at the *ma'had*, her father serving as the office manager and her mother as the cook and matron for an initial group of thirty or so students. Her brother, a trained accountant, and his wife, a trained secretary, added their services in support of the project. Staying at the *ma'had* with her students was the only way she could gain the trust of their parents. By the time he died two years after the establishment of the *ma'had*, her father's deep faith that the future was in the hands of the younger generation had become an additional inspiration for Mudira. As the *ma'had* expanded, Mudira came under increasing pressure to get married; her mother articulated received cultural values in maintaining that an unmarried woman should not be managing an institution. She did eventually marry, and fortunately for her, her husband became an additional important partner in the *ma'had* project. With the moral support and blessing of her Lamu family, and the logistical support of her family and friends in Nairobi, then, the *ma'had* took off and became an institution of national pride among Muslims of Kenya.

Mudira also acknowledges that the moment, the mid-1980s, when she launched the *ma'had*, was of significance in the success of her venture. The Khomeini-led Islamic revolution of Iran in the 1980s that affected Muslim youth across Muslim societies even within strong Sunni strongholds like Kenya (Bakari 1995) was part of the cultural context that favored Mudira in her vision for the *ma'had*. This period also coincided with the biting effects of structural adjustment after the Cold War and the assault by the neoliberalism of the 1990s on the social fabric of society that led to the disintegration of the middle class and to high unemployment, especially among Muslim populations that lagged behind in Western education. The ratio of Muslim students who earned the Kenya Certificate of Primary Education in 2011 was a clear demonstration to many of how dismally low the education standards are in the regions of Kenya that are predominantly Muslim (Kenya Institute of Education 2012). These wider historical forces have had an impact on gender relations in most Muslim societies, sometimes inadvertently creating the opportunity for Muslim women's mobility and their participation and access to resources in the public domains.

The *Ma'had*

Mudira calls her institute a *ma'had*. Here she is applying a symbolic demarcation between the madrasa (school), or the old educational institution that excludes young women once they reach *balaagh* (puberty), and her school, which opens its doors for advanced Islamic learning to girls who have at least attained the age of puberty. Thus, Mudira's *ma'had* represents a female-centered modernist project that essentially reforms Islamic education in Kenya by gendering it, thereby challenging the authority of the traditionally powerful spiritual leaders, the ulama, and their expectations that women should simply be passive recipients of basic ritualistic knowledge on the lines of one *madhhab* (school of thought) or another.

The Student Body

The *ma'had* recruits are mainly students with at least a high school diploma whom Mudira considers ready to undergo training in *akhlaq*. Mudira believes that the development of Islamic character will make them more rounded Muslims even in their pursuit of the secular knowledge necessary for the developmental needs of Muslim communities from an Islamic perspective.

Consonant with her ethnically diverse background, Mudira makes every effort to make the composition of her student body as ethnically and racially diverse as possible:

> My students come from diverse communities and backgrounds even within the same community. When I sit for selection . . . I make sure that I have a student from every community: I must have a Kikuyu, I must have a Luo, I must have a Luhya, I must have a Nandi. You see, I try to have a Kalenjin, Swahili, and Arab. I try to get Indians also because, with our Indians, I want them to mix with our locals. I want to do away with this idea that we are [distinct] communities. We are Muslims. It is a bit difficult with our Indian communities, but they have given me girls and they have graduated.

Partly because of their own internal hierarchies—some of which are rooted in the history of caste—and partly because of the juxtaposition of pyramidal racial hierarchy of British colonialism that resulted in racially zoned residential areas, the small but economically strong minority of South Asian origin—often called Indians in Kenya because the majority comes from the Indian subcontinent—including those of Muslim origin, have tended to remain relatively insular (Seidanberg 1983, 7; Warah 2011, 107). It is the attitudes arising from this history and structures that Mudira seeks to break in her attempts to increase the proportion of Kenya Indian Muslims in the *ma'had*'s student composition. Because of the historical marginalization of the Northeastern Province, Mudira also makes special attempts to recruit students from there and offer them "remedial" training to put them on par with more educationally advantaged students.

In addition, Mudira makes the question of ethnic/racial intolerance and *ubaguzi* (discrimination) part of the learning process. Emphasizing that *ubaguzi* is anti-Islamic, she points out that Allah (God) created ethnic and racial differences only "li-taarufu," or "to enhance" (Qur'an 49:13) human understanding of others and mutual tolerance.[2] She guides the students to place primacy on their Muslim identity:

> Yes, they come from different ethnic communities, but they come here for their Islamics. But they also have their culture and this is the first thing I fight. I tell them, "Yes, you are Luo. But don't bring *ubaguzi* [here]. Don't bring barriers; we are Muslims. . . ." And I tell them, "Don't teach discrimination. This is not a place for racism." [When you graduate] you are going to go back and teach

the Luos, teach the Baluhyas, or the Kikuyus or teach even the Swahilis—I have
lots of Swahili girls who come. You know, when they come here and they notice
that you are very strict in those lines, they don't bring their traditions.

In a country like Kenya, which has repeatedly exploded into bloody violence
along ethnic lines, Mudira's attempts to forge an interethnic Muslim consciousness is often seen as especially appealing. What is yet in the womb of
time is whether her strong emphasis on Muslim identity will ultimately
encourage sectarian tensions in a climate and context where Christian evan-
gelicals have become especially aggressive in their work.

Mudira maintains a very high level of discipline at the *ma'had* and demands that her students work hard:

> We have very strict regulations that the girls usually from morning till evening,
> they are studying. They hardly have time. Some of the girls who graduated say
> that *wallah(i)* ("I swear to God"), if we had the same type of vigorous training
> in form 4 [the last year of secular secondary schools], we should have had an
> A, the way we push them in studies. We really push them, we really monitor
> them. We really put it into them, but they have to study. They have not come
> for anything else here. I keep my regulations. I don't want very close friendship.
> I don't want a girl to misuse her time. You see, this is an honor when her par-
> ents brought her to me. I have to make sure that she got the right type of edu-
> cation, and goes back.

Equally significant, Mudira guides the students to be monitors of their own
conduct, to develop a sense of responsibility for their actions and behaviors.
Partly as a result of this social orientation of the college, some community
members have sometimes wrongly regarded it as a "rehabilitation center" or
"boot camp" where delinquent girls are reformed and trained to be "better"
citizens at home and in their communities.

The Curriculum

The *ma'had* curriculum is designed to focus primarily on the study of tawhid,
the *akhlaq* that is necessary for building a moral Islamic personality, *sira*
(biography of the Prophet Muhammad), hadiths (sayings and traditions of
the Prophet), qasida (Islamic poetry), *tafsir*, and the different *madhhab* within
Sunni doctrine. The four, within which *fiqhi* is framed, include the Hanafi
school founded by Abu Hanifa An-Nu'man, the Maliki school of Malik ibn

Anas, the Shafi'i school founded by Imam al-Shafi'i, and the Hanbali school founded by Iman Ahmad ibn Hanbal. The *ma'had* also offers courses in how to conduct *da'wa* (proselytizing) for the graduates who choose to preach or recruit more believers or keep the Muslim communities in spiritual focus. In addition, Mudira takes advantage of the fact that her students all reside at the *ma'had* to engage them in a variety of extracurricular activities.

> I have tried to keep them in a hostel in the sense that what I cannot offer during the daytime, I offer it at night. I was training them in *swalat* (prayers) practically. I was training them in *da'wa*.... I would go out with them. At that time I did not have a driver. I would drive. I used to drive. Take them myself. We would go to programs. We introduced Islamic seminars for women. We introduced Islamic teenage week for young girls. We introduced Islamic *qasidas*. We were the ones who introduced Islamic songs. We would act them out. We take them to Mombasa, presented them to the people to show that we have come up as an Islamic revival again from women.

Between the classroom and the dormitory, then, Mudira kept her students focused on Islamic education as a doctrine as well as a lived experience.

In addition to content courses, Mudira also offers pedagogic training, guiding her students in approaches and skills appropriate to the teaching of Islam and Islamic studies.

> I [also] give them methodology, teaching techniques. How to teach to children, how to teach to women, and we test them on it practically. We place them into madrasa and see whether they can teach. They have to present teaching aids with it. So basically I try to do anything that a teacher training college will do with the techniques and everything. Afterwards, we will think of how we will be accepted by the government.... But for the moment, we have tried to make our syllabus suitable in the sense that if this girl comes out, she can either go for further studies or she will be able to teach. That is the basic, that she must be able to teach.

This emphasis on teaching, which was part of her own training at Umm al-Qura University, is a direct response to a problem connected to the teaching of religion that has arisen in the educational system in Kenya. The Kenya educational system requires all elementary school students to take a course on religious studies. But, because of the dearth of teachers of Islamic religious education, many schools have not been offering Islamic religious education as an option. So critical has this shortage of qualified teachers of the Islamic religion been, in fact, that the Muslims for Human Rights have long contemplated taking the Ministry of Education to court to challenge the continuation of the religious education requirement that has decidedly worked to the great disadvantage of students of Muslim faith. The result is that in many schools the only option that Muslim students have to fulfill this requirement is a course on Christian religious education. With her *ma'had* training, then, Mudira was hoping to fill the gap by producing female teachers of Islamic studies who could be properly certified by the Kenya Ministry of Education.

The medium of religious education is also an issue that the *ma'had* has been trying to address. How can Muslim women use Islam to fulfill their Islamic obligations or to seek their rights when they are not competent in the Qur'anic language of their Islamic law—the Arabic language? It is true, of course, that the language of oral proceedings in the kadhi courts is primarily Kiswahili, and records of the proceedings are usually kept in English. The proceedings, however, are invariably based on an Islamic law maintained primarily in Arabic. In offering training in Arabic, then, Mudira is trying to help her students secure access to the law in its original language of composition and avoid exclusive reliance on the mediated Islamic bodies of knowledge through male ulama interpretations and translations. At another level, of course, Mudira is also motivated by the belief that Arabic is a potential language of Muslim unity:

> I want Arabic to be revived. I believe that Arabic could bring us all together and also because it is the Qur'an language. It is the hadith language. If we could get Arabic revived, people will go back to the sources. . . . Look at me dealing with schools from diverse communities, and [my students] being from diverse communities. I couldn't take English, I could not take Swahili. Arabic is the best choice and also it is the religious language of Muslims. It was part and parcel of an idea to revive Arabic so that they could unify with one language.

In conceptualizing the curriculum for her *ma'had*, then, Mudira seems to have taken into consideration a range of issues related to content and methodology as well as the controversial issue of medium of instruction in an Afro-Islamic context.

The *La-Madhhab* Approach

According to Mudira, the *ma'had*'s curriculum seeks to reform the tradition of *taqliq*—submission to the classical teaching of a specific *a'lim* (Muslim classical jurist within one of the four *fiqh madhhabs*)—that limits the reception of religious knowledge to only one interpretative authority by exposing her students to the four different Sunni *madhhabs*. *Taqliq* often does not permit *ijtihad* (independent reasoning) nor does it make any reference to the wide array of Islamic schools of legal thought. Mudira created the *ma'had* with the goal of propagating mass theological training of Muslim women, in the hope of producing a group of female ulama who would be able to contribute to the reform of Islamic social practices in Kenya and beyond. Her concern with gendering the composition of the ulama in East Africa has already begun to bear fruits in Kenya, the Middle East, and the Western world, with the Pangani Ma'had graduates opening their own *ma'had* in these locations (I address this transnational propagation of Mudira's vision in a subsequent section on the inspiration for Mudira's *ma'had*).

A fundamental goal of teaching at the *ma'had* is to ensure that the students are rationally taught the fundamentals of Islam in all branches, as well as the four leading schools of thought within Sunni doctrinal Islam, without influencing their inclination. This is a departure from the traditional madrasa approach whereby knowledge of Islam basically amounts to the disciples knowing the particular views of the ulama they follow.

The *la-madhhab* tradition was, in fact, part of Mudira's training in Saudi Arabia through her engagement with transnational Muslim women colleagues from South Asia and other parts of the Muslim world. But she embraced it partly because of its scholarly appeal and partly because she was persuaded that the paradigm gave women greater interpretative leverage. Introducing a "*la-madhhab*" perspective in a *madhhab*-centered East Africa and dominated by the Shafi'i school was, of course, a major challenge that required careful strategizing in instructional approach. In the process, Mudira attempted to give her students the pedagogical tools appropriate to the Shafi'i orientation of the communities within which they would be working. This approach was based on a curriculum in which the study of Maliki, Hanbali, and Hanafi was constructed around that of Shafi'i, allowing Shafi'i to maintain at least a centrality with respect to trans-*madhhab* learning outcomes.

As a Muslim woman, Mudira was particularly concerned that what for East Africa amounted to a revolutionary paradigm shift would not be a cause for new intrareligious tensions in the community.

So I decided that I did not come to separate the *umma*. I did not come to do that and I don't want to fight with the ulamas, but to teach the right way. Even with the traditional ulamas I don't want to fight, right? So I told the girls, "You have to teach Shafi'i in the madrasa area wherever Shafi'i is going on . . . and don't go and compete with the sheikh who is already there. Don't fight. You are supposed to blend in with the *umma*." So, *Alhamdulillah*, after some time I also give them the reference books. In fact, [I give them] the names of the books they should follow, because once I give them basic *fiqh*, now they can follow any book, and they have their Arabic with them.

Mudira, then, is clearly a reformer who believes that gradual diffusionism rather than a dramatic paradigm shift that could cause tension and lead to the failure of her initiative is the best strategy. While pursuing a trans-*madhhab* approach, she is careful not to allow it to be a cause of trouble for her graduates once they go out to face the challenges of teaching Islamic studies in the "real world."

This trans-*madhhab* approach to learning about Islam proved to be quite popular with and an eye-opener for women:

In fact, it is an elderly lady . . . [who] made me realize the problem. . . . She in her old age, she decided to take two classes. After she finished she told me, "You know what, my daughter, something that is closed to us and we were made to fear that. We were not supposed to know. It is a closed thing. Today you have opened it up to us. And we are now realizing that Islam is a way of life. Otherwise, we have been in something like a cult where there are some things you just believe in and you don't ask. And when you ask the *mwalim*, he does not want to open it up for you."

In short, working strictly within an Islamic framework, the *la-Madhhab* paradigm was opening new vistas of knowledge and understanding for Muslim women, though the full meaning of this knowledge is still unfolding.

The relevance of the trans-*madhhab* approach to the current Kenyan context can easily be appreciated from two recent debates, one concerning the issue of whether women can take up public leadership roles, including that of the kadhi, and the other concerning the practice of female genital mutilation. The Shafi'i school of Islamic jurisprudence that predominates in much of Kenya takes a more literal reading of some of the Qur'anic verses and hadiths mentioned in the introduction, seeing men as "custodians" of women in both the domestic and public spheres. The Hanafi school, however, restricts the supposed custodial role of men to the domestic sphere alone. Hanafi canonical texts do not bar women from holding judicial or any other kind of position of public leadership (Hashim 2010). With respect to FGM, the Maliki School seems to provide women with an interpretation against the practice under its *diya* (blood money) provision, which prohibits harming any healthy part of the human body (Abusharaf 2006; Badawi 2000; Hicks 1996).[3]

In a sense, then, the *la-madhhab* approach used in Mudira's *ma'had* provides ample space to Muslim women educators and Muslim women rights activists to navigate between doctrinal readings of different *madhhabs* and to come up with Islamically framed positions that are empowering to women and protective of their rights. Maryam Sheikh Abdi, director of the FGM program of the UN Population Council, for example, has repeatedly invoked a reading consonant with the Maliki interpretation that FGM is not permissible in Islam (Askew 2009; my interview with Abdi, 2006).

Government Response

During the colonial period in Kenya, the colonial government often acted in a way that validated male Muslim authority in cultural and religious affairs. The postcolonial government responded to Mudira's *ma'had* project in a similar way. Because of her gender, youth, and unmarried status and in spite of her university credentials as a graduate in Islamic studies, Mudira's reformist call for a feminine presence in higher Islamic studies through the training of Muslim women in Islamic theology did not initially receive favorable support from the secular state in her bid to register the *ma'had*. In her opinion, this is because the state recognizes only the authority of the male ulama emanating from the traditional Sunni hierarchies of Kenya Muslim communities.

> Yes, the *umma*. I got a lot of problem. I was young. I was not married. I was very fresh in the field. But I was very determined. I approached very many organizations, internationally and locally. Even, I had approached the Aga Khan Foundation to give me a building that they had empty. I was not successful. Everywhere I would go it was like "What? What do you want to do? Islamics for women? You want to actually educate girls in being ulamas?" and I would joke and tell them, "Yes, I want them to be a challenge to men" [*laughs*] . . . "What do you want to get out of this?" and I would say, "I want teachers. I want outreach *da'wa* professionals and at the same time I want a certificate that people would recognize."

Mudira's goal was to have a *ma'had* accredited by Kenya's Ministry of Education as a teacher certificate–granting institution in the area of Islamic studies. But this was not to be; in the end, Mwalim Azara could only register the *ma'had* as a private enterprise without the provision that its diploma would carry the government seal of approval in the job market. As a result, in the realm of Islamic education, which has been Mudira's primary focus, her graduates have only been able to be employed as UTs—untrained teachers of Islamic studies in elementary and high schools whose salary scale is substantially lower than that of graduates of accredited teacher training colleges in the country.

Even Muslim organizations such as the Isma'ili Aga Khan Foundation did not support Mudira's vision for her *ma'had*, partly because of its proposed curriculum focus on advanced Islamic theology for women. The Aga Khan Foundation's mission is fundamentally different from Mudira's; it promotes integrated madrasa education, which frames the teaching of nonreligious content from an Islamic perspective at the primary level in low-income Muslim societies. The lack of support from the Aga Khan Foundation also stems in part to Mudira's *la-madhhab* (*madhhab*-free *ma'had* approach to training its students. But for the Sunni *umma*, breaking away from the male control of Islamic learning was a novel idea that they were not prepared to embrace, given its potential to vex the authority of the traditional ulama, both from early reformist households and from the Sufi aristocracy.

Mobilizing the Community

In her quest to realize her vision of a *ma'had* for Muslim women in Kenya, Mudira strategically embarked on mobilizing members of the broader Muslim *umma* who were ready for a women-inclusive modernist Islamic reformation through *ijtihad*. It is significant that she made her first public declaration of intent to open a *ma'had* for Muslim women on the Kenya coast, which is historically known as the cultural headquarters of Sunni Islam (Oded 2000). Mudira was able to strategize effectively and thereby convince the Muslim constituency—the *umma*—to give her a chance to implement her idea of running a reformist Islamic school not for girls but for young women. That fact that Mudira sought legitimacy for her vision at the coast is demonstrative of her bold courage, given the history of the power of the religious aristocracies of Mombasa and Lamu. Considering her gender and young age, she faced an uphill battle; what she did have on her side to convince the *umma* and the "traditionalist" ulama about the need to feminize the teaching of Islamic studies was her determination, her educational credentials, and the young women who decided to give her a chance by being part of the first experiment.

Mudira was up front with the members of her audience, informing them that her graduates would not get government certificates. But she assured them that during the two years that their daughters would be enrolled at her *ma'had* she would provide them with quality education that would prepare them for life. She allayed their fears that the *ma'had* experience would compromise their daughters' pursuit of more marketable certificate programs, by arguing that, on the contrary, Muslim women would make better professionals in any field once they had gone through the *ma'had* experience.

Mudira pays special tribute for the help she received not only from her father but also from Kenyans of Christian faith in her efforts to register the *ma'had*. Here again, Mudira's case is like the cases of Abida Ali (see chapter 4) or Mama Halima, discussed in the introduction of the book, who created a hospice in Pumwani's slum quarters for Muslim women in charge of giving a proper Muslim burial to poor elderly Muslim women. We see Muslim women leaders reaching out across faith boundaries to mobilize support for establishing welfare programs for the common good of all Muslims. This cross-faith networking is another contribution of Muslim women, one that helps overcome the traditional insularity of male Muslim leadership and that reflects the agency of Muslim women leaders in going beyond identity politics to respond to community needs and relate to other citizens of the nation. This leadership quality of Muslim women dispels two myths. One is the idea, rooted in conservatism, that the outside world can only have a "corruptive" influence on women, and the other is the non-Muslim stereotype of the Muslim woman as non-independent and entrapped by Muslim cultural conservatism. In chapter 1, Muhashamy-Said discusses both the support from the Goan Catholic schools that pushed her to succeed in education as a Muslim girl during the colonial period and her appreciation of Christian educationist reformers in the 1990s who saw her integrated madrasa curriculum as a model to copy for reforming the Christian schools in Kenya.

Mudira talks about the support she received from senior professional secularist women, whose *hikma* (wisdom) was instrumental in helping design strategies for confronting the Muslim patriarchy in her quest to implement her vision. This collaboration between religious women activists and secularist women activists offers yet another concrete example of the blurring of the boundaries between secularism and religiosity, at least in the African landscape. More important, it demonstrates that Muslim women too can rise and build coalitions beyond boundaries of ideological difference in their struggle to achieve certain rights, in this case the right to Islamic education: "Some of the ladies who were educated secularly came up actually and gave the support: 'We support your girls. We will support your programs. We want to be with you and come seek advice.' I had Islamics, [but] I had no practical experience. How do I go about teaching women? I don't know, I was still young then. I was in my twenties. So, I needed these women; they would guide me."

It is also noteworthy that Mudira highlights the support she received from the new, educated ulama for her *ma'had* project. These contemporaries of hers are the beneficiaries of postindependence mass education programs in formal secular education and have also been abroad in countries like Egypt, Sudan, Malaysia, Kuwait, Saudi Arabia, or Indonesia for their Islamic studies. Through these transnational educational experiences, the new male ulama have been exposed to Islamist (reformist) thinkers such as Tariq Ramadhan, whose books and recorded lectures on cassette tapes and DVDs are popular in Islamic mosque bookstores like the one at the Jami'a shopping center in Nairobi. Although there are some traditionalist ulama who are sympathetic to women's issues to the point that they have been referred to as "women's kadhis," as demonstrated in Susan Hirsch's insightful study of Muslim women's agency in the kadhi courts in Mombasa (1998), they have generally remained averse to the idea of opening the gates for women's participation as religious authorities in Islam. So the fact that there had already emerged a new Muslim ulama capable of relating to her vision worked immensely in her favor.

While the *ma'had* received support from a range of community members, it also had its detractors. In particular, the *ma'had* has become a challenge to the male ulama not only on the question of gendering Islamic voice of authority but also on gendering of (employment) opportunities. Although there are a few women Qur'anic teachers, Islamic teaching has always been dominated by men. Despite the ideology of gender segregation, males still dominate the teaching of young girls in madrasas, be they of the traditional "chuo" type or the modern types. Consequently, the production of Muslim women *walimu* represents a conflict of interest further tied to opportunities. Moreover, although gender segregation is common in educational settings, the new trend of women *walimu* in the madrasas for girls and women poses a problem for male ulama who teach both male and female students. Mudira predicts a time when the traditional male *walimu* will no longer be teaching girls "because we are going to replace them": "My girls will replace them finally. They were teaching males and females, isn't that so? Now my girls are going to take over teaching females. So what happens to their jobs?" Resistance to Mudira's graduates was also initially strongest among male *walimu* who were insecure about their own knowledge of Islam. But partly because of her reassuring demeanor, this class of teachers too came to be more and more comfortable with her initiative and to appreciate the important role it has in the community. They became increasingly persuaded that once girls reach puberty, there are areas of Islamic life that they can best learn about from female teachers. In addition, her graduates began to establish an excellent record of instruction in areas like tawhid. In a sense, then, the *ma'had* was beginning to reconfigure the space of Islamic teaching.

When engaging men who were comfortable with her initiatives, knowledge of Islam, and leadership, Mudira would take the opportunity to show them that what they thought were their rights as a matter of Islamic principle were in fact deeply embedded in non-Islamic culture. Her view is that "it is not Islam, it is culture. It is either African culture that is demeaning women, or it is Asian culture that is demeaning women, or it is an Arab culture, because those are the types of girls I was getting. And they have been made to believe this is Islam because the husband is a Muslim. So now I was separating [the two]: This is culture, this is Islam, and in Islam we have the rights." Mudira's emphasis on the rights of women in Islam would at times be carried home by the women who studied with her, which in turn sometimes precipitated new gender dynamics in the domestic space.

In the heat of the national debate on reforming the kadhi courts, new roles may also be emerging for graduates of the *ma'had*. Some of them may, of course, pursue further Islamic studies abroad and vie for kadhi positions in the future. For the time being, however, the graduates can play a crucial role in raising awareness among Muslim women and girls throughout the country about their rights within kadhi courts and the wider framework of shari'a (Islamic law based on the Qur'an). They could initiate a grassroots women's network for the transformation of the traditional paradigm of learning about Islam that submits to the authority of one or two ulamas and contravenes the spirit of *ijtihad*. One of the recommendations at the conclusion of "Access to Justice for Women in Kenya," a UN-sponsored conference held in December 2010, was the formation of shari'a centers that would help Muslim women understand the functioning of the kadhi courts. Were these centers to materialize, the *ma'had* graduates would be suitable and probably ideal officers to run them. Such centers could provide opportunities for the *ma'had* graduates to work with Muslim lawyers to promote legal literacy to the Muslim women they serve.

The Inspiration for the *Ma'had*

Just as Mudira received inspiration from an Indonesian friend studying with her in Saudi Arabia, she hoped to be an inspiration to others without them feeling pressured to conform to her views, opinions, or ideas even within the framework of the *la-madhhab* vision. The last thing Mudira wanted to see in her educational mission was simply a reproduction of herself: "I didn't want to be the only one. I wanted there to be many of us. I didn't want me to be the last. There should be some others, more than me. Like now there is this student whose Arabic is better than mine because she got a degree in Arabic. So she actually guides me in my Arabic syllabus. So this is exactly what the idea was: To be me so that she could be better than me so that we could take this ideal ahead."

What Mudira means by saying that she does not want to produce "duplicates" of herself is that she does not want to produce followers like in the old tradition of *madhhab*. The graduates of her *ma'had*, having acquired knowledge of Islam in all schools of thought, must develop their own independent thinking and shape their teaching or preaching based on their own intellectual visions. This is a new articulation of Islamic reformism. Partly because of its success in inspiring and empowering, the *ma'had* attracted students from all over Eastern and Central Africa and beyond.[4] And for the same reasons, the *ma'had* vision spread quickly through the work of Mudira's graduates in East African countries like Tanzania and the Comoro Islands and in Central Africa in the Congos and Rwanda, Middle Eastern countries like Dubai with large foreign expatriates, and Western countries like England and Australia.

Mudira notes the institutional restrictions that her graduates had to overcome in places like Dubai where foreigners are not permitted to open Islamic schools catering to Dubai citizens. The strategy adopted by one of her graduates was to open a *ma'had* in Sharjah (United Arab Emirates) for teaching Islamics to Muslim women expatriates from African and South Asian countries. But word of it eventually reached women citizens of Dubai, who became interested in this new female institution of Islamic learning derived from East

Africa. The creation of *ma'had* in East London and Australia is clearly demonstrative of the global reach of Mudira's vision.

Because of the dearth of women teachers of Islamic studies, Mudira initially relied extensively on male teachers who believed in her mission. In time and through her own network, she was able to obtain sponsorship for a number of her graduates to pursue further studies at the African Islamic University in the Sudan. The fact that her students were already trained in Arabic language made it possible for them to adjust easily and to maintain an excellent performance record, opening up additional opportunities for future *ma'had* graduates. Several of the graduates from African Islamic University then went back to teach at the *ma'had* in Pangani, Kenya, gradually increasing the ranks of women instructors, as Mudira had always intended. With her encouragement, this new pool of faculty came to assume an expanding role in the academic and administrative affairs of the *ma'had*.

As the ranks of the *ma'had*'s instructional staff filled with its own highly qualified graduates, Mudira transformed it from a two-year to a four-year institution of study. This allowed the *ma'had* to begin offering more in-depth study of the various subjects in its curriculum. In addition, in response to community demand and requests, she introduced a separate continuing education program focused on Islamic studies as well as, for interested women, subjects related to home economics:

> I now have Saturday women's classes. I do it personally. You see, the working ladies are very good potentials [*sic*] of the *umma*. They are interested in knowing more, but they don't have the time. So we take one subject like *aqidah* [creed] and teach it a whole year because they only come once a week. We have now started a new series. We are now doing *sira*, *sira* of the Prophet. We have finished *aqidah*, then *akhlaq*. We have done some *tafsir* of the laws, the shari'a rulings in the Qur'an. Recently, I finished the forty hadith after two years.[5]

In this way, mothers and daughters come to be mutually reinforcing parts of the *ma'had* experience.

Given how qualified her instructors are, offering salaries that are competitive enough to ensure that she does not lose them has been a challenge. Tuition from the students is one source. The introduction of the vocational training program has also been a help. In addition, however, Mudira is constructing apartments and business premises for rent in an attempt to increase *ma'had* resources. In this regard, she is very conscious that competitive remuneration of the instructors is crucial in giving the profession the kind of worth that would make it valuable in the eyes of the communities of the instructors.

Mudira is also an experienced family counselor who regularly counsels women on a wide range of marital problems—such as coping with polygyny—and on how to manage their financial affairs. Helping women cultivate better and more fulfilling relationships with their children, and children with their parents, is part of the counseling services she provides to the community. She also runs weekly seminars for youth intended to inculcate an Islamically inspired understanding of the challenges and opportunities before them. But Mudira is firm in keeping the *ma'had* experience separate from her own outreach work with women and families in the community.

The success of the Muslim *ma'had* experiment for women and girls brought a growing number of requests from Muslim parents for Mudira to open a *ma'had* for boys as well.[6] She agreed, with the support of the community, to open a boys institute for Islamic studies, which she named Al-Furqan (another Arabic name for the Qur'an), in a town called Namanga in the Rift Valley Province at the border with Tanzania.[7] With the mushrooming of *ma'had* and other Islamic schools in Kenya, Mudira urged Muslim educationists to form an umbrella organization for Muslim educational institutions that would have a board of governors to oversee educational standards and be a stakeholder in national education decision-making and policy implementation processes. She proposed the name Iqra Literacy Foundation for the umbrella organization ("iqra" means "read"). Moreover, the success of her work has attracted the interest of Muslim education investors and has generated more demand for managerial accountability, which so far has been handled voluntarily by Muslim professionals vested in the *ma'had* vision.

CONCLUSION

The analysis in this chapter provides insight into the new ways in which reformist Muslim women educated within the Islamic framework, such as Mudira, use their knowledge to critically develop autonomous paradigms for acquiring knowledge about Islam that destabilizes the patriarchal status quo and sectarian politics internal to Muslim politics while also trying to break down barriers erected by Arab-Muslim slavery and European colonialism in Kenya that divide Muslim women's communities. Mudira addresses discrimination along racial and ethnolinguistic lines within Muslim communities through the constructive deployment of Islam as a religion that celebrates *lita'arafu*, a concept related to tolerance and mutual respect for multiculturalism, and ethnic and linguistic diversity against *ubaguzi*, as clearly stated in the Qur'an, chapter 49, verse 13: "O people, we have created you from a male and a female and made you into races and tribes so that you may know each other. Surely the most honored of you in the sight of God is the one who is the most righteous of you."[8]

Furthermore, she endeavors to cultivate a culture of tolerance and respect among Muslims by democratizing the learning process and by exposing the students to the diversity in Islamic philosophical and legal thought. This is why she opted to frame her *ma'had* within a *la-madhhab* approach whose intention is to prevent any one theological teacher from having an interpretative control over the minds of the students enrolled in the program. Mudira exposes her students to all Islamic school of thoughts in order to enable them to develop autonomous interpretations of Islam as required within the principle of *ijtihad* and as stipulated also in *Al-Ma'idah* 5:48: "To each among you have we prescribed a law and an open way. If Allah had so willed, He would have made you a single People, but (His plan is) to test you in what He has given you; so strive as in a race in all virtues. The goal of you all is to Allah; it is He that will show you the truth of the matters in which ye dispute." Thus, this principle of *ijtihad* enables individuals and communities regardless of their gender, race, class, and other backgrounds to become autonomous thinkers who might differ from others in their views. By the same token, Mudira uses Islam and knowledge of the Arabic language, the language of religious unification, as the vector for building a common Islamic *akhlaq* that has the potential to foster continued interchanges across Kenyan Islamic cultural diversity and beyond.

Ultimately, another of Mudira's goal is to serve as an education interventionist who genders Islamic higher education in Kenya by producing a contingent of female *walimu* with an autonomous understanding of Islam, a goal she is achieving as these new female ulama begin to have an impact on the mass education of young generations of Muslim girls. And by injecting into her curriculum subjects other than religious topics, Mudira is able to set higher practical goals for her *ma'had* graduates so that they navigate the modern world with relevant skills.

Finally, this chapter provides a concrete illustration of the success of Islamic reformist Muslim women such as Mudira in using strategies of social networking rooted in their cultural frameworks and beyond. These social

networks have been fundamental in mobilizing support for women reformists from both female and male kin, friends, and power brokers within local
and global Muslim communities seeking to implement their own women-
centered reformist agenda. The analysis also illustrates both the global transnational and local dimensions of an initiative driven by a Muslim woman's
determination to alter the status quo and bring about real social changes.

3

Muslim Women Legislators in Minority Status

Contributions to Representative Politics

I was coming in an avenue, a career [Parliament] that people think
is reserved for men. . . . The only thing I had was a good education.
But everything else from me was wrong. I was single, I was from a
marginalized community, I was a Muslim, and I was a woman. . . .

—MP Amina Abdallah

INTRODUCTION

Until 2012, the Kenyan legislative body, known as the Parliament or National
Assembly, had a total of 210 electoral seats that accommodated the *elected*
representatives of the people from 210 constituencies in the country that had
been established by the Electoral Commission. Furthermore, it provided for an
additional twelve seats for *nominated* MPs. These were often used to increase
representation from marginalized minority groups and/or to bring on board
relatively well-known citizens with skills, experience, and training that were
deemed valuable to the business of the legislative body. There were also two
seats of ex-officio (nonvoting) members, occupied by the speaker of the
National Assembly and the attorney general.

Before the minimal constitutional revisions that accompanied the 2002
electoral process, the selection of nominated MPs was exclusively in the hands
of the president from the ruling party, hitherto KANU. This often led to
abuse, with the president electing officials only to increase the number of MPs
from his own political party and subsequently his party's voting power in
favor of or against specific motions and bills. Since the Ninth Parliament
(2002–7), however, the seats for nominated MPs have been divided propor-
tionately between the political parties with the largest number of electoral

seats, irrespective of whether a party is in power or in the opposition. For the Ninth Parliament, the nominated seats were primarily divided between the National Rainbow Coalition, KANU, and the Forum for the Restoration of Democracy-People. In the Tenth Parliament (2007–12), six of the nominated seats went to the ODM, three to the People for National Unity, two to the Orange Democratic Movement–Kenya (ODM-K, a splinter of ODM), and one to KANU.

Kenya's First Parliament was constituted immediately after the country gained its independence in 1963. In that entity, which was the result of a multiparty election, there was not a single woman. Women did not have a significant presence in the Kenyan Parliament until the general election of 1974. By then all political opposition had been banned and electoral competition took place between individual politicians within the same single, ruling party KANU.[1] Three women were then voted in: Grace Onyango, a former mayor of Kisumu town, Julia Ojiambo from Nyanza, and Chelagat Mutai of Rift Valley. Significantly, Ojiambo was appointed as assistant minister, becoming the first woman to occupy a cabinet position. In addition, there were two other women who joined the house as nominated MPs: Eda Gachukia and Jemimah Gecaga

The 1979 elections for the Fourth Parliament and the first elections under Moi's presidency saw an increase in the number of women elected to Parliament. Grace Onyango, Julia Ojiambo, and Chelagat Mutai were all reelected in their respective constituencies, and Ojiambo was reappointed as assistant minister. In addition, Phoebe Asiyo was elected for the first time. In the next two Parliaments, the fifth (1983–88) and sixth (1988–92) parliaments, there was, however, a significant drop in the number of elected women MPs. This coincided with what has sometimes been described as Moi's "reign of terror" (UMOJA 1989). The violence that accompanied the elections made it difficult for women to participate effectively in them. In addition, Moi introduced the *mlolongo* system. Under this system, whereby voters had to queue up behind photos of candidates they were supporting in the primaries, outright intimidation of both the candidates and their supporters reigned supreme. Compared to the two previous elections, the number of women politicians willing to stand for elections was reduced by more than 50 percent in spite of the increase of electoral constituencies from 158 to 188. The women elected in these two elections included Phoebe Asiyo and Grace Ogot.

In the 1997 general election for the Eighth Parliament, women achieved another historical milestone, though not necessarily in the number of women elected to Parliament. The number of registered political parties had now increased to fourteen. Two of these, the Labor Party of Kenya and the Social Democratic Party, nominated women as their presidential candidates, Nobel Peace Laureate Wangari Maathai and Charity Ngilu, respectively. More relevant for this book, during this election, the first Muslim women vied for national electoral office, both on the KANU ticket. These were Sophia Abdi Noor, a Kenya Somali from the Northeastern Province, and Marere Mwachai, a Digo from the Coast Province. While Abdi Noor was pressured to withdraw before the elections ended, Mwachai went on to win her seat, becoming the first elected Muslim woman in the Kenyan Parliament. Mwachai made additional history when she was appointed assistant minister in the Moi government.

Two of the most important women ministerial appointments following the 2002 elections were those of Charity Ngilu as minister of health and Martha Karua as minister of water management and development. Hitherto, women ministerial positions had been limited to posts that had to do with women issues, children, culture and social services, and youth. Now, for the first time, they were taking on very critical core ministries. During the 2007 election, yet another woman vied for presidency: Nazlin Omar Rajput. A Muslim, Rajput ran under the ticket of yet another new party, the Workers Congress Party of Kenya. Rajput was the only woman in a total of nine presidential candidates. Though in the end she won neither the presidential seat nor the parliamentary seat of her constituency, Rajput was influential in making the Muslim community in Kenya more integral to the national political process, as reflected in a summary of presidential candidate performance provided by the Electoral Institute for the Sustainability of Democracy in Africa (see top table on page 87).

In addition to the increase in the number of elected women MPs to nine and nominated women MPs to nine—including three of Muslim faith: Ummi Naomi Shaban, Amina Abdallah, and Shakila Abdallah—the number of women cabinet ministers expanded. These included Martha Karua, who until her resignation in 2009 was minister of justice and constitutional affairs; Ngilu, minister of water and irrigation; Shaban, minister of special programs; Ester Mathenge, minister of gender and children's affairs; Beth Mugo, minister of public health and sanitation; Helene Sambili, minister of youth and sports; Sally Kosgei, minister of higher education, science and technology; and about seven other women (see bottom table on page 87).

Candidate	Coalition/Party	Votes	% Votes
Mwai Kibaki	Party of National Unity	4,584,721	46.42
Raila Odinga	Orange Democratic Movement	4,352,993	44.07
Kalonzo Musyoka	Orange Democratic Movement –Kenya	879,903	8.91
Joseph Karani	Kenya Patriotic Trust Party	21,171	0.21
Pius Muiru	Kenya People's Party	9,667	0.10
Nazlin Omar	Workers Congress Party of Kenya	8,624	0.09
Kenneth Matiba	Saba Saba Asili	8,046	0.08
David Waweru Ngethe	Chama Cha Uma	5,976	0.06
Nixon Kukubo	Republican Party of Kenya	5,927	0.06
Total		9,877,028	100.00

Sources: Commonwealth Observation Mission 2008, 16; European Union 2008, 37; Office of Government Spokesperson 2007.

Year	Assistant Minister	Name
2007	Assistant Minister of Transport	Cecily Mbarire
2008	Assistant Minister of Tourism	
2008	Assistant Minster of Home Affairs (she was killed in a plane crash together with the Minister of Roads)	Lorna Labosa
2008	Assistant Minister for Nairobi Metropolitan Development	Elizabeth Ongoro Masha
2008	Assistant Minister for Cooperative Development	Jebii Kilimo
2008	Assistant Minister for Housing	Bishop Margaret Wanjiru
2008	Assistant Minister of Youth and Sports	Wavinya Ndeti
2010	Assistant Minister of Mineral Resources	Margaret Jepkoech Kamar

Proportionally, however, this increase is still small; women still constitute less than 10 percent of the House and the Cabinet. This explains why Kenya women were calling for the enactment of the Quota Bill, which the patriarchal political structure resisted until it finally became integrated into the new 2010 constitution of the country. The new constitution now provides that women hold at least 30 percent of the house seats in electoral or nominated status.

Since, prior to 1997, the nominated seats were allocated at the pleasure of the president, these nominees are excluded from the list on page 89, which comes from the Electoral Institute for the Sustainability of Democracy in Africa.

MUSLIM WOMEN MPS:
A MINORITY WITHIN A "TRIBE" OF WOMEN

Few Kenya Muslim women have seized the opportunity for pluralistic representation opened up by the democratization process to commit themselves as active political participants vying for executive seats in the government, the parliament, and municipal councils. Of the 210 electoral seats of the Ninth Parliament, there were a total of nine women and about twenty-four Muslims. Of these, only one, Ummi Naomi Shaban—a dentist by training, representing the Taveta constituency on a KANU ticket—was both a Muslim and a woman. Of the nine nominated women MPs, the only Muslim nominee was Amina Abdallah, also on a KANU ticket. By this time, KANU had an affirmative action seat that, in Abdallah's words, was intended to "give minority groups and special interest groups a chance to come to Parliament so that they can use it as a stepping-stone to get back to elected members of Parliament or use this opportunity to raise issues about minorities here." And it is through the affirmative action plan that Abdallah was nominated to Parliament.

In the Tenth Parliament, Muslim women's representation in the list of nominated MPs increased substantially. Abdallah was renominated by KANU for a second term. But she was joined by two other Muslim women, Abdi Noor (ODM) and Shakila Abdallah (ODM-K). The nominations of Mohamed Abdi Affrey (ODM-K) and Mohamed Dori (ODM) brought the total number of Muslim-nominated MPs in the Tenth Parliament to almost the same as that of non-Muslims—perhaps indicating rising sensitivity to the marginalization of Muslims in the country.

On the electoral side of the Tenth Parliament, however, there were minimal gains. The number of Muslim officials elected was more or less the same

Year	Directly elected			Party nominated			Total seats		
	Seats	Number of women	% of women	Seats	Number of women	% of women	Seats	Number of women	% of women
2007	210	15	7.12	12	6	50.00	222	21	9.46
2002	210	9	4.29	12	8	66.67	222	17	7.66
1997	210	4	1.90	12	5	44.67	222	9	4.05
1992	188	6	3.19	—	—	—	188	6	3.19
1988	188	2	1.06	—	—	—	188	2	1.06
1983	158	2	1.31	—	—	—	153	2	1.31
1979	158	5	3.16	—	—	—	158	5	3.16
1974	158	4	2.53	—	—	—	158	4	2.53
1969	158	1	0.63	—	—	—	158	1	0.63
1963	124	0	0.00	—	—	—	124	0	0.00

Sources: Constitution of Kenya, 2009; Women's Shadow Parliament, Kenya, "Rapid Gender Assessment and Audit of Political Parties in Kenya" (2006), 17; Women's Shadow Parliament, Kenya, "The Elusive Quest for Women's Empowerment in Electoral Politics: A Synopsis of the 2007 Electoral Year: Second Rapid Assessment and Gender Audit of Electoral Processes in Kenya" (2008), 16, 17.

as in the Ninth Parliament. And of the thirteen women elected (in contrast to nine in the Ninth Parliament), there was only one Muslim, Shaban. Rajput, the other Muslim woman political figure, campaigned for both a parliamentary and a presidential seat but was not successful in either of her bids. Given the long history of patriarchal opposition to the inclusion of Muslim women in public politics, it is surprising that as the political space has become more pluralistic, more Muslim women candidates have not entered the fray to vie for political office.

The two Muslim women MPs I interviewed identified themselves as Muslims, allowing them to take advantage of the new politics of pluralistic representation both as women within their parties and as Muslims in the wider polity to gain new appointments in leadership positions. They take a wholly secular approach to politics, however, in order to broaden their potential electoral constituency. That is why they sought (and continue to seek) political leadership through secular political parties like KANU rather than through a faith-based political organization like the Islamic Party of Kenya (IPK).

The limited number of women MPs in general and the gender bias of the media coverage in favor of male MPs has significantly reduced the degree to which women's voices in Parliament are heard.[2] Muslim women MPs, however, have also had to confront a stereotype, held even by fellow women MPs, that they are essentially "voiceless," timid, and unable to make parliamentary contributions. Referring to the first time she and Shaban attended a meeting of the Kenyan Women's Parliamentary Association, Abdallah remarks that "somebody described another Muslim woman saying that 'some people get to Parliament and don't utter a word.' So for me it was a big challenge because they perceive us as very timid and as people who cannot represent ourselves. So I think that in some way I have gone on overdrive to deal with that issue because I talk too much so that I can cleanse that stereotype. . . . [laughs] . . . It is an issue. It is a big issue for us."

The women's parliamentary association is the women's caucus within Kenya's legislative body. Given prevailing stereotypes within the caucus, then, speaking for Muslim women and inscribing their voices in national politics is one of the major priorities of both Muslim women MPs. Moreover, women parliamentarians have to confront the coalition of multiple patriarchies, which cuts across religion, ethnicity, class, and party affiliations.

Furthermore, as both MPs suggest, although women constitute 54 percent of Kenya's voting population, they occupy only 7.8 percent of parliamentary seats. On August 7, 2007, local and international media reported that ten thousand Kenyan women marched through the streets of Nairobi seeking one million signatures needed for the adoption of a women's MP quota bill in the National Assembly to bridge the gender gap. In this regard, the European Parliamentarians with Africa news observes:

> The purpose of the campaign was to gather a million signatures in support of the amendment of a Constitutional Bill that was to be discussed in Parliament on August 14, 2007, to campaign for the allocation of 50 women's seats in the Kenyan Parliament. The campaign was initiated by the Kenya Women Parliamentarians Association (KEWOPA), women professionals, civil society activists and politicians drawn from various political parties and was supported by UNIFEM. The creation of the 50 special seats for women was aimed at raising Kenyan representation in the legislature. Only 8 percent of parliamentary posts in Kenya are occupied by women. The Bill was discussed on August 14, 2007, and rejected in its entirety the same day to the dismay of over 2,000 women from across Kenya who had camped in the surroundings of Parliament to lobby legislators to vote in support of the Bill, which would have guaranteed at least 17 percent women representation.[3]

Until the enactment of the 2010 constitution, the Kenyan Parliament had failed to respond to the UN Platform for Action (1995) for governments to ensure "women's equal access and full participation in power structures and decision-making."

Both Abdallah and Shaban denounce how the male-dominated media reinforces patriarchal discrimination of women in political executive positions by either refusing to grant them fair coverage of their political achievements or by portraying them through negative stereotypes. This is why they celebrated the appointment of Martha Karua, a woman, as Kenya's minister of constitutional affairs.[4] In her position, Karua received frequent coverage in both the print and electronic media, putting women's executive abilities and achievement in "high" politics in the limelight. As Shaban explains:

> The women of Kenya, because of the marginalization of women in the country and voting trend in this country, when a woman comes to Parliament, they really work very hard to retain their seat because you are perceived as ... [pause] ... they look at you as the weaker sex and also people who cannot make decisions. So we are all, by society at the same level, at par. In our Parliament, the

standards of performance where women are concerned have been very high. They have been very good. Except that because of the general misconception that women are nonperformers, you find that even the media is not concerned about what women [parliamentarians] talk about or what they say and their contributions. So you find that their only interest is . . . I will put it this way: even the lousiest of the male [Parliament] members, when he says something, it will be reported all over. Yet when a woman gives a contribution it is not reported. . . . But we are lucky this time because the deputy leader of government business happens to be a woman [Martha Karua] who is a minister of constitutional affairs. It is a plus. It has never [before] happened and to us it is a plus. And at least every day we get to hear her talk. We believe that as time goes on, people will appreciate women more, and more women will be elected in the next general election because, without blowing trumpets, I believe our women have really worked, including the nominated women. The elected and the nominated women, we both worked in our own areas of interests.

In Shaban's view, then, the media has been complicit in erasing the contributions of women in Parliament and in making them "invisible." Consequently, women MPs have to work twice as hard and perform immensely better than their male counterparts just to be visible. Both Muslim women MPs' take on the mainstream media bias supports Joyce N. Omwoha's insightful analysis in "Media and (Mis)representation of Women in Political Leadership Positions in Kenya" (2011) into how the media uses humiliation and ridicule to negatively depict women political leaders and/or deliberately fail to report their accomplishments to the public. Omwoha provides concrete examples of negative media coverage of prominent women political leaders such as Martha Karua, former minister of justice and constitutional affairs, and Margaret Wanjiru. Such media (mis)representations suggest that Kenyan women are simply "unfit" for public political leadership. As Omwoha points out, "In Kenya newspaper cartoons, the ladies on 'political satire' in what could be a first for freedom of expression litigation in the country, Ms Martha Karua, former Minister of Justice and Constitutional Affairs and arguably the most high profile female politician in Kenya, sued the *East African Standard* over a caricature of her that appeared in the April 25, 2010, issue of *Penknife*" (2011, 143). Elsewhere in the article she adds that "in a robbery incident in 2003, Kenyans really got excited and amused when the Minister (Ms. Martha Karua) was carjacked at around midnight and the only person she was with at the time was one Catholic priest father Wamugunda. Caroline Mutoko, a presenter in a popular radio station in Kenya had a field day asking her eager listeners all sorts of hypothetical and hilarious rhetorical questions addressing the mystery as to what the minister may have been up to with the father before they were carjacked. A newspaper article published by the *Daily Nation* on December 12, 2003, was headlined "Martha: I owe no one an explanation" (2011, 143).

Such awareness of media misrepresentation of women in public office has led some Muslim women political leaders such as Shaban and Rajput to invest energy in persuading reporters who are sensitive to gender mainstreaming to publicize their achievements in legislation and their success in securing resources for the development of their electoral constituencies. In addition, as I have demonstrated elsewhere (Alidou 2011), the political liberalization processes of the 1990s resulted in the intensification of Muslim minority efforts to gain greater political representation as equal citizens within the Kenyan nation through effective use of Muslim-owned print and electronic media such as Radio Rahma, Iqra, Radid Salaam, FM Pwani, and others.[5] These Muslim-owned media outlets have increasingly become a venue in which Muslim women political leaders and community activists can present their agenda for women, the Muslim communities, and the nation at large to the public.

Muslim Women Parliamentarians Confronting Adversity within Muslim Communities

Although all the political parties discriminate against women, the Muslim women MPs argue that they stand a better chance of achieving their leadership goals through secular organizations than through faith-based organizations. For example, among the numerous Muslim women who were behind the success of the IPK, not a single one of them rose to a position of executive leadership within the party, and their chances of rising had the party been registered were very doubtful. The continued patriarchal interpretation of Islam, even within the context of political pluralism at the national level, constrained leadership opportunities for Muslim women in Kenya. Global *ijtihad* that seeks to reread Islam in a way that empowers women to succeed in their goals and aspirations is not the ideological paradigm framing the orientation of IPK and other Muslim organizations.[6] Ironically, the formation of IPK during the democratization era contributed to the political radicalization of Muslim communities, on the one hand, and to greater women's marginalization, on the other hand. Even as the momentum for pluralistic representation continued to grow, many Muslim men, some Muslim women supporters of IPK, and the predominant conservative Muslim organizations in Kenya continued to believe that political leadership in the public sphere was an exclusive preserve of men. Shaban recounts how culture and Islam were invoked in order to prevent her as a Muslim woman from vying for a parliamentary seat in the Coast Province and describes the types of violence unleashed against her as a result of her resistance:

> The first time I tried—I tried to compete in a by-election in my constituency— was when my former MP had resigned. That was in 2001. But culturally it has taken a long time for people to realize that even women should try to compete for such a position. First of all, the first resistance I felt was from the males, the male elders who sent a delegation to come and tell me [as a woman] to stop doing politics. So you can see where we started. But of course, if you are focused and you want to be there, it is difficult, it is not easy. You will be insulted. I was insulted. But, fortunately, I had the support of the women and the youth.
>
> [In the process of campaigning] my car was broken into pieces. I had another car and the second car was burnt. A friend's car—he had lent me his car for campaign—it was burnt. My home was almost burnt, for they poured the petrol all around it. But they did not burn it. That was in 2001. But again, that did not deter me. So the following year again, I was there on the spot again to try. This time around, I made it, I made the points. And of course, the insults were fewer because they thought, this one will not stop. The insults got less, they were less interesting.

New to the game and with cultural forces against her, Shaban lost in her first bid. But refusing to be intimidated and having learned some important strategic lessons from her first experience, she went on to compete again for the same seat in the 2002 general election, and this time she succeeded. Even after her election, however, Shaban continued to experience the hostility of men and women; both genders believed that on religious and/or cultural grounds she should not be serving her society at that level of legislative leadership:

> But for the Muslim women, of course, you realize that because people want to keep off the women, they also misquote the Qur'an saying that women are not meant to lead. They misquoted it because I have not seen it anywhere, retained anywhere; they misquoted it. But again, this is just to lock out the women. Again like I am saying, [in] African culture, not only in East Africa, but in West

Africa as well, the women have always been looked at as children. They are supposed to be children and looked at as minors. But as time is getting on, we are trying to get our rights in the society and we are going to stay, we are here to stay. We hope we will be able to carry on board other women, the youth also to include them on board.

Abdallah likewise notes the opposition of conservative Muslim women to women's public political leadership, remarking how the roles played by people like her and Shaban could help transform prevailing attitudes for the better:

[If] there is a chance that we have two Muslim candidates, a man and a woman, it is the women who are saying, "In fact, we can't support her. Islam does not allow for women in leadership." So for me, I think if I win, when I win, I think I will be doing them a service because they would see me not only as a nominated MP, but an MP they did not vote for, but who is bringing them development. That would be more effective in convincing them [that women can be effective leaders], like what has happened with Naomi. Now it is going to be very hard for some religious radical to come and say that a woman cannot lead. They have the record to show. They will start to list what Naomi has done for them.

In a sense, then, both Shaban and Abdallah seem to be strong believers in the power of example, seeing their personal records of achievement as key to founding a new political culture within the Muslim communities that would be more respectful of women's leadership potential in the public sphere. This belief also explains why the two feel a great sense of responsibility not only not to fail but to perform at the exceptionally high level.

Of course, their own individual and collective efforts on behalf of the advancement of Muslim women's causes should have been immensely aided by the existence of a Muslim women's movement. But, as Abdallah suggests, such a movement has not survived as an enduring phenomenon:

There is no Muslim women's movement in Kenya, whether secular or religious, as it exists in other African countries. I think it will not happen until the Muslim women themselves see the need for that, and a leader that is emerging from her action. You know, most of the time we are having failures in establishing these Muslim women's organizations because they don't come up from grassroots needs. They come up because maybe we are near election and there is this thing that women candidates would be assisted. So we establish a Muslim sisters' network so that it can channel the money, and when the elections are over it dies. The next time, there is an HIV thing, we start something else and it dies. Even now there is something else that is in existence. But that is an individually driven initiative to increase my visibility or something like that. But once they see that this person can do for both Muslims and Christians, especially in Nairobi.... Because Naomi is more active in Taita, it is less visible to an outsider. It is more visible to guys in Taita. So if you come to Nairobi, because everybody comes to Nairobi for one reason or another, and we have a successful Muslim woman candidate who has gone to Parliament elected and is doing actual work, the ripple effect would be bigger.

In Abdallah's view, then, Muslim women's organizational initiatives are ad hoc and sometimes even opportunistic. But she continues to hope that a record of effective and successful leadership of Muslim women in Parliament, as in other domains, will begin to stimulate more sustained organizational efforts driven by a broader vision rather than single issues and moments.

Unmarried Young Muslim Women in Parliament

While senior or married women have been more acceptable in a male-dominated public politics, the fact that Abdallah was a young unmarried woman in Parliament was a major source of pressure for her. The Muslim community in particular put pressure on her because it saw it as its responsibility to monitor the moral and sexual conduct of a "never married" Muslim woman. A young Muslim woman must uphold family honor through the preservation of her virginity until her first marriage. Failure to obey this code of honor has been the source of family psychological and/or physical violence against young women among the conservative Muslim families to which Abdallah belongs. This patriarchal cultural concern regarding family honor is at the root of long-standing cultural practices such as FGM among Muslim Boranas and Somalis in Kenya and Somalia. Furthermore, given her nonmarried status, Abdallah constantly feels pressed to demonstrate that her nomination to Parliament was based on the merits of her candidacy and not on some undeserving favoritism based on personal association with one of the powerful politicians within the nominating political party:

One of the biggest challenges that I got the first week that my name was announced was "Who is she? Whose girlfriend is she? Why is she here?" For me, I already had plans to do whatever I was going to do. But I thought that now that I have issues, I have to reduce my problems because I was coming in to an avenue, a career that people think is reserved for men. And then, not only I was coming to the career reserved for men, I was coming to a career that stereotypes the community that I come from, not only the religion, but the region and tribe I am supposed to have come from.

Abdallah is a Kenyan of mixed descent: her father came from Yemen, and her mother is from the northeastern region of the country and of Borana descent. Abdallah grew up in the town of Moyale in the Northeastern Province, which she describes as "a very marginalized post of the country" that is hardly accessible due to very poor infrastructure. It is impoverished and has literacy rates that are very low. In the imagination of many Kenyans, all these factors—questionable citizenship, poverty, and illiteracy—are linked to the predominantly Muslim upbringing. Compounding all these "negative" factors at the time she was first seeking office was the fact that she was young and single: "The only thing I had was a good education. But everything else from me was wrong. I was single, I was from a marginalized community, I was a Muslim, and I was woman. So I was combining too many negatives and I needed to neutralize some issues. So although I was single, I had to very quickly make the decision to change that. And I think that helped a lot." So soon after her initiation into parliamentary politics, Abdallah proceeded to get married to someone to whom she was already engaged. Like Azara Mudira, she decided to get married earlier than she had planned in order to gain some cultural capital and legitimacy to better pursue her chosen career in politics.

What is remarkable about both Abdallah and Shaban is the sisterhood that binds them in their struggle as Muslim women in public politics as they confront all sorts of adversities. Being senior in age, profession, and public politics, and having gone through the violent experience of fighting for a legislative political seat as a divorced woman, Shaban offered herself as a mentor to Abdallah. She helped Abdallah to develop strategies for winning the confidence of the electoral constituency in the upper Eastern Province she was running in. Some of these strategies included getting married in order to "neutralize" political opponents who might use her unmarried status for negative attacks. Aspiring to a parliamentary seat made Shaban a target of disparaging patriarchal attacks because she was a divorcee and single mother. She did not want her mentee to undergo similar experiences:

As the community kept talking about [Amina], even the members of Parliament who were Muslims were not amused about the fact that she is basically
the one who is being nominated. She is on the top of the list of the nominees.
But for my part, that time I had to talk very forcibly [in support of] Amina
because I had looked at her CV. I knew what she has done for the party, and
I thought this girl is meant to be here, she is meant to be with us. . . . But of
course, I was one of the people who were telling her, "Get married and very
fast. Since you are engaged, can you do that?" [*laughs*] . . . "Can you do that? By
the time you are going for election, I do not want you to face what I faced. It
is not a good thing."

Shaban was then divorced and was living as a single parent of two children
and a guardian to an orphaned cousin. This again is a combination of cultural factors that works to the disadvantage of women seeking to be MPs.
She notes that as a result,

as much as one would like to do certain things, all female members of Parliament do not have a social life. Socially, you don't have a social life whether
married or single. You don't have that social life. You can't afford to have it
because everybody is like in a telescope. Actually they put you under a microscope and they have to look at each atom in your body and think "Have you
done the right thing today?" So there you are, you are put on the spot. You
have to know how to carry yourself morally [to know] what kind of respect
you command from the people. It is like you are put on that lens by your constituency and also nationally.

Abdallah finds that Muslim men and women, in fact, are the worst offenders
against their fellow Muslim sisters who are presented with leadership opportunities that could advance their collective cause:

Yes, whether or not it matters, she is right: you are put under the microscope.
For example, as she was telling you, the Muslim members of Parliament were
bigger opponents of my nomination than non-Muslims. Then, when you come
to the women's movement, Muslim women were the first to say, "We don't
want her. She does not represent us." Even if they are not in the same party as
you. So, that in itself, you have to be ready for. You have to be ready for criti-
cism on things you have done and things you have not done. Even if you are
married, even if you try to remove the loopholes as much as you can, politics

is such that we operate on rumors, rumors to finish your opponent or potential opponent. Every day you wake up, you say, "Oh God, I am keeping this marriage, so that nobody says anything about me." They would still say something about you. You cannot be too happy. If you laugh too loudly with a guy, you are having something with that man! [laughs] So for a woman, in this profession, you have to do a hundred and fifty percent better than a man and you have to do things that would divert people's attention from you, the social being. And even when you do well, they would still find something bad to say about you.

For Abdallah, it can be harder to cope with the problem of stories made up to disparage women politicians in societies that are primarily oral. This is especially true of nomadic communities of the Northeastern Province, where oral art forms are alive and well. Orality itself becomes a fertile condition for reimagining reality in the image of one's value system (Hayward and Lewis 1996; Jama 1991; Kapteijns 1995; Samatar 1992):

> For a Muslim woman, it is even worse because you are from a community that is very oral, especially like the Somalis. Most people who have not gone to school are very oral. So, they have so much to talk [about] and to come up with . . . anytime you don't overfocus on making sure they don't have other issues to talk about you. . . . [laughs] It is only that we have gotten that opportunity [that we continue to work hard on it] and if we do not build on that opportunity, the ones behind us would not have the same chance as ourselves.

Gender-based discrimination and harassment within the Muslim community was also reported by Abdi Noor, who was eliminated from the process by influential male leaders of her region who used religious arguments despite her winning the nomination of her party during the 1997 elections in Kenya (Maoulidi 2011). The public harassment of women parliamentarians that Abdullah and Shaban recount recalls Aili Tripp's account of the myriad cultural prohibitions women in politics in neighboring Uganda and Tanzania confront that their male counterparts do not confront (2003; 2009, 229).

How Muslim Women MPs Transform Parliament and Schools

Both Abdallah and Shaban see their roles not only as serving their constituents but also as transforming the culture of their space of work. Muslims, who observe a ritualistic bodily hygiene and insist on the gendered separation of cleansing spaces, have been instrumental in ensuring that their faith-based ritualistic and gender needs for infrastructural accommodation are addressed in the Parliament building. A separate bathroom for women was thus installed in the Parliament. On the basis of this parliamentary experience, the two MPs proceeded to raise government and public awareness about the need to have separate latrines and bathrooms for girls and boys in schools. Lack of separation between boys' and girls' bathrooms is one of the reasons that many Muslim conservative parents do not allow their girls who have reached the age of puberty to attend schools; they fear their daughters

Picture of Muslim female bathroom taken in Kenyan Parliament, 2006

will become sexually active and/or get pregnant out of wedlock.[7] This is unacceptable to them given that the preservation of family or clan honor is strongly tied to the success of Muslim girls in keeping their virginity until their first nuptial encounter with their husbands, who are not subjected to the same obligation.

Another gender-related issue of concern for the two MPs is tied to motherhood. Throughout the world, motherhood has been a mixed blessing for women, especially for professional women and those who would like to hold executive political seats. In fact, in many patriarchal contexts, childbearing is used as a mechanism for keeping women out of the public sphere and in "the house." After giving birth to her baby as a married woman, Abdallah, with the support of other women MPs, was successful in her efforts to get Parliament to provide medical coverage for pregnant MPs and to grant maternity leave. This led to the passing of a Parliament motion to provide medical insurance for their children, to subsidize the cost of diapers in Parliament, and to build a nursery in the Parliament building where MP mothers could breastfeed their babies. As Abdallah explains:

> In the past, parliamentarians have been menopausal women! [*laughs*] Naomi is not one. [*laughs*] . . . [So] we never had women of childbearing age [in Parliament]. So I was the first one to have an official baby in Parliament. Parliaments had no system for pregnant people. I had to struggle to have maternity leave and to have maternity medical coverage. Fortunately, that is getting very good. People are [now] encouraged to have more babies because we have maternity leave, we have medical coverage for maternity, we have insurance coverage for the child that is very lucrative because it starts when the child is born rather than when the child is six months old, which is the usual case. What else? We are going to have a playroom in the Kenya Women's Parliamentarian office where we are going to breastfeed our babies. So I think my battles have been good. [*laughs*]

Each successful struggle for achieving access to resources for women MPs is used as an opportunity to further address concerns related to women in general and the girls in particular. Next, Abdallah led the fight for the reduction of the price of diapers nationally and for the provision of diapers in Parliament offices. With the support of fellow women MPs she and Shaban also lobbied for the free provision of sanitary napkins for girls in public schools:

There is also something else that we have worked on as women parliamentarians, in general. It has to do with the sanitary napkins for the girl-child in schools. You know most of them will be dropping out [of school] because of not having proper facilities. It [our campaign] is working and also encouraging communities to consign development funds to build enough latrines and toilets so that girls can feel safer, and more private, because in most schools you will find that they don't have latrines. So the girl-children would run away at the time when they are supposed to have privacy. So we finally got the sanitary napkin to be reduced, maybe their prices to be zero-rated, no taxes on them. It made them cheaper. [The manufacturing companies] are making it easier for the girl-child. Kenyan women parliamentarians are also encouraging the government to put sanitary kits for the girl-child as part of the free primary education's incentive because the need of the girl-child is different from the need of the boy-child.

In addition to poverty, a low level of health literacy and taboos surrounding sex education represent some of the major reasons why menstruating girls, especially in the Muslim communities, drop out of school. Thus, as Shaban points out, their advocacy for free sanitary napkins followed by effective community sensitization efforts became imperative:

But I think in general the communities themselves and even us as women at home, we have difficulties talking to our husbands about our children's menstruation. You know, it is supposed to be a kind of secretive thing and we are not supposed to be discussing it. I was telling our community, the difference between our African set-up and the white man's set-up is that a white man, when their daughter gets her first menstruation, they even celebrate and they discuss it as a family. So that they know that this girl is becoming mature and everybody should look at her as somebody who requires her privacy and should understand her situation. And yet, in our African culture, it is supposed to be a daughter-mother secret.

Shaban goes on to explain that in many Kenya African communities the subject of a daughter's menstrual needs is a taboo subject of conversation even between husband and wife. If the wife does not have an independent income and relies exclusively on funds provided by the husband, then catering to the needs of a menstruating child becomes a tricky affair, especially if the girl is in boarding school. This culture of secrecy over the subject of menstruation, then, sometimes fosters an environment in which husband and wife cannot totally agree with each other on the issue of the monthly domestic budget. The wife is under pressure to "misappropriate" part of their budget to provide for her daughter to ensure that her menstrual cycle will not result in embarrassing moments that could encourage the girl to quit school.

Dress Politics in Parliament: Inscribing Kenya Muslim Diversity

Muslim women MPs often use dress politics in order to fight the stereotypes and discrimination they face by virtue of their faith-based minority status and to mark their participation in national politics. They employ dress politics to resist assimilation to the dominant non-Muslim majority's adoption of a Western-inspired dress code, on the one hand, and to raise national consciousness about the diversity of Muslim communities within Kenya, on the other hand. In Kenya, Muslims are found in virtually every ethnic group, sometimes constituting the majority (as in the case of the Digo, Somali, and Swahili) and sometimes a minority (as among the Taita, Kikuyu, and Luo). Some call themselves Muslims by birth and others refer to themselves as reverts. Being a Muslim in a predominantly Muslim area has different implications for Muslim women and men than being a Muslim in a predominantly non-Muslim area. Coming from a minority position (as women) within both Muslim-majority and Muslim-minority communities, respectively, both Abdallah and Shaban challenge the homogenizing tendency of the politics of representation in Kenya.

In the case of Shaban, dress politics has an additional meaning partly because of her popular middle name, Naomi. This is a name she was given by a woman neighbor and friend of her mother, and it stuck. Though born of Muslim parents, then, Shaban is widely referred to by a name, Naomi, that is not Islamic and that is not common among Kenyans of Christian faith either. For non-Muslims who know little or nothing about her background, her name often raises questions about her faith. Instead of adopting the *buibui* style of dress of the Swahili or the more modern abaya type, however, Shaban gets her dress inspiration from West Africa, which, in her opinion, expresses the union of Africa and Islamic culture, on the one hand, and neutralizes too overt expression of religious identity, on the other. In her words:

Again, the way Amina and I myself dress has made a bit of a difference in Parliament. A bit [of a] difference because we see people dress more like us. [*laughs*]

Yeah! [*laughs*] Before, people were used to suits and what have you; we are seeing a difference in leadership. Now you have a function, you go there. You can't
tell who is a Muslim, who is a Christian. You can't tell because morally the culture is all the same. I think our African culture and Muslim [culture] are interrelated. They are interrelated. For instance, if you go to West Africa, you can't
really tell who is Muslim and who is a Christian by the way people dress. Among
the women, you can't tell and even among the men, you can't tell.

In a sense, then, Shaban has adopted a mode of dress that makes her
comfortable with both her Muslim and African identity and that at the same
time does not mark any sectarian distance from Kenyans of non-Muslim
faith. Coming from a constituency where Muslims are a minority, her religiously neutral dress allows her constituents of non-Muslim faith to be comfortable with her and to trust her ability to represent their interests without
religious bias.

Abdallah, on the other hand, has adopted a modern dress style for her
public appearance that is clearly associated with Muslim faith and identity.
It strongly affirms the continued need for greater representation of the Muslim minority in Parliament. Because she comes from a predominantly Muslim constituency, her dress satisfies the moral standards of her constituents.
Just as important, it is seen as an act of courage for her to mark her Muslim
identity in an institution of power controlled almost entirely by Kenyan of
non-Muslim faith.

The decision to mark Muslim identity by wearing modern Muslim attire
is particularly significant in light of the derision their Islamic dress has elicited
from some non-Muslim citizens, including national leaders. For example,
Minou Fuglesang points out the public attempt of Christian-centric Kenya
president Daniel arap Moi to humiliate Muslims by demeaning coastal Swahili
Muslim women's wear of the *buibui* in a 1985 speech delivered in Mombasa.
According to the *Message*, a local newspaper, "President Moi in his recent
tour of Mombasa asked Muslim women not to wear the *bui-bui* as it did not
reveal their beauty. The president said, 'Women in Mombasa should not
wear the *bui-bui* because if you cover your faces with the *bui-bui*, nobody will
know if you are beautiful. You will also miss the chance of someone to marry
you'" (qtd. in Fuglesang 1994, 205).

In light of such pronouncements and the attitudes that underline them,
one can appreciate why Muslim women politicians take it on themselves to
signify their Muslimness through dress discourse in Parliament, a site whose

defining principle of composition is representativeness. The semiotics of this dress act becomes significant not only for political relations within the August House (Kenyan Parliament) but also for how the constituents see themselves (re)presented. Mary Porter (1998) also elaborates on the politicization of Islamic dress as school uniform in public schools in Mombasa to mark the Muslim distinctiveness of Swahili adolescent girls. In sum, what this discourse suggests is the tension between belonging to a community of faith, with its internal histories of hierarchies and normative gender ideology, and belonging to a country as members of a religious minority that Muslim women continue to experience.

In spite of their overt display of Muslim women's identity through their mode of dress, however, the Muslim women MPs adopt a secular politics as parliamentarians. Both MPs stress their commitment to serving Muslim and non-Muslim constituents through the adoption of secular politics, for secular politics is strategically necessary for broadening their electoral constituency, which is multiethnic and multireligious. This is crucial especially because very few Muslims participate as candidates in electoral politics, even in communities where they are the majority. Both MPs have well-thought-out strategies for winning or retaining parliamentary seats.

Secular politics is deemed important even in constituencies where Muslims are the majority. According to Abdallah, there is a general tendency among Muslims in many parts of the country not to register as voters because of what she calls "a slum upbringing." As underprivileged minority, many Muslims in her constituency live in slums where bread-and-butter issues take precedence over all else. In such a situation, Muslim MPs cannot rely exclusively on the Muslim vote and have to adopt a politics that appeals to Muslims as well as to constituencies of other faiths. For Shaban and Abdallah, the strategy of secular politics is as effective as it is necessary for their work.

For Shaban, who represents a Christian-majority constituency, the imperative of secular politics applies not only to her work in Parliament but also to her regular engagement with her constituents. Though a Muslim, she may on occasion even be required to support the construction of a Christian church. Such action on her part may upset some of her Muslim constituents, and she finds that she has to rationalize it to them as much as to herself:

> If I can add, the other problem we face because of our secular nature of the country generally, even if you start home, most of the constituencies even where I come from [Taita in the Coast Province] is Christian. There is no way I will

be told "Look, [Christians in your area] are building a church" and I look the other way. You understand. So I must give them some of my contribution because I think that basically we are praying to the same God, although they use a different route. I should also encourage them their own way.

Shaban sees hope in the young as well. Increasingly the young are crossing religious boundaries in their relationships. Interreligious marriages are rising. And even though one of the spouses ends up converting in order to bring up the children within one faith, the growing incidence of Christian-Muslim marriage is defusing religious tensions and is making it easier for her to support the religious aspirations of her constituents who belong to a different community of faith.

Even more than Abdallah, Shaban, who comes from a Muslim-majority coastal constituency, is always walking a tightrope between her Muslim community of faith and her non-Muslim constituents without whose support she could never have gotten voted into Parliament. It is partly for this reason that a culturally neutral attire worn widely by Muslim women in West Africa plays out well in her area. A dress that places emphasis on her Africanity essentially reinforces her embrace of secular politics in the public arena.

Achieving Success within Their Constituencies

Throughout the period before President Kibaki came to power, MPs saw themselves and were certainly seen by their constituents as primarily agents of development and only secondarily as enactors of laws. They thus spent a good deal of their time and energy mobilizing human and material resources toward the social and infrastructural advancement of their constituencies. Notwithstanding the massive corruption often involved, the MPs were more likely to be reelected by their constituents for having built a new clinic or school here, a social hall, mosque, or church there, and/or transport infrastructure within the precincts of their constituencies. Because of these demands on the MPs, their legislative responsibilities were often neglected, and MPs with more material resources generally fared better in election than those with less.

When President Kibaki came to power in 2002, he tried to change this equation by introducing the constituency development fund. This is a grant given by the Kenyan government to individual MPs to help them address the specific developmental needs of their constituents. The MP is required to set up a committee that identifies and prioritizes the needs of the constituency using the framework of a four- to five-year plan, coinciding with his or her tenure. These needs may range from water resources and public health to education and sports. In the case of Shaban and Abdallah, the large portion of the constituency development fund they received was injected into the promotion of education, health, and civic literacies.

Within the Parliament, Muslim women MPs must dispel prejudices against them from both (Muslim and non-Muslim) male colleagues and non-Muslim female colleagues regarding their capacity to perform as effective legislators. Outside Parliament they use their national prominence as legislators to address specific needs and concerns of their constituencies. Education is prominent among these. The educational disparities between Muslim and non-Muslim children is huge, with Muslim girls occupying the bottom rung of the educational ladder (Chege and Sifuna 2006, 41). This is the result of both cultural and religious conservatism within their own Muslim communities and their economic marginalization by successive regimes in the postcolonial dispensation (Oded 2000, 91–99). Muslim women MPs feel a great responsibility to alter this educational equation, at least within their constituencies if not at the national level, without neglecting the developmental needs of their non-Muslim constituents.

One of the major problems facing Kenyan Muslims, especially women, is that they lag behind in literacy in Roman script and secular education. Many Muslim parents are reluctant to enroll their female children in schools, and even those who do attend secular schools often drop out after high school (Chege and Sifuna 2006, 41). Early marriage in order to ensure that brides are virgins when they marry and thus preserve family honor is one of the leading causes of female illiteracy among Kenyan Muslims. Both Shaban and Abdallah use their position as political figures to raise consciousness about the need for their Muslim constituents to embrace education, especially the education of girls:

> In my constituency, I have personally tried to make sure that our girls, the girl-child, especially the Muslim girl-child, is making the right decision about their lives and their professions. Now they are going into professional fields. Some of them, some years back, had even been called to university and they had refused. They declined. But I have gotten them back to go to the university. I have talked to them. I have gotten some sense [in]to them. I have told them that they can't get where I am if they don't do the right thing and the right thing is to know that "the only weapon you have is education."

Shaban, then, has assumed the role of a mentor, encouraging girls—as well as boys—to take advantage of every educational opportunity and work hard at it. Girls have spent years of their lives exposed to local traditions and practices that have fostered a culture of low expectation in an increasingly competitive world, and so Shaban works with them and counsels them to aim for the very top, always drawing from her personal professional journey to inspire them.

The question of professional expectations, of course, is not unrelated to family pressure to get married. An issue that is always coming up in my interviews with young women is that the further they progress, the more anxious their mothers become. Their mothers are concerned that by the time their daughters have completed their educations, they may be too old to find a spouse. This anxiety is perhaps influencing the professional path that young women are taking, since it stands to reason that if becoming a doctor takes a very long time, then the shortcut to the medical profession for the Muslim girl would be to become a nurse. Shaban thinks that if parents were encouraged to send their children to school on time—that is, to begin elementary education at age six—then there would be no problem of delayed marriage. For then it would be possible for a young woman to complete her university education by the age of twenty-two. She would then be ready for marriage and, equally important, be better placed to help her family financially in a new Kenya where the salary of a husband alone is proving increasingly insufficient to cater to the necessities of daily life. As Shaban explains:

The other thing I tell parents, especially in my area [Coast Province], "Who wants a woman who is not going to school? Who wants a woman who is not working? Really, let's ask." Today, it is not easy. In the past, a woman's place was in the kitchen back home. But as time is passing, life has become so difficult. Even the man is expecting to receive some economic assistance from the wife. It is not easy anymore, it is rough. So nobody would look forward to being married to somebody who is not working. That thing is a thing of the past where you tell a woman, "Now that I am marrying you, you should quit your job." Those are things of the past. It is no longer what is practiced today. Most of the people would want someone who comes and who would be a kind of financial help towards that family, not to be a burden for that family. OK, their needs are more today. . . . Even for our age group, the ones who got their wives and decided that their wives should not be working, right now they are busy running around looking for jobs for their wives because that is the only way they can [meet their needs].

In the wake of the success of the sensitization campaign for girls' education, Abdallah also warns of the danger of neglecting the boys who are falling behind in education. It has been observed that the patriarchal preference for Muslim boys often means that boys do not get proper educational supervision at home, which in turn makes them vulnerable to the culture of drugs and juvenile delinquency, which is rampant in Muslim communities.[8] She points out that gendered discordance in educational attainment, with girls increasingly performing better than boys on the average, could inadvertently generate another social problem for educated Muslim young women, who may now experience problems finding compatible husbands:

> There is another challenge also. . . . We should not be overtargeting just the girl-child. We have some situations now of having the girl-child moving very fast and actually reinforcing the parents' fears because there are not sufficiently educated Muslim men to go out with. [laughs] . . . I mean it is serious. There is actually a shortage of eligible Muslim men. [laughs] . . . I went to Majengo and Pumwani where I want to stand. You find so many girls with Bs. We are trying to get them into colleges. We are trying to advance them in careers. But when it comes to the boys, they are all chewing miraa; the best they can get is D+. So if this girl goes out, the chances of coming back to marry anybody there is very hard because these guys are not eligible. So we have to have a balance, a balancing act, so that we do not leave those men of ours behind. I personally think they are really lagging behind. They need to wake up.

Miraa (also referred to as chaat) is a leaf drug that is widely chewed in Kenya, especially among the Somali and Swahili. It is expensive and addictive. It is also a "social" drug in the sense that those who are addicted to it enjoy chewing it in the company of others while engaged in hours of free-flowing conversation on topics that range from the philosophical to the absurd. But for the Muslim women MPs, the woes of drug culture have now been multiplied tenfold by the introduction of hard drugs (Beckerleg 1995, 2005).

Besides poor education, in fact, exposure to both soft and hard drugs is contributing to an increase in sexual violence against both girls and boys within families as well as outside. During the time of my fieldwork, the rape of children and women and incest that pervades both Muslim and non-Muslim communities was highly denounced even in Muslim communities that in the past had kept silent in order not to dispel the myth of Muslim moral immunity to sexual misconduct and violence. Muslim women MPs and other

Muslim women politicians, such as the vocal Nazlin Umar Rajput, the subject of chapter 5, were strong advocates for the enactment of a sexual offenses bill that laid down severe punitive sentences for perpetrators of sexual violence in all communities. Muslim women MPs and other politicians like Rajput have been remarkably successful in educating legislators about the ways in which culture and religion can be effectively deployed legalistically to address offenses or rights related to such social problems.

Public Health Education: The HIV Pandemic and Community Sensitization

Kenya is one of the countries in Africa with the highest rates of HIV/ AIDS, and women and children are the most affected. Although also affected, Muslims were in denial for a long time, claiming immunity based on their "sexual morality." Given the ravaging effects of the HIV/AIDS pandemic even among the Muslim communities, Shaban and Abdallah are investing a great deal of their energy in public health sensitization and health literacy. Partly because of poverty and a lower level of (secular and religious) education among Muslims, there is little awareness about the causes of the pandemic and the best means to manage it once one is infected and/or affected by it. Consequently, Shaban and Abdallah also allocate a great portion of constituent development funds to developing health awareness, holding public health literacy workshops, and mobilizing Muslim and Christian clergies to join in the fight against the HIV/AIDS pandemic.

Their first goal was to assist Muslim communities in becoming actors in the fight against the disease by first rejecting the attitude of denial that prevents them from acknowledging that the disease is present in their communities as well: "Of course, now as we are organizing people, it just occurs to me, coming from a medical background, I realize that if a Muslim was passing on a message about HIV/AIDS to a fellow Muslim, they would understand more. So I had to organize people in community-based organizations to be able to carry out this message of HIV/AIDS awareness to them."

Community-based organizations are some of the most effective structures for reaching people at the grassroots. Shaban channels some of the constituent development fund monies to community-based organizations so they can hold workshops, carry out campaigns, and engage in other activities to raise awareness about HIV/AIDS and the fatal danger of not owning up to its existence in the community of Muslims. She gets community-based organizations to underscore that message that the worst that can happen to a girl who is not in school is not becoming pregnant but becoming infected with HIV/AIDS. For Shaban, then, it is crucial that parents realize that as much as it is frowned on by their communities, premarital sex is a reality. And instead of forcing their children to engage in premarital sex "underground," they would be doing them great service if they taught them about safe sex and HIV/AIDS management and engaged with them on these topics, even if cautiously.

Sexuality, sex education, and HIV/AIDS sensitization are not an easy topic in most Muslim communities and other faith-based communities, and the ulama and other religious leaders are not at ease with these subjects: "HIV/AIDS was a very big problem and its main stumbling block was, whereas other communities have taken drastic measures to combat HIV/AIDS, the religious communities, both Muslims and Christians, were quite adamant not to act. They were in denial. Yet our community, as much as you know what we should tell people, is about abstention." When religious leaders decide to talk about it at all, it is always in terms of sexual abstention. In the process, young people keep dying, and the religious leaders are forced to conduct one funeral service after another:

> And this is why HIV/AIDS is a disaster that has taken so long in being con-
> trolled, simply because we have been in denial. I asked myself, "How come the
> Western countries have been able to control it and we in Africa have not been
> able to?" Yet, morally, they are not more moral than the African society. What
> is it that we do that is not correct? Of course, it is the message that we are car-
> rying across—denial and abstention rule. That is the way I have looked at it.
> It is because of the message. That is a big, big problem because every day the
> reverends and the sheikhs are busy burying. Every other day, you find you are
> in a funeral service. Every other day, you find yourself in a sermon because this
> person has gone, you can't bring them back, and you can't wish it away.

The religious leaders not only refuse to discuss matters of sexuality and HIV/AIDS but also campaign vigorously to prevent any introduction of sex education in schools. As Shaban explains: "And even family health life education was supposed to be introduced in our schools in the early 1990s, but it got a lot of resistance from the religious leaders, both Muslims and Christians, who argue that you cannot teach people about sexuality. That is the way they are looking at [it]."

In spite of these cultural and religious constraints, Shaban sees a silver lin-ing: more and more members of the Muslim clergy are coming to terms with

HIV/AIDS reality, partly because of the success of their campaigns and partly because the problem is so pervasive that the clergy can no longer pretend it does not exist:

> But now, we seem like we are talking one language. You go to a church, you find the story, there is HIV/AIDS. Even when people are getting married, the religious leaders are passing on that message. You go to a Muslim function, you find there is a message about HIV/AIDS. They have finally accepted it. Although they don't talk about condoms, they actually caution people to be careful. As much as it is godly to abstain, my question to some few religious leaders I have come across is that "OK, I am married. But I know my husband is married somewhere else because our set-up is polygamous. So, am I going to tell him, 'People, keep off because you have been involved somewhere else, I am not going to be involved with you or are we going to be more careful.'" That is when they say, "Yeah! That is the catch." But I tell them you must pass on that message to the community, otherwise they would go home and say, "The religious leader said it is forbidden."

The prevalence of HIV/AIDS has, of course, been aggravated by the rise in gender-based sexual violence. Muslim women are subjected to sexual violence constantly, which pushed the Kenyan women MPs across faith lines to call for the Sexual Offences Bill that passed into law in 2006. Njoki Ndung'u—another woman MP—introduced the Sexual Offences Bill into Parliament in response to the upswing in sexual crimes such as rape, incest, and pedophilia in Kenya. The two Muslim women MPs joined their non-Muslim women MPs in sensitization campaigns, especially in the slums, on the legal protective measures proposed by the Sexual Offences Bill:

> We have also the issue of rape whereby young boys come and gang-rape their own sisters, gang-raping their sisters. Let me tell you we have become a cursed community. It is terrible. Right now I am dealing with a case of a young girl. Let us say a baby who was raped by a forty-year-old. . . . [The rape of girls] is a phenomenon that cuts across the board. It is just that with the Muslim community there is also the problem of cover-up once the rape occurs. There is a cover-up by members of the family. There is less reporting of the number of Muslims doing it, because our community is very protective. Maybe that is why it is not showing in the statistics. It is just like with HIV/AIDS: they want

Workshop on sexual offenses against women and legal defense support for women
facilitated by Njoki Ndung'u and Amina Abdallah

Njoki Ndung'u and Amina Abdallah with workshop participants

to wish it away and deny that it is happening. Given the social factors that contribute to rape that cut across the board, the incidents also cut across.

CONCLUSION

The narrative analysis of the interviews with the only two Muslim women MPs in Kenya until the end of 2007 reveals that the 1990s democratization process opened up doors of opportunity for women in general and for Muslim women in particular, giving them the chance to participate as political actors in public politics in the nation. However, that process has not been able to transform the patriarchal ideology rooted in all Kenyan communities, which prevent women from participating in electoral politics and from seeking executive political seats, such as the Parliament, on equal terms with men. Despite the constraints of patriarchy, Muslim women who experience multiple, gendered marginalization as members of a religious minority and as ethnic minorities contend that the democratization process offers them a terrain on which to contest these negative forces within their communities as well as within the nation at large. Both MPs also stress the crucial role of literacy and mass education, which are key to political consciousness-raising regarding civic rights and obligations among Muslims. They contend that addressing the Muslim educational gap in general and that of Muslim girls in particular is crucial in the struggle to achieve equal rights and opportunities for greater participation in the democratic sociopolitical transformation of the nation.

This analysis also highlights the ways in which Muslim women MPs subvert patriarchal representations of women in order to achieve some practical gains on behalf of women and girls and themselves as political leaders. Furthermore, it offers an explanation of why they opt more for a secular rather than a faith-based politics, namely, that they are seeking to reach out to and win the support of their multiethnic and multireligious constituencies. The 2010 constitution itself defines Kenya as a "secular state," but one within which all communities of faith are to be treated equally and protected. This is a provision that provides ample room for advocating for the rights of Muslims in Kenya without resorting to a faith-based politics of the kind that inspired the IPK and that could potentially threaten religious coexistence in this multireligious nation.

4

Judge Abida Ali-Aroni

First Muslim Woman Justice of the Kenya High Court

My agenda really is the agenda for women generally speaking and the agenda for the Muslim community.

—Abida Ali-Aroni

INTRODUCTION

The increase in the proportion of Muslim women in the Tenth Parliament was partly a product of the gains from civic and political struggles for constitutional reform in Kenya. As Willy Mutunga (1999) demonstrates in his insightful study, these struggles go back to the final years of Daniel arap Moi's presidency, during which civil society, under the leadership of the National Conference Executive Council, put pressure on the government to constitute a national conference. And when the government would not submit to popular pressure, except by way of making changes in electoral laws and procedures to level the playing field, the council went ahead and drafted a symbolic constitution.

It was not until the post-Moi era and under Mwai Kibaki's first term as president that the process of constitutional review was finally taken over by the government (Katumanga 1996; Mutunga 1999). Mwai Kibaki himself understood only too well the need to move quickly to put a comprehensive constitution review process in place. After all, it was the same civil society forces pushing for constitutional reform that put him in power. So in 2003 the Kibaki government established the Constitution of Kenya Review Commission under the chairmanship of Yash Pal Ghai. The constitutional conferences organized by the commission used to meet at the Bomas of Kenya—essentially a modern village that serves as a tourist attraction—and documents arising from it are widely known as the Bomas Draft Constitution. The first and most popular of these documents was known as the Ghai Boma Draft. Further negotiations and compromises, after Yash Pal Ghai, a Kenyan of Asian origin of Hindu faith, resigned from the commission in protest against the Kenya government's alleged tampering with the constitution-making process (Rutten 2006) and was replaced by Ali-Aroni, resulted in the second Bomas Draft. This document was then further doctored by the then attorney general, Amos Wako, resulting in the Wako Draft. And it was the Wako Draft that was rejected in the 2005 constitutional referendum (Rutten 2006).

The dispute over the results of the 2007 presidential elections exploded into weeks of widespread violence in the country. This situation resulted in the negotiations headed by former UN secretary-general Kofi Annan, which led to the national accord and a power-sharing formula between the contending parties. A key requirement of the accord was a new constitution for the country. As a result, Parliament enacted the Constitution of Kenya Review Act in 2008, appointing a committee of experts to solicit the views of the citizens on various contentious issues and produce a new draft constitution that was finally adopted after receiving overwhelming support of Kenyans in the 2010 referendum.

The imperative of representation along gender, religion, ethnicity, age, and disability lines consistently framed the constitutional struggles in Kenya. This demand naturally led to the participation of several Muslim women at the center of the constitutional reform movement, representing one civil society constituency or another (Cussac 2008, 295; Kabira 2012). Indeed, a number of "minority" representatives rose to sudden visibility during this period. Among those Muslim women who became very involved in the process was Sultana Fadhil. With Naima Bin Daghar, she was among the very few Swahili women to be trained in and enter the practice of law, serving first at the bench as a magistrate and later at the bar with her own chamber in Mombasa, Fadhil and Kilonzo Advocates. Fadhil was a founding member of Muslims for Human Rights and for a while served as the chair of its executive board. Partly because of her training in law, her human rights and women's rights work, and her community orientation, she was among the first Muslim women whose participation in the constitution review process was sought after by Muslims on the Kenyan coast.

Another Muslim woman similarly sought after for the review process is the one who is the subject of this chapter, Abida Ali-Aroni, a lawyer by training and a judge of the High Court of Kenya since June 2009. In fact, Ali-Aroni is the first Muslim woman ever to be appointed a judge of the High

Court in Kenya. Prior to this most recent national judicial appointment, she had achieved public prominence in 2005 after her appointment in July 2004 as the second chairperson of the Constitution of Kenya Review Commission. Given the tendency toward the ethnicization of politics and religion in Kenya and the tendency of many African governments to be ethnocratic and sectarian, the appointment of Ali-Aroni, a Muslim woman from a minority community that wields no power in majoritarian political calculations, is a demonstration of a certain political consensus reached between the state and the civil society in the democratic quest for neutrality and fair play in the process of constitution making. Ali-Aroni, however, does not feel that her Islamic background has ever been a liability to her; indeed she feels the opposite is true:

> I told you I had never felt discriminated against and this I am telling you from the bottom of my heart. I have never felt discriminated because I am a Muslim. I don't see it. I refuse to see it. I have refused to see it. And it has always worked to my advantage. Now, this is now hearsay for me because I was never consulted when I was appointed chairperson of the commission. One, I was a vice-chairperson of the commission. So it did not just come from out of the blue. And for my friends, the reason why I ranked high is because I was a Muslim; two, because you could not strictly tie me to any tribal affiliation because Muslims in Kenya are identified as "Muslims" first and then your tribe comes second. So . . . when we have two big tribes fighting in this country. . . . We have the Kikuyus who are at the helm of leadership and then we have the Luos who have always been competitive with the Kikuyus. And then we have this political divide strictly speaking based on tribal affiliation. I couldn't fit anywhere. I have given you my background. So that was a plus for me. So that is why I tell you that my being a Muslim, my being a Muslim woman has always worked, it has always worked in my favor.
>
> In many other positions that I have held, people say, "We have never seen a Muslim woman. Why don't we try her?" It has always worked for me. So that is why I say that there is a great potential for the Muslims and the Muslim woman in this country if only we could find our space, because we have it in this country.

Ali-Aroni's refusal to acknowledge discrimination is generally a strategy for subverting it; she turns a blind eye to it so that she can place herself at the center of the struggle to achieve justice for marginalized women and minorities within the national democratic process while also making personal political gains as a Muslim woman lawyer. This tactic is significant especially given both the long history of exclusion of Muslim women within the principal male-centered Muslim organizations and the absence of a strong Muslim women's sociopolitical movement. As a professional lawyer with the necessary legal tools and skills, she seized the opportunities afforded by the democratization momentum to propel herself into leadership positions in institutions hitherto not open either to (Muslim) women or minorities so that she might effectively advocate for the rights of women, especially of Muslim women.

This chapter offers an analysis of Ali-Aroni's personal account of her family background, her educational and professional journey into spaces culturally restricted to men, the development of her political consciousness through her involvement with Muslim politics during the constitution review process, and her contribution to reform movements focused on (Muslim) women's rights through coalitions with national non-Muslim activist women's organizations such as the International Federation of Women Lawyers and with the support of progressive Muslim men lawyers engaged with the dominant Muslim organizations, the MCCK and SUPKEM. This chapter also brings to light her perspective on how the interplay of multiple levels of structural marginalization on the ground of religion, ethnicity, race, gender, age, and class have acted in concert to undermine the potential for the emergence of a strong sociopolitical movement among Kenya Muslim women in spite of the opening up of the democratic space.

A subject of critical importance that Ali-Aroni addresses is the status of the kadhi courts in Kenya's judicial system. While both Muslim men and Muslim women agreed on the need to retain the kadhi courts in the constitution, it is Ali-Aroni's view that Muslim men and Muslim women each want a different type of court. The goal for Muslim women is to overhaul the kadhi courts in order to free them from excessive patriarchal control and interpretation. Finally Ali-Aroni offers an important critique of the culture of political activism of Muslim women in Kenya. She sees it as unduly sporadic and narrow in its focus and generally operating under the patronage of Muslim male organizations.

Muslim Women's Rights Activist of Mixed Heritage within Kenyan Ethnic Politics

Ali-Aroni describes herself as a product of a mixed ethnic, racial, and religious family heritage. Her identity is a testimony of the long and sustained historical interactions between and *brassage* (ethnic blending) of Africans, South Asians, and Arabs on the two sides of the Indian Ocean. This is a blending that even British and French colonial projects did not succeed in breaking. The Comoro Islands, a predominantly Muslim country where her father comes from, is a former French colony, whereas Kenya, the birthplace of her mother, who is of mixed African and Goan (South Asian Catholic) descent, is a former British colony. Born in Nairobi, Kenya in 1961, Ali-Aroni received her education in the country of her birth and completed her law degree at the University of Nairobi. Later in life she crossed yet another identity boundary when she married a Kenyan of Kisii ethnic affiliation, adding another layer of complexity in the identity of their three children.

Although a Kenya citizen, Ali-Aroni maintains ties with the birthplace of her father, the Comoro Islands, a phenomenon of transnational allegiance that is very common throughout the world with people born of such rich, multiple heritages. Her allegiance to her father's homeland explains why she once thought she would end up becoming a Comoro consular officer, in which capacity she could have assisted Comorian citizens living in Kenya who face problems that require the intervention of their consular office. As she puts it: "Before I joined the reform movement, I wanted to be the consular for the Comoros. The current consular who has been consular for over ten years is Asian-Kenyan. But the local Comorians—we have a community here, although not very big, but it is there. . . . He did not take our interests to heart. Most of them still keep their Comorian nationality at heart. I don't. I am a Kenyan by virtue of being born in Kenya. So they wanted a Comorian-Kenyan to represent them." Ali-Aroni even received a letter from the president of the Comoros appointing her as the country's consulate officer. But partly because the incumbent consular was not willing to relinquish the position, partly because she was an expectant mother, and partly because of the increasing pull of Kenyan politics, she did not pursue the matter to its conclusion.

Ali-Aroni sees herself as a cosmopolitan Nairobi Muslim woman and contends that her cosmopolitanism and multiple ethnic and religious heritage helps her to be a cultural bridge builder and provider of an understanding of how laws and policies may affect minority (Muslim) constituencies differently from dominant groups. For Ali-Aroni, therefore, being a Muslim woman lawyer of mixed ethnic background married to a Kisii husband with whom she bore three children legitimizes her as "a citizen of consensus" among diverse constituencies with competing interests over political power

Justice Abida Ali-Aroni in her law office, standing by her reference law books, including a book from India on Indian shari'a, 2006

and control of national resources. Thus, Ali-Aroni argues that both her belonging to powerless marginalized groups that do not threaten the power equation in the country and her having achieved educational and professional success as one of the very few Muslim women lawyers have been great assets in positioning her, within the democratization era, as a leader in the national political arena defined by identity politics.

In her advocacy for Muslim women's education and women's rights, Ali-Aroni discusses the ways in which her access to higher education and her professional achievements in law practice—a field highly dominated by men of all ethnic and faith backgrounds—have significantly contributed to minimizing gender politics within the two male-dominated Muslim organizations involved in the constitutional review process: the MCCK, a group of Muslim rights activists who lobbied in the late 1990s for a Muslim-friendly constitutional change; and the SUPKEM, the umbrella body of all Muslim organizations in Kenya. Both the MCCK and the SUPKEM felt the urgent need to include Muslim women, who they believed could be instrumental in advocating for the right to maintain the kadhi courts (Cussac 2008). It is within this context that in 1997–98, they called on professional Muslim women to create the Muslim Women Sisters Network (Cussac 2008, 295). Ali-Aroni was then selected by the same male-dominated Muslim councils as their spokesperson during the constitutional review process to represent Muslim women's position on issues. She believes that the fact that the Muslim community allowed her the chance to be the spokesperson helped in getting her nominated as the chair of the review commission:

> So my getting to that position, one would like to credit it to the community because they gave me an opportunity from the beginning to represent the Muslim woman, especially when the government was trying to understand why there was a lot of agitation over reform. I went in as a representative of the Muslim women. The community allowed me to go in. . . . So I went in. I had no idea about politics. I got a lot of assistance from the Muslim Consultative Council's officials and SUPKEMs who were already involved in the agitation. I went in to give the representation of the Muslim women. Then from there I joined other women. But even from there I kept representing the Muslim community. When we were amending the law that was the backbone of the review, I represented the Muslim community in a small committee of five people to amend the law and make it acceptable to civil society and religious organizations.

It is significant that her designation by the MCCK and SUPKEM to play this prominent public national role as a Muslim woman did not raise any protest from the wider Muslim communities, even though she is a strong supporter of a secularist system of governance and administration of justice. This is partly due to the fact that the leaders of these two organizations belong to the traditional Muslim hierarchy, and their main political concern during the debate for constitutional reform was to have a spokesperson in "a secular educated Muslim woman" who could effectively advocate not only for the retention of the kadhi courts, within the secular Kenyan constitution, but also for upgrading of the status of kadhis within the state judicial system (A. Mutua 2005, 2006; M. Mutua 2009). As a secularist advocate for Muslim women's rights, Ali-Aroni used the SUPKEM's and MCCK's mandate to advance Muslim causes in the debate on constitutional reform and as a window for negotiating the gendering of the councils themselves through the admission of Muslim women members in Muslim organizations, for centering the Muslim women's rights agenda, and for calling for the reform of the kadhi courts by challenging traditional patriarchal control of the shari'a and interpretation of the Qur'an.

Lessons from the Muslim Women Sisters Network

Majoritarian politics is ultimately a by-product of identity politics and is tied to the control of power and distribution of resources that matter not only in electoral competitions but also in arrangements related to communities and the nation as a whole. The struggle for political and economic power within minority groups, then, often collides with gender and class interests in representative politics, group decision-making processes, and distribution of resources. Furthermore, it may have a negative impact on the potential for qualified members of marginalized groups within minority constituencies, such as women and members of low social (or economic) status, to emerge as leaders of political organizations. In general, traditional elite control of the power of representation and decision-making processes might hamper reforms, especially those related to the "woman's question."

The question of the right of representation is one of the constraints faced by Muslim Women Sisters Network, which lacks infrastructural capacity for functioning independently since it is a women's organization initiated from the top down by patriarchal organizations committed to maintaining the status quo of gender relations within Muslim communities as they bargain for the constitutional retention of the kadhi courts. In fact, at a certain point Ali-Aroni had to tell the MCCK to "let go" of the Muslim Women Sisters Network, because the organization was not able to grow under the MCCK since it itself was not growing. In her opinion, these constraints are due to a number of factors. One is that the majority of Muslim women in both secular and religious organizations are not well educated. Another is that the ratio of professional Muslim women who struggle to maintain their social and professional mobility is tiny (having a profession is a privilege rarely enjoyed by educated upper-class Muslim women, who are more often bound to domesticity once they have married Muslim men from traditional elite backgrounds). Yet another is that the social class allegiance of educated upper-class Muslim women to the traditional Muslim elite prevents them from participating fully in advocating for reforms that might challenge the authority of that elite within the social hierarchy of Muslim communities. It is against this backdrop that Ali-Aroni laments about the Muslim Women Sisters Network, noting that "we have gone back to our cocoon because I am not hearing Muslim women talking anymore. Probably it is just a phase and we will reemerge and join the women's movement to agitate for reform of the rights of women in Kenya." Socialization into a belief system that it is not important to educate girls and that the woman's place is in the domestic sphere are two of the reasons that the Muslim Women Sisters Network lost steam prematurely:

> In a way, I think because the socialization of the Muslim women in Kenya is such that you would rarely find them actively involved in social matters due to the customs that we have adopted, we Muslims. Even if you look at traditional contexts, it is very difficult to find women agitating, especially from the predominantly Muslim areas. If you talk of the coastal area, a Muslim woman is normally in the kitchen. Women are married off at very early ages. They are hardly given education. So it is really difficult for them to be at par with the rest of the Kenyan women. If you look at the Northeastern Province, it is a similar issue.

As long as Ali-Aroni provided leadership, the group continued to maintain significant momentum. Though she was not "political" initially, her experience working with the International Federation of Women Lawyers, of which she was a founding member, and her national visibility helped her provide effective leadership to the emergent Muslim women's movement. As she explains, through her work in the federation, "I was able to participate in activism. So for me it wasn't new and even when I joined the Muslim Women Sisters Network it was against that background. I was a familiar face in Kenya, I was a familiar face in the women's movement, although I wasn't really politically oriented until I entered the Muslim Women Sisters Network and we got involved in reform and other political activities." Ali-Aroni even provided office space in her chamber for the Muslim Women Sisters Network to use.

Once Ali-Aroni was appointed to chair the constitutional review commission, she could no longer creatively participate in the work of Muslim Women Sisters Network. She no longer had the time and as a result, without her direct leadership, the organization began to fade:

> So, when I joined the commission formerly, I could not participate fully in the movement that we had begun for the Muslim women. It is very involving. There is the issue of donor funding; there is the issue of attending all sorts of civil society meetings and a lot of people couldn't do that. With my exit to the review commission, it kind of died off and I kept hoping that other people would pick up, but it really did not pick up. So you will not find that systematic progression of that movement. Although we have small groupings of women within different areas depending either on the profession they have or the locality, it is so low and so disorganized they are unable to be heard at the national level. That is the most unfortunate thing.

The lack of resources that would permit growth independent of patriarchal Muslim organizations was an additional factor behind the inertia of the Muslim Women Sisters Network. The same observation has been made by Nazlin Omar Rajput, who in protest against Muslim men's control of organizational leadership went ahead and founded the National Muslim Council of Kenya (NMCK), which has an overwhelming number of Muslim women from a low-income background and the slums. In the absence of an independent women's group, upper- and middle-class professional and educated Muslim women interested in reform have generally joined professional women's organizations or political parties that absorb women of all classes and ethnic and religious affiliations (the IPK is one group that does not absorb all women, since its membership is based on religious identity [Oded 2000]).

Partly as a result of her experience working with Muslim women through the Muslim Women Sisters Network, then, Ali-Aroni became highly discontented over the lack of dynamic political involvement on the part of educated and professional Muslim women who embrace Muslim identity politics in a national women's movement. However, it is important to point out that her pessimistic view is countered by the dynamism of other Muslim women activist leaders such as Maimuna Mwidau, the cofounder and director of the Kisauni-based League of Muslim Women of Kenya, the late peace activist leader Dekha Ibrahim of Wajir, MP for Wajir Sophia Abdi Noor, Somali Muslim women of the Wajir Women for Peace, and Amina Zuberi, chair of the Mombasa-based Tangana Women Development Group, chair of the Caucus for Women's Leadership, and board member of Muslims for Human Rights. Muslim women activists across the nation have persisted in imparting civic education to grassroots Muslim women constituencies, leading to a critical mass participation in local and national politics and gender justice activism. Their impact in advocating for (Muslim) women's social and political rights has earned them international recognition. Maimuna Mwidau, for example, was the first Muslim woman to receive the Charles T. Manatt Democracy Award from the International Foundation for Electoral Systems for her significant work in advocating for women's empowerment and greater representation and participation in electoral politics. Her leadership role in the constitutional review process is highly praised by Wanjiru Kabira in her *Time for Harvest: Women and Constitution Making in Kenya* (2012). She also moderated the April 2010 National Women Constitution Conference at Bomas of Kenya attended by more than one thousand participants. Like Nazlin Umar Rajput featured in chapter 5, Mwidau organized radio programs to raise awareness of the importance of the Sexual Offences Bill.[1] She is an advisor in major international forums related to women's participation in governance.

After her political awakening, Ali-Aroni joined other non-Muslim women's advocacy groups such as the International Federation of Women Lawyers, using her professional skills to bring Muslim women's perspectives to the national struggles for women's rights. She used the space opened up by the national democratization momentum to strategically carve a path for herself for pursuing her activism on behalf of (Muslim) women, including herself.

The significance of Ali-Aroni's role as the chair of the Constitution of Kenya Review Commission must be appraised in the context of the wider movement for constitutional reform in Kenya that began in the early 1990s, and whose study constitutes an important dimension of Kabira's *Time for Harvest* and Mutunga's *Constitution-Making from the Middle*. After all, the Bomas of Kenya meetings of the commission were themselves a culmination of several years of a political struggle that has appropriately been called Kenya's second liberation struggle, second only to the militant struggle for political independence from Britain in the 1950s. In importance, the demonstrations, gatherings, conferences, and conventions that resulted from the constitution review movement were akin to the Lancaster House conferences of the early 1960s that ushered in the so-called independence constitution. These popular efforts during which several Kenyans lost their lives and many more were injured, permanently maimed, or imprisoned, aimed at redressing some fundamental limitations of the independence constitution, some aggravated by subsequent amendments that more and more concentrated power in the presidency and diluted basic provisions of the bill of rights. As the collection of essays in Wanyiri Kihoro's edited volume (2002) demonstrates, this was a pivotal moment in the country's long journey, as the nation took stock of the turbulent road it had traveled and the lessons it had learned and considered the path it wished to follow toward a new and different future. It is quite telling of this moment's value, in fact, that the draft constitution that was produced in 1994 by the Citizens Coalition for Constitutional Change—the civil society umbrella organization for local human rights NGOs and church organizations—was titled Kenya Tuitakayo (meaning "the Kenya we want").

Because the question of representation was so central to this moment of struggle, it opened up new opportunities for participation and leadership from a range of communities and organizations that had hitherto been marginalized and disenfranchised. Trade union organizations, youth groups, associations of the disabled, religious bodies, ethnic minorities, and so forth all became an integral part of the movement for change, galvanizing their members and constituencies into a formidable popular force for change. In the forefront of this reform movement and process were women's organizations like the International Federation of Women Lawyers, the National Council of Women of Kenya, and the League of Women Voters that fought endlessly to ensure that women's political empowerment was part and parcel of the vision and practice and culture of the Kenya Tuitakayo. Individual women leaders like the late Wangari Maathai, Maria Nzomo, Tabitha Seii, Nazlin Omar Rajput, and Wanjiku Kabira were incredibly successful in giving voice to women and women's concerns in the constitutional review process. The National Women's Convention was crucial in initiating the momentum for reform that the convention insisted must include women and women's agendas. It was an unprecedented gathering that "brought together women from all walks of life—the young and the old, the educated and the uneducated, rural and urban, and women from all ethnic groups," determined to make a difference in the creation of a new Kenya (Nzomo 1997, 244). And with the rise of a new Muslim political assertiveness in the country that was partly spearheaded by the controversial Islamic Party of Kenya, the context was ripe for the leadership of those who, like Ali-Aroni, had the necessary professional skills, the personal attributes, and the iron determination to contribute to a new future for Kenya. Given her participation in the constitution review process and her leadership in the Constitution of Kenya Review Commission at a great sacrifice to her future, Ali-Aroni is bound to go into the annals of history as among the important figures of Kenya's second liberation.

In 2011 Ali-Aroni was made the resident judge of the High Court in the city of Kisumu in the Nyanza Province, a region of the western part of the country that is predominantly non-Muslim. The position of High Court justice in Kenya is a lifetime leadership appointment that grants Ali-Aroni great powers and leverage to work toward human rights gains on behalf of (Muslim) women, a cause to which she seems committed.

Secular Accommodation of the Kadhi Courts

One of the most controversial areas of the constitutional review process that Ali-Aroni participated in as a member and leader of the Muslim Women Sisters Network and had to mediate in her capacity as chair of the Constitution of Kenya Review Commission was the debate over the future of the kadhi courts, the question being whether or not they should continue to be a provision of the new constitution. This debate was partly a product of the natural contestation precipitated by the new politics of pluralism in the country and partly of the growing force of Christian evangelical activism globally (Chesworth 2006; Kelley 2010).

The kadhi courts existed in East Africa, especially along the "Swahili" coast, long before the inception of British colonial rule in the region, although they were perhaps less structured than they are today. For a while the East African coast was part of the dominion of the sultan of Zanzibar. When the region fell under British colonial rule around 1895, the coastal strip of Kenya remained the "property" of the sultan but was now administered by the British as a protectorate, separately from what became known as Kenya Colony. In this arrangement, the sultan of Zanzibar and the British colonial government came to an understanding that the kadhi courts would be maintained under a new judicial, albeit colonial, set-up. In time, the colonial government came to institutionalize a tripartite system of law—common law (inherited from Britain itself), customary law (to cater to certain African traditions), and

Islamic (personal) law under the jurisdiction of the kadhi courts—which has persisted in one form or another to this day.

As the countries approached full independence, an agreement was reached between the then prime minister of Kenya, Jomo Kenyatta, and the then prime minister of Zanzibar, Mohamed Shamte, that, subject to certain provisions, the sultan would relinquish sovereignty of the coastal strip, allowing it to become fully a part of the independent country of Kenya. One of those provisions was that the kadhi courts in the judicial system of the new Kenya would be preserved and that Muslims throughout Kenya would be allowed to use the structure in seeking justice and arbitration in matters of personal law. Until the constitutional review debates erupted several decades later, then, the kadhi courts in Kenya were not only protected by the constitution and the successive governments but were also allowed to grow in number and consolidated in institutional structure.

Of course, the existence of the kadhi courts does not preclude litigation among Muslims in matters of personal law in the magistrate's or high courts of the country. In these instances, as much as within the structures of the kadhi courts, lawyers have the opportunity to draw on a wide range of precedent sources from other parts of the world. As Ali-Aroni points out, "India also is part of the Commonwealth. So if you want to persuade the court, we do rely on Indian law from India in Kenya because their system is British system like ours," adding that "we also borrow when we apply the Islamic shari'a. You see, we have a problem here because the Islamic jurisprudence hasn't grown in Kenya. If we want to use persuasive authority, we use Indian authorities for Islamic shari'a in Kenya." By "Indian," however, she does not mean "Hindu," but "Islamic": "In India the Islamic law is codified and is applied to a large extent and they have jurisprudence. So we do that as persuasive because there is no other jurisdiction that has Islamic shari'a within a secular context other than Indian. So we do apply Indian authorities as persuasive authorities in Kenya."

The constitutional review debates, however, soon revealed that Muslims could no longer take their kadhi courts for granted. It became an open secret that a section of the Christian clergy, purportedly supported by U.S. evangelical Christians, was determined to have a constitution that was free of any provision for the kadhi courts. Fortunately for Muslims, they had the support of radical Christian clergy like Reverend Timothy Njoya, many lawyers of Christian background, many non-Muslim intellectuals, as well as secularist women's organizations like the International Federation of Women Lawyers (Mutua 2007).

As expected, the new proposed constitution quickly came under attack from the U.S. Christian right. The *Daily Nation* reported on July 12, 2010, that

> Conservative American Christians assisting the "No" campaign [against the new proposed constitution] are focusing at least as much on the kadhis courts issue as on the proposed constitutions' provision regarding abortion. "On websites and in opinion pieces" the *Washington Post* reported last week, "conservative US Christian groups have denounced the proposed constitution. They are opposed to the kadhis courts provision, and they see other aspects of the constitution as being pro-abortion. Some have organized petition drives against the courts." Prominent among those groups is the American Center for Law and Justice, founded by right-wing evangelical Christian leader Pat Robertson. (Kelley 2012)

However, even in the face of intense and at times acrimonious opposition, much of it fired by the Christian evangelical zeal, Kenyans succeeded in making the kadhi courts a continuing part of their constitutionally mandated judicial system.

Ali-Aroni's remarks underscore the transnational operation of Kenya personal law that has defined citizenship and identity in the African space that we call Kenya from the colonial era to the present. The multiethnic, multiracial, and multireligious composition of Kenya as a postcolonial secular state is continuously being refashioned through legal precedents from other nations, such as India, which share the same colonial history. A positive outcome of this judicial transnationalism is that progressive lawyers, especially progressive Muslim lawyers, can now find support for their arguments and support in law from places like India, which has already made great strides in establishing precedents in favor of minorities and Muslim women's rights within the shari'a.

Muslim women lawyers advocating for women's rights and progressive Muslim male lawyers are seeking to transform the patriarchal interpretation of the shari'a, the patriarchal consciousness of the kadhis, and the way the kadhi courts are run. Notwithstanding her support of both the shari'a for personal law and the kadhi courts, Ali-Aroni also calls for the urgent need for the state to reform the kadhi courts by requiring and supplying adequate training of the kadhis in Islamic jurisprudence and by upgrading of their status within the civil court:

> Look at what the kadhi does. His role is not specified. He is an imam in a mosque. He will be there preaching on a Friday. I have no problem if he is an imam in a mosque. He is the spokesman of the Muslim community politically and socially. He conducts marriages and divorces and sits in arbitration. I don't think he can be effective because this is not the role of a kadhi and a chief kadhi. He cannot be effective because if you are a judiciary officer, then you should be an adjudicator, period. You should not be a spokesman of the community. You should not be conducting marriages. You can have a registrar who does that work. They are doing other things. They should not be in the mosque preaching because then you have so much that you are not effective. So those are some of the things we were trying to request during the review process.

In Ali-Aroni's opinion, many kadhis are semiliterate in Islamic jurisprudence and are not competent in the Arabic language with all its denotative and connotative meanings; furthermore, they operate using patriarchal gender ideologies often rooted within traditional conservatism. As a result, their capacity to arbitrate fairly is often compromised, and women and children pay the price. Ali-Aroni provided some examples in areas pertaining to *siri* (secret) marriages, which violate an Islamic requirement that marital contracts be publicly proclaimed.[2] Community members witnessing a marriage contract is significant for litigation related to a child's right in cases of contestation of paternity and protection of a wife's rights in case of widowhood. Other areas of concerns to Ali-Aroni are the "justification" of the rite of female genital mutilation, the denial of the rights to (higher religious and secular) education, and the right to employment outside the domestic space for Muslim girls and women. She elaborates on issues related to marriage:

> Polygamy is there and there is lot of what is called secret marriages and the wives don't have to know. There are a lot of secret marriages among the Muslims in Kenya. I have witnessed quite a number. . . . And even when they do it publicly, they don't care. They don't notify [the previous wife]. Again they don't apply the equality rule among the wives. [*laughs*] . . . The majority of them [women] do not understand their rights within the shari'a. The majority of them have no idea what their rights are within the shari'a. Number two, they

don't support [*siri*] marriage, but they don't have a voice. The kadhis, I am sorry
to tell you that the majority of them do not help women.

Overt polygyny predates Islam in African societies and is a contemporary
cultural practice in many Muslim and non-Muslim societies. The case of *siri*
marriage in Kenya mentioned by Ali-Aroni is distinct from *mut'a* (temporary marriage), over which there is a doctrinal contention among Sunni and
Shi'a, especially with regard to the shari'a's requirement of the presence of
witnesses and the question of the legal status of the woman and the offspring
born out of such relationships. Sunni Muslims generally believe that *mut'a*
predates Islam and was banned during the lifetime of the Prophet (Haeri
1989, 4, 20). *Mut'a* is most commonly practiced by the Asian Ithnasheri Muslims of East Africa (Richa Nagar 2000, 2004), who are greatly influenced by
Iranian Shi'a (Haeri 1989).

A contradiction between doctrine and practice emerges in the fact that
Sunni Muslims in Kenya do in fact engage in *siri* marriages. Sunni Muslim
women interviewed contend that in general, *siri* marriages are undertaken
between well-to-do Sunni Muslim men and (Sunni) women generally of less
privileged background. However, although gendered power relations define
the practice of *siri* marriage among Kenyan Muslims, economic class is not
necessarily the main determining factor. According to some interviewees, some
educated Muslim women of means who are party to *siri* marriage justify it
as "more religiously proper" for protecting their *sitara* in a female-male relationship, given the cultural inappropriateness of engaging in sex outside marriage. Furthermore, age and reproductive concerns are among the reasons
for highly educated (or well-to-do) Muslim women in premenopause to be
siri wives.

Female interviewees also mentioned that some educated Sunni Muslim
males have *siri* marriages because they desire to be on the same footing with
non-Muslim professional colleagues married to educated wives who can con-
verse in English and engage in mundane life conversations at professional
social gatherings. As my research assistant, Shamsiya Ramadhan, puts it, "*Siri*
marriage is practiced among the educated to address the issue of the 'educationally discordant' couple."

The need for Muslim women's education in both the religious and the secular domains cannot be overstated, especially as scriptural knowledge becomes
crucial for engaging with (Muslim) women's rights and responsibilities within

the shari'a and other civil laws. Because the majority of Muslim women are illiterate both in Islam and secular law, a nonreformed kadhi court will continue to make them vulnerable even in claiming their rights as granted to them by Islam. According to Ali-Aroni:

If you look at the hierarchy of the judiciary system in Kenya, the post of the kadhi is the lowest. The lowest of the low is the position of the kadhi. So you do not have a progressive kadhi in Kenya. OK, now we are changing a little bit. But before, we did not have a properly trained kadhi. Because for me it is not enough that you know the Qur'an; you must possess a judicial mind, you must be trained as a jurist. You must have a legal background so that when you sit there you are able to adjudicate because that is not an easy thing. So when you have a kadhi that may have the knowledge of the Qur'an but has not been properly trained into the adjudication of such matters and sits as a kadhi, sits as an African man, sits as a Muslim man and you are there as a woman, he will not see your point of view.

And I tell you that a lot of Muslim lawyers would rather not appear before the kadhi especially if you are appearing for a woman, because you do not get justice. And I am not embarrassed to tell you that if I have a Muslim woman coming before me now, I would rather go to a secular court and argue the shari'a there. Because there, I am sure, the woman, the child would get justice. I am not sure of the kadhi's court.

Although the trend is moving—when they advertised for the post of the kadhi, you see they asked for a graduate in Islamic law. But you see a graduate in Islamic law is not trained as a lawyer to practice. But somebody who did a bachelor of arts in Islamic law, you know, you are doing theory of Islamic shari'a. For me, you need further training the way other justice systems do, which is not happening as far as kadhis are concerned. Then you do not get properly trained kadhis because their payments are the lowest within the hierarchy of the judiciary. Then you look at the location of the kadhi's court, you really would see the problem. It is really very different. Right now it has been thrown into a funny place where nobody has access [to it]. An ordinary Kenyan woman would not have access to that place, that one. Even when they are set up within the normal court, they do not have adequate facilities, they do not have clerks, they will not have secretaries. And the community here we have not been able to agitate administratively to be able to have proper qualified kadhis and properly remunerated. Then you attract qualified people. So we can have facilities that others have.

In a recent announcement of a position of a kadhi, the following were listed as the minimum requirements:

For appointment to this grade, a candidate must have:

(a) A degree in Islamic law or its equivalent from a recognized university/institution;
(b) Profess the Islamic faith;
(c) Demonstrate ability to effectively communicate in English, Kiswahili, and Arabic;
(d) Have good conduct in accordance with the Islamic faith; and
(e) Have proficiency in computer application (*The Standard* [Nairobi], March 24, 2010, 50).

As Ali-Aroni indicates, these requirements represent progress. Kadhis in the past did not need to be university graduates. The trilingual requirement is in accord with the new status of English and Kiswahili as the co-official languages of the country and of Arabic as the language in which the major sources of Islamic law are composed. And consonant with the technological age, kadhis too are expected to be proficient in computers.

Conspicuously absent in the list, however, is the requirement that the candidates for the kadhi courts must have undergone the necessary training in legal and judicial application. All members of the bench—magistrates and judges—in Kenya must have a first degree in law from an accredited university. In addition, however, they must attend a law school—most end up going to the Kenya School of Law—where they receive practical training in such matters as litigation, legal drafting, conveyancing, and professional ethics and practice, to name a few. Subsequent to this, they must serve in internships in an established legal firm for at least a year before they can receive their license to practice law. As Ali-Aroni suggests, neither of these two requirements that are so essential to the administration of justice has been made mandatory for the appointment to a kadhi court.

The process of selecting a kadhi is overseen by the judicial service commission, the body that appoints or makes recommendations for the appointment of all judicial officers. In the case of kadhis, the chief kadhi, the person who heads the entire institution of kadhi courts in Kenya, is a key participant. But here too Ali-Aroni has her reservations. According to her, "The chief kadhi should be strictly speaking from the rank of High Court justice, even superior. Right now the chief kadhi's position is probably at the middle cadre of the judiciary."

The urgency for these reforms was first brought into sharp focus by the League of Muslim Women of Kenya in December 2010. This was during a UN-sponsored conference titled "Access to Justice for Women in Kenya" in which then acting chief kadhi—Sheikh Ahmed Muhdhar—and other kadhis participated. At the end of the conference, three critical recommendations were made. The first was that there ought to be a concerted effort to help Muslim women understand their rights both generally as well as under Islamic family law (one participant specifically recommended the establishment of "justice centers" in areas with high Muslim populations). Second, women should be given education on the process of accessing the kadhi courts and the limits of the courts' jurisdiction. Finally, the government ought to recognize the kadhi courts as part of the formal justice system in the country, according them the same facilities, resources, and staff training opportunities as other sections of the judiciary so that they are able to play their part as a conduit for access to justice ("Enhancing Access" 2011). While the modalities for implementing these recommendations were not specified, it is significant that the conference took place about three months after the promulgation of the constitution, when the government of Kenya had begun to consider formulas for implementing various acts of the new constitution.

The question of the reform of the kadhi courts acquired additional momentum in late September 2011 when Chief Justice Willy Mutunga was reported in the national media to have publicly sanctioned the appointment of women as kadhis (in *The Standard*, September 29 and September 30, 2011, and at allAfrica.com, October 4, 2011, to cite two).[3] As I indicate in the introduction, Muslims themselves came to be divided on this question, based primarily on differences of interpretation of Islamic texts. Ali-Aroni, however, introduces a new argument—that the position of the kadhi ought not to be seen as a religious one at all, that matters of faith and religio-cultural practices ought to be separate from the judicial responsibilities of the kadhi. This argument, in fact, came to be adopted by the Mombasa-based group Muslims for Human Rights, as reflected in a statement by Hussein Khalid, its director (Lornah 2011). In its support for the right of women to serve as kadhis, the group has insisted, along the lines argued by Ali-Aroni, that the office of the kadhi is *not* a religious one but a judicial one. It is true that whoever holds that office must be very knowledgeable about Islamic law. But equally important, the person must be a professional, properly trained in the practice of administration of justice:

> We were trying to see whether the position of the kadhi can be elevated to that of justice of the High Court. We failed on that. But we were also trying to see whether we could have some reform. For instance, when you are at the lower court, we have the Islamic justice, not properly schooled if you asked me. On appeal, you have an ordinary justice who is secular, and then the chief kadhi may be invited, just maybe. Or a Muslim scholar may be invited at the discretion of the justice, and his opinion is not binding. So we were trying to see whether we could get there. But we did not manage even at the level where we were at the first or second draft of the reform.

Ali-Aroni's general assessment of the patriarchal hold on the kadhi courts seems to corroborate the conclusion reached by Susan Hirsch (1998) in her fascinating study of Muslim women's use of the kadhi courts in Mombasa.[4] Muslim women use the kadhi courts to publicly expose domestic abuse in a marital setting, thereby challenging the normative cultural silencing of women, commonly referred to as "heshima" ("respect"). Muslim women's agency is circumscribed within a regulated framework of patriarchal culture. As a result, although women may challenge power structures by coming forward as individuals with their complaints, ultimately through what they say and the way they say it, they may help reinforce collective gender roles operating within and beyond public institutions. This is why in his review of Hirsch's work, Snajdar comments that "the women in Hirsch's cases are also limited to performing within formalized religious and legal institutions run by men. Thus, the question of women's power remains framed by the particular social and political context that ultimately structures any 'pragmatics of inclusion' within it" (2005, 294). The contradictory outcomes of women's acts of resistance make the acquisition of critical knowledge and (legal) literacy skills within both the religious and secular realms therefore even more urgent for Muslim women.

Bargaining with Patriarchy

In the context of Muslims' engagement with identity politics in a predominantly non-Muslim nation-state such as Kenya, the wearing of the hijab by Muslim women has become a symbol of the Muslim identity rather than necessarily a testimony of one's modesty. Muslim women's bodily presentation becomes a matter of intense public scrutiny. As Minou Fuglesang rightly concludes regarding the hijab controversy in Kenya, "Veiling has become a body technique intrinsically linked to political and cultural struggles. Women, their bodies, dress, and actions have, more than ever, become symbolic representations, expressing concerns that lie far beyond them" (1994, 211). This phenomenon of patriarchal exploitation of religious symbols and rites leads feminist geographer Richa Nagar, who studied the imposition of hijab and *mut'a* on women by the Tanzanian Asian male Ithnasheri, to remark that "the discussion of [hijab] and *mut'a* reveals how religion, a category that is not always salient in Western contexts, can profoundly reinforce and complicate racial and class-based distinctions and provide one of the main nodes around which heterosexual relations and everyday gender politics are played out. The regulated and mediated nature to sexual boundaries in a community, then, must be understood in relation of how that community negotiates its socioeconomic and spatial boundaries vis-à-vis other social groups in the specific context within which it is situated" (2004, 35).

In spite of the high-profile position of public leadership that she had come to assume, along with the powers that came with it, Ali-Aroni too found it necessary at times to take into consideration this identity politics, often rooted in Muslim male sensibilities, in the way she presented herself publicly. For her and for many other professional Muslim women, wearing the hijab became a careful strategy in the process of accomplishing "higher" goals:

> Let me tell you this. I easily fit in the secular world. Maybe you wonder why I am not veiled. [*laughs*] I veil when I am in public and I did. When I was in the commission I always had a headscarf because I knew how much that meant to the community. The biggest problem they had with me is: "You do not portray yourself as a Muslim woman." So for the sake of the community even today if I were to go public, I would get the scarf just to get everybody comfortable. But I fit in very easily because I did not make my name as a Muslim woman per se. I made my name as a professional. So I enjoyed both worlds: I enjoyed the world of being a Muslim and I fit in the professional world easily.

As we approached the end of our series of interviews, I asked Ali-Aroni if I could take a picture of her for possible inclusion in my book: "It is all right. But let me get a scarf because a lot of people are very concerned about this. Both Muslim men and women are concerned about my public appearance. I said to them, 'Thank you I heard your concern and I have taken note.'

[*laughs*] . . . So it is a major issue. It is a major issue." This response triggered a long conversation between us about recent and old hijab "traditions" in African Muslim societies. When I pointed out that in Niger only married women were veiled before the 1990s rise of Izala, a Wahhabist brand of Islam (Alidou 2005, 159–62), and that we often tied the scarf in the turban style she used, she immediately recalled her childhood memories of the Comoros, where women were also not veiled. We contrasted the traditional *buibui* style of the Swahili women with the new fashionable abaya style imported from the Middle East Gulf countries.[5]

This issue of wearing or not wearing the hijab must be assessed through the lenses of what the Turkish feminist sociologist Deniz Kandiyoti has called "bargaining with patriarchy":

> I will argue that women strategize within a set of concrete constraints that reveal and define the blueprint of what I will term the *patriarchal bargain* of any given society, which may exhibit variations according to class, caste, and ethnicity. These patriarchal bargains exert a powerful influence on the shaping of women's gendered subjectivity and determine the nature of gender ideology in different contexts. They also influence both the potential for and specific forms of women's active or passive resistance in the face of their oppression. Moreover, patriarchal bargains are not timeless or immutable entities, but are susceptible to historical transformations that open up new areas of struggle and renegotiation of the relations between genders. (1988, 275)[6]

Given that patriarchal Muslim institutions are the ones that propelled her to a position of national visibility, Ali-Aroni carefully uses her agency to choose her battles so that she can continue to contribute to the wider mission on behalf of the Muslim community and Muslim women more especially. Precisely because she is the only Muslim woman of that stature, all eyes have been on her, publicly scrutinizing her moral integrity and wondering what public image of a Muslim woman she will present. What may appear as compromise or opportunism is, in fact, a personal sacrifice that Ali-Aroni, like many other women pioneers, has had to make for advancement of the common good.

The Kenyan experience of patriarchal policing of Muslim women's dress appearance is quite similar to the experience of Ithnasheri Asian women of Dar es Salaam in neighboring Tanzania studied by Nagar (2000, 2004). With regard to veiling, Nagar points out that "in reinforcing the identities of women and men as Shi'tes and Muslims and in urging them to resist the pressures of Westernization, the Shia male leadership of both local [Tanzania] and international organizations underscored the importance of *hijaab* and constructed women's 'natural role' as keepers of home and family. But this increasing regulation of gendered bodies and sexualities during the 1980s was simultaneously marked by the emergence of a new feminist Islamic consciousness among [Ithnasheri] women, which led upper class women to demand greater participation in communal affairs and direct representation in the Jamaat" (2004, 41).

It is the struggle to contest such policing of Muslim women's bodies through the politicization of religion and race and class to which Nagar draws our attention: "Sociospatial practices and choices surrounding dress and veiling, for instance, reveal how 'different, spatially realized sets of hegemonic rules and norms' regarding women's bodies are 'themselves produced by specific constellations of power' and result in different degrees of formality, enforcement, stability, and contestation. . . . It also attends to the ways that specific nexus of racial and class-based oppressions reinforce group identity and the manner in which femininity becomes both a tool and a source of women's disempowerment in constructions of racial and cultural homogeneity at the margin" (2004, 33). In spite of Ithnasheri male leaders' dismissal of their protest, educated and intellectual Ithnasheri women persist in overtly expressing their discontent on Islamic grounds. Moreover, they call for the greater need to include women in decision-making processes of the Jamaat. However, Nagar also points out how feminist Asian Ithnasheri women's consciousness has fallen short of developing a broad transracial and class solidarity with Ithnasheri African women converts, Arab (Sunni) women, and Chautara women who are affected by the same hegemonic norms and rules (2004, 41), especially with respect to the institution of *mut'a* commonly practiced among Shi'a Ithnasheri.[7]

Unlike the Ithnasheri women that Nagar discusses, Ali-Aroni is not seeking a greater role and voice in organizations of Kenyan Muslims. Her essentially secular orientation would not allow her to seek positions in the SUPKEM or the MCCK. On the contrary, it is the Muslim organizations that sought her participation and leadership in the constitutional review process. In this sense, Ali-Aroni was in a position of power of not having to negotiate with patriarchy at all. Nonetheless, her commitment to representing Kenyan Muslims as a marginalized minority, taking with her the collective will of that constituency, ultimately meant adopting a strategy of careful negotiation with the authority and sensibility of Muslim men.

GENDER AND THE DIALECTICS OF RELIGIOUS AND
SECULAR LITERACY

While Muslim women in influential leadership positions like Ali-Aroni can choose the areas to be negotiated with the patriarchy, she is deeply disturbed by the social exclusion of Muslim women resulting from oppressive traditionalism embedded within Muslim communities, which hampers their public participation in national politics and prevents them from accessing public resources such as education and employment. She is concerned about the ways in which patriarchal interpretations of fundamental Islamic texts are used by patriarchal men in order to justify cultural rites such as female genital mutilation whose raison d'être is the control of female sexuality:

> The marginalization of the Muslim women is historic. Let me look at it from tradition—like in the majority of African cultures women have no say. That is similar in Kenya. In most of the African communities in Kenya women have no rights at all. And as much as the shari'a gives us rights, conveniently there is double [standard in its] application. There is the shari'a when it suits them and then [they] turn back to our traditional life when it suits them. One notable example is female genital modification. FGM, you will not find it in coastal Kenya. But you will find it in other communities, the Somali communities, for instance, and in the other communities like where I am married—it is predominantly a Christian Kisii community. The Nubian community, for instance, they do it. Literally every other community [does it]. Kikuyu, there are Muslims and [they] would use the shari'a to justify why they are doing FGM. The Somali community does it and you know they use the shari'a to justify it.
>
> When it comes to inheritance, there is no application of the shari'a. People go back into African traditions where the woman inherited nothing. Those are some of the issues of self-marginalization.[8]

Of course, there are coastal communities like the Digo, for example, who practice FGM. Though predominantly Muslim, the Digo do not justify FGM on grounds of Islamic faith. It is also true that there are Muslims of Kikuyu backgrounds. Again, FGM among the Kikuyu has been linked to traditional Kikuyu culture rather than to Islam and was a major bone of political and cultural contention between the Kikuyu and British (Keck and Sikkink 1998; Pedersen 1991). But Ali-Aroni's general point is how "Islam," on the one hand, and "African traditions," on the other hand, are often invoked in an opportunistic manner to deny Muslim women their rights. When the men cannot find a justification for their discriminatory practices against women in an Islamic text, they will resort to cultural traditions; and where they cannot find support in cultural traditions, they will revert back to Islam.

Ali-Aroni also points out how Muslim traditional conservatism and misinterpretation of Islam, rather than Muslim marginalization by the state, is often what accounts for Muslim women's exclusion from secular as well as advanced religious literacy. As a result, women become passive agents in understanding Islam and recipients of patriarchal interpretations of Islam and Islamic texts. Muslim women's lack of religious literacy prevents them from knowing their rights within Islam, which would assist them in fighting against the violation of their human rights: "The shari'a does not stop girl's education. If you look at the Qur'an, the hadiths, from Islamic history, nothing stops women from being educated. The Muslim woman in Kenya is denied education beside basic Qur'anic school [training]. . . . You are married off. You do not have the opportunity to study Islamic shari'a. You never get to understand your rights. Secular education is out. So you are absolutely marginalized in terms of literacy. You have no idea. They believe what the men tell them. They read to them the shari'a, and they believe [it]." In other words, keeping women uneducated is an integral part of patriarchal structuring of society and from which it builds its legitimating ideology.

BUILDING WITH PROGRESSIVE MUSLIM MALE LAWYERS AND OTHER WOMEN'S RIGHTS ADVOCATES

According to Ali-Aroni, education and literacy among Muslim women can be important sources of power and a means by which to challenge patriarchal control of Islam and the misuse of religion that holds back Muslim women and prevents them from participating in public democratic processes and from gaining employment. As her comments reveal, the limited literacy of kadhis and ulamas in *fiqh* has severe consequences for women and girls, and such blatant incompetence on their part can be used by educated women as a platform for disrupting male control of religion. Therefore, she stresses the importance of producing educated Muslim women who are engaged in critical Islamic literacy even if that literacy is mediated through translation in local languages and/or English. In her work in connection with the 2000 Affirmative Action Bill, which called for the application of quota representation of women and marginalized groups in every key decision-making sector and all sectors of the workforce, and the 1999 Equality Bill, which called for nondiscrimination on the basis of sex, faith, and other factors, she employed mobilization strategies involving legal literacy with the support of resourceful progressive Muslim male lawyers and other non-Muslim women lawyer-advocates of women's rights in order to engage and win the support of conservative Muslim clergy.

The Affirmative Action Bill was designed to guarantee minority groups, including disabled people, a minimum of 33 percent of representation in Parliament and on local town and city councils. Immediately, the Muslim community of Kenya went to war against the bill without fully understanding its provisions and the contexts of its application. With funding support from the Federation of Kenya Women Lawyers and Urgent Action Fund-Africa, which was established in Kenya in 2001 to support the work of women in Africa and which was then under the directorship of prominent Kenya lawyer and activist Betty Murungi, Ali-Aroni enlisted the support of progressive Muslim male lawyers to launch a civic education campaign in the Muslim communities in Kenya. With her team, she moved from one Muslim community to another to explain to them what Muslims, as a minority community, stood to gain from supporting the Affirmative Action Bill. She challenged those who opposed it to present a single Islamic source that would preclude better representation of minorities in forums that could help shape a better destiny within the nation-state. Some were suspicious of her motives, believing that she ultimately intended to vie for political office:

> You know, many people think that I would like to be a politician, which is not true. I have no interest in being a politician. And I said after a lot of discussions with them and what they start to ask is that "you can be anything, but you can't be a president." And I said to them, "No Kenya Muslim woman wants to be a president. Let's cross the bridge when we get there. But look at this bill and tell me how it negatively impacts on the Muslim community?" And I told them the "affirmative action does not talk about women per se. It talks about marginalized groups. We are marginalized. If this bill passes, you as Muslim men would be catered for." So after that the Muslim community supported that.[9]

Again, we see here how Ali-Aroni's understanding of the patriarchal hold on the Muslim community helped her to employ strategies of constructive engagement, including that of enlisting the support of Muslim male lawyers knowledgeable about Islam and the shari'a, to mobilize for what she perceived to be in the community's best interests.

A similar Muslim opposition erupted when the Equality Bill was introduced. The part of the bill that was seen to be particularly repugnant to Muslims was that related to inheritance, especially because this is provided for in the Qur'an itself with specific, often gender-based, ratios of inheritance allocation. Again, Ali-Aroni became actively engaged in dialogue with members of the Muslim community across the country in an effort to understand the basis of the opposition. Eventually, she was able to mediate in the process and introduce an exclusionary clause in the bill that would exempt Muslims from sections of the bill that were deemed contrary to the shari'a. In this way, many Muslims were eventually persuaded to support the Equality Bill also.

Of special significance for Ali-Aroni in these struggles on behalf of Muslim women is the support they have enjoyed from other Kenyan women of non-Muslim background. Once they are made to understand that the shari'a is not the beast they were made to believe it is, they are quick to come around and provide their unconditional support:

> And let me also tell you this. The rest of the women are truly sympathetic to the Muslim women. Once we speak to them and tell them, "The notion that you have is wrong. The shari'a does not marginalize us. It is the negative practices of our people." And you know once you—we show them that indeed we have more rights than they have even under the secular law, they support us. They all come up to support us, and they come out in support. The problem is within us. But for me the sky is the limit.

Her Muslim background, on the one hand, and her national stature as a successful woman lawyer, on the other hand, have enabled Ali-Aroni to serve as an important cultural bridge-builder that brought women of various faiths together in a joint struggle for a common good.

CONCLUSION

When I began research on Muslim women public figures in Kenya since the 1990s, Ali-Aroni's name kept coming up over and over again. Muslim women take pride in seeing her eloquently speak or write from the standpoint of a field that is highly male-dominated and intimidating to Muslim women in general, and more important, in the fact that she held a very powerful position then as chairperson of the Constitution of Kenya Review Commission. Whether or not they agreed with her politics, Muslim men are quick to point out the significance of her position from the perspective of Muslim political life in Kenya as a community that experiences structural discrimination on the basis of its faith, and it was male-dominated organizations like the SUP-KEM and the MCCK that were partly responsible for getting her to serve as a voice for Muslim in the constitution review process. Ali-Aroni clearly demonstrates her strong bond to her Muslim heritage and her commitment to advocating on its behalf through the rule of law for its rights to equal treatment and access to resources. By the same token, she is committed to reforming the problematic areas of Muslim culture that violate Muslim women's rights. A close reading of how she addresses issues affecting Muslim women's lives also reveals Ali-Aroni's commitment to coalition building with other non-Muslim women and progressive Muslim men on the basis of political interest rather than simply on identity politics in order to achieve her goals of defending (Muslim) women's rights. This is crucial, especially given the almost complete nonexistence of an active sociopolitical Muslim women's movement in Kenya. Today, Ali-Aroni has crossed a new bridge for a Muslim woman in her appointment to her lifetime position as a judge of the High Court of Kenya. This is a role that she can use to make a difference for other (Muslim) women and Muslims in Kenya.

5

Muslim Women and the Use of New Media

Inscribing Their Voices in Rights Discourse

INTRODUCTION

The proliferation of private media broadcasting stations, private newspapers, and magazines resulting from democratization processes in most African countries has created an outlet for the many voices in various national constituencies and has also allowed for ideologically divergent affirmations in Muslim polities. This development in old and new information and communication technologies—radio, audiocassettes, television, satellite, Internet, and magazines—plays a key role in shaping the sociopolitical discursive practices in Muslim societies (Alloo 1999; Eickelman and Anderson 1999; Haenni 2002; Salvatore 1999; Schulz 2005, 2012). This interplay between democratization and the media is especially significant as educated Muslim women become active agents as media producers, hosts, and consumers (Alidou 2005; Mernissi 2005; Nouraie-Simone 2005; Skalli 2006) because it offers a platform for advocating for their rights within the nation.

In this chapter, I illustrate this trend with two case studies in Kenya: a Muslim women's magazine titled *The Nur* (*The Light*) produced in Nairobi and a women's radio program, *Ukumbi Wa Mamama* (*Women's Forum*), hosted by the Islamic-oriented Radio Rahma (Voice of Mercy) in Mombasa. I show how secular learning and skills have been mobilized by certain Muslim women for religious and sociopolitical ends on behalf of Muslim women in particular and the Kenya Muslim community at large in the political context of the nation in transition. These Islamist women's voices challenge prevailing and deeply entrenched orthodoxies that have defined relations not only between men and women in Muslim communities but also between Muslim women and non-Muslims, including their non-Muslim "sisters." "Islamist women" in the Kenyan context refers to Muslim women whose activism is shaped by an Islamic framework rather than by secular reasoning, which they reject as a constituent of Western colonialism. Partly as a result of their Islamist orientation, they are strong supporters of the continued existence of the kadhi courts, but within a reformed framework sensitive to women's rights.

As in other African countries, Kenya's adoption of a mass education policy in the postcolonial era produced a great number of educated young women, among them Muslims. This education allowed young Muslim women to develop skills in information and communication technology. Combined with the introduction of domestic satellite dishes and Islamic electronic commodities from all over the world, these skills have helped Kenya Muslim women connect with the *umma*—the global Muslim community. In the process, this new technology-based networking and the knowledge arising from it have created a space for an alternative women's understanding of Islam and Islamic discourses regarding gender identity. Furthermore, global Islamic education exchanges at the tertiary level (U.S. college-equivalent level) have become much more common over the last thirty years. Many Kenya Muslim students, including women, who were interested in Islamic studies benefited from Islamic scholarships to study abroad.

The process of democratization that began in the early 1990s affected Muslim women in two ways. First, it liberated both print and electronic media from excessive state control, making them more open to use by different constituencies. Several FM radio stations, some ethnic based, some religious in focus, emerged as a direct expression of the national mood for democratic pluralism. Among Muslims, the first was Radio Iqra (Radio Recite), which aired from Nairobi. This was followed by the establishment of Radio Rahma (Radio Mercy), and more recently Radio Salaam (Radio Peace), both in Mombasa. Invariably, these radio stations host programs catering to women or focus on women's issues. Second, democratization has fostered a pluralism that has included female articulations of political Islam. Whether framed within secularism or Islamism, these new Kenya Muslim women activists are using their advanced literacy in English, Arabic, and Kiswahili and their competency in the old and new information and communication technologies to provide and debate distinct ideas about Muslim women's lives.

Until recently, virtually all Muslim organizational structures in Kenya, such as the SUPKEM and the National Union of Kenya Muslims, were entirely male-centered and male-dominated. The founding of the NMCK, which Nazlin Omar Rajput chairs, marked a clear departure from this patriarchal tradition. NMCK has clearly signaled the determination of Muslim women activists to transform the gendered structures of Kenya Muslim organizational leadership.

The primary mission of NMCK is to solve the problem of women's underrepresentation in male-dominated Muslim organizations. More important, its goal is to provide an effective mechanism for addressing major societal issues affecting Muslim women and children, including HIV/AIDS, gender disparities, the role of religion in women's rights, and social justice in their own communities and the nation at large. NMCK is also active in providing a Muslim women's perspective on governance. As Rajupt points out,

> The situation of Muslim women is made all the more invisible due to the lack of accessible information on their status, their priority needs, and the factors that contribute to their marginalization. Without reliable gender sensitive information, awareness-raising on persistent gender inequalities is undermined and the development of effective "action for change" programs is constrained. Also, while a small number of Muslim women community groups exist, they are geographically scattered, not well organized, and are not linked through formal networking arrangements. Instead the interests of Muslim women tend to be represented by male-dominated and gender-blind organizations acting as umbrella bodies for Muslims, which have no interest in, nor programs targeted specifically for, Muslim women, nor any representation of women throughout the nation. (Rajupt 2005, 5)

Because Muslims are a minority in Kenya, avoiding dissent among Muslims and instead promoting Muslim unity has been seen as the best means of dealing with the perceived challenge of the non-Muslim majority. Some Kenya Muslim women, however, are beginning to refuse to be part of the patriarchal vision of the unconditional unity of Muslim polity. In their view, Muslim unity cannot be secured only by confronting the non-Muslim "other" on questions of distributive justice but also requires the promotion of a more just relation across the genders within the Muslim *umma* itself.

However, because of their limited economic resources, Muslim women activists and producers of magazines or electronic programs centered on women's issues often have to adopt a strategy that entails accepting co-optation by (religious or secular) male media sponsors who use religion as a platform for advancing their agenda. A close analysis of Muslim women's media discourses reveals that while on the surface Islamist women identify with the broader Muslim male clergy's denunciation of the state's discrimination against Muslim people, they diverge on questions related to Muslim women's rights in Muslim communities resulting from patriarchal misrendering of the shari'a. Consequently, Muslim women public figures are resorting to new Muslim women's magazines, such as *The Nur*, electronic venues like Radio Rahma's program *Ukumbi Wa Mamama*, and websites to present a critical look at political Islam and secularism and their shortcomings in adequately addressing the rights of Kenya Muslim women within the Muslim communities and the nation at large.

The Nur Magazine: Islam, HIV/AIDS, Sexuality, and Women's Rights

In 2005 the NMCK launched a triannual magazine called *The Nur*. It is a publication of about twenty pages produced in Nairobi under the chief editorship of Rajput, who is its founder. By the time I was conducting my research in the winter of 2005 and the spring and summer of 2006, two issues of that magazine had been published. *The Nur* is the first Muslim women's magazine of its kind in Kenya; it focuses on issues of sexuality and HIV/AIDS in Muslim communities within an Islamic spiritual framework.

Rajput is a Kenyan with a complex multiracial and ethnic heritage, a descendant of Asian (Afghan-Indian) and Kamba people. Born in 1967, she is a woman of modest Western educational accomplishment, having gone no further than high school level because of family pressure to marry early. In spite of her background, she is clearly a brilliant person who is widely read in both the Western and Islamic traditions. In the process of educating herself in both secular and Islamic subjects, she has acquired a degree of consciousness and skills in critical literacy that seems to be rare for Muslim women of her level of formal education. Her personal history has made her particularly sensitive about the interplay between culture, gender, and identity and the way that interplay in turn defines power relations between constituencies in the nation. Highly articulate, with a record of activism that goes back to her high school days, she quickly rose to national prominence as an advocate of Muslim women's rights within Islam within both the Kenya Muslim community and the wider national context. She was a presidential candidate in the 2007 Kenyan national election and is currently the chairperson of the National Muslim Council of Women of Kenya. Her bold public image and mastery of Islamic discourse in both Kiswahili and English—the two

Cover of *The Nur*

most important transethnic languages of the country—defy the traditional image of the nonvocal and submissive Muslim woman.

Rajput did not choose HIV/AIDS as the primary subject matter for *The Nur* magazine in order to attract funding by capitalizing on one the greatest tragedies of our time. Rather, she chose it in order to provide space for the interrogation of issues of sexuality that are central in understanding the power relations between Muslim women and men as well as the discourse of morality that is often used by patriarchal Muslims to draw a distinction between the self and the other. With respect to the discourse of morality, *The Nur's* report on the NMCK's projects is seen to be not only an educational forum for Kenya Muslim women but a bridge-building device between Muslim women and men, on the one hand, and between Muslims and non-Muslims, on the other.

Breaking traditional taboos on open discussion of sexuality and challenging the denial and stigmatization of Muslim people infected and affected by HIV/AIDS, *The Nur* promotes sex education within an Islamic spiritual framework as a fundamental component of Islamic human rights and a tool for combating the epidemic. Lengthy essays by Rajput dealing with the interplay between HIV/AIDS, Islam, and women's rights fill more than half of the magazine. In addition to summary reports of regional HIV/AIDS activities and workshops sponsored by the organization, *The Nur* features "coming-out" stories by HIV-positive Muslim women who are overcoming societal stigmatization and discrimination as a result of their participation in NMCK sensitization workshops organized under the project named "Breaking the Silence: Behind the Veil."[1] According to *The Nur*, the central objective of this project is

> to create critical awareness among the male and female Muslim population of the prevalence of not only the disease but also the stigma and discrimination within the community and further train the Muslim leadership (imams, kadhis, women's leaders, and madrasa teachers—male and female) on the proper application of shari'a on AIDS prevention. This will hopefully stop the pointing of fingers at PLWHAs [people living with HIV/AIDS], which in turn will contribute to the eradication of the disease. At this point, it is expected that at the end of eleven months' project, an open dialogue amongst the local communities and regional PLWHA support networks will contribute substantially to eliminating HIV/AIDS stigma, and discrimination. (Rajput 2005, 7)

In other words, the project essentially serves as a forum that brings together women living with HIV/AIDS for workshops facilitated by health experts, religious bodies, and social workers with the aim of providing resourceful and supportive Islamic network.

The first issue of *The Nur* appeared in December 2005, featuring a cover page showing two Muslim women in hijab (one of whom is Rajput herself) hugging the other and accompanied by a headline that says "Breaking the Silence: Behind the Veil." The headline is flanked between two iconic HIV/AIDS symbols forming the shape of a heart, signifying love and compassion for, rather than rejection of, the Muslim women affected by the lethal virus. Reflecting on the mission of *The Nur* in her first editorial, Rajput asks, "What strategies does Islam have in its coffers that we can . . . share with the rest of the world to contain the pandemic? What is Islam's response to sexuality, stigma, disease and gender disparities? What are the injunctions and strategies that would provide the response that AIDS could respect, AIDS could submit to, and . . . would in turn shake its very foundation and bring it crushing to a rubble dust?" (2005, 7).

She then chastises the Muslim community and its leadership for both marginalizing the infected and remaining silent about the spread of the disease in the communities. Rajput also addresses the problematics of the discourse of Muslims' exceptionality—that is, the idea that the Muslim community is somehow protected from HIV/AIDS because of its presumed "Islamic morality." "Our greatest challenge," she notes,

> is the blanket silence, denial, marginalization and poverty. A great majority of Muslims are also a third world people who lead a poor and unhygienic life plagued with endemic disease and malnutrition. Some experts argue that the real problem of Muslims is not really AIDS. This kind of thinking is supported by the fact that many Muslim communities are protected from the massive spread of HIV because of whatever is practiced by them with respect to the Islamic way of life. Many Muslim communities, thus, also believe that AIDS is not their major concern, not only because of this belief but also because concerted efforts to sensitize and target them in the programs have been largely lacking. (2005, 7)

Such discourse is commonly heard in mosque sermons and public presentations by Muslims that are reported on by the media. Because it comes from the religious authorities, this is a message blindly internalized by the majority of Muslims, even the educated ones. Unlike the ulamas in Muslim countries such as Senegal who have used the mosques as part of the larger community effort to sensitize their citizenship about HIV/AIDS, the Kenyan ulamas have been comparatively slow in assuming leadership to combat the multifaceted dimension of the disease. The discourse of Muslim exceptionality also serves to validate the Muslim "self" vis-à-vis the non-Muslim "other" almost as a silent declaration that the Muslim moral code on sexuality is somehow superior to that of non-Muslims. This state of denial is aggravated by inadequate local resources for engaging in effective sensitization advocacy work:

> In Kenya, the scourge has not spared the Muslims; this is reflected in the high prevalence of HIV in Muslim populated areas such as Tiwi in Mombasa district, parts of Malindi, and Majengo Village in Meru district among others. The situation is further compounded by the taboo status of the disease, the silence surrounding the virus, and the false fallacy within the Muslim community and the general society. . . . We must wake up from this deadly slumber of silence and denial. We must build our capacity in understanding the greatest enemy of humanity, look at the virus in the face, and brace ourselves for battle. It is here among us, in our brothers, our sisters, our babies and our loved ones, and in many of us. We must break the silence within the grassroots, our youth, homes, and families. We must reach out to our loved ones and help them survive. I cannot stress the point harder that if we don't break the silence and don't apply Islamically oriented preventive actions immediately and continuously, we may soon see in the global Muslim community the tragedy of the decimation of whole villages and townships. (2005, 7)

The Nur, however, not only offers a critique of the ulamas' silence but also tries to reach out to them in a programmatic manner, offering them training for effective participation in the fight against the HIV/AIDS pandemic. In these workshops, the NMCK implores the Muslim clergy to draw upon their Islamic understanding for the promotion of creative anti-HIV/AIDS strategies that will be acceptable to the Muslim communities. These initiatives by the NMCK that seek to engage the Muslim clergy have also been the subject of *The Nur*. Pictorial coverage of events where such collaboration has taken place bears witness to the emergence of a new culture within Kenyan Islam, with Muslim women as leaders and active catalysts. As much as it is a product of the wider democratization process in the country, the new gender collaboration at both the organizational level and within the leadership ranks of the Muslim community is now contributing in important ways to the "multiculturalization" of Kenyan democracy and civil rights discourses.

Using an Islamic spiritual framework, *The Nur* invokes the Qur'an as the platform for interrogating Islamic practices that render the community and women especially vulnerable to HIV/AIDS infection. These include Muslim marriage and divorce practices and parental complicity in the early marriage of their children and early termination of their education. There is some debate among Muslims about whether the spirit of Islam, if not its letter, permits the practice of polygyny. Rajput clearly adheres to the school of thought that sees polygamy as licensed by Islam. However, she points out that this is an Islamic institution that is overwhelmingly abused by what she calls "unscrupulous" men who engage in serial marriages and divorces that expose the community to HIV and who refuse to undergo voluntary counseling and testing:

Kadhi of Mombasa, Sheikh Twalib & Halima Kulowe, Chief of Tudor, member of NMCK-NUR, Coast Province- tackling HIV/AIDS Stigma workshop.

The Chief Kadhi of Kenya (left), Sister Nazlin Umar, and Sheikh Swaleb Kwatemba at an open forum at the Coast on HIV/AIDS. Involved were the Ministry of Health, the Policy Project and various muslim leaders.

First national Muslim Women Leaders forum in Kenya, Thika; Feburary 2004 and the launch of the NUR network. Chief guest of honor nominated M.P. Hon. Amina Abdallah.

Nazlin Umar Rajput's HIV/AIDS workshop involving Islamic clergy

The unchecked abuse of polygamy where women are misused by being married at the convenience of unscrupulous men and then divorced and/or abandoned at the whim of her husband is negative practice that is rising at an alarming rate and exposing the community to HIV and immorality. . . . In fact, it is to protect women from unnecessary complication and misuse, to maintain integrity and minimize evil that Islam has allowed recourse to polygamy with reservations and conditions. Further, much as polygamy is part of the solution to combat HIV-AIDS, its abuse and the failure of the marriage partners to undertake voluntary counseling rapidly increases the infection rates within families. (2005, 10)

Quoting Qur'anic verse 2:195 of *Al-Baqarah* ("The Cow")—which says "And do not throw yourselves in the path of destruction"—Rajput makes women aware of their right within Islam to refuse partnership with any Muslim male whose HIV status they do not know. Using the same injunction, she questions the ethics of parents who blindly subject their children to arranged marriages without insisting on an HIV test. She also speaks of the rights to self-protection of divorcees and widows in Muslim societies. She argues that when partners do not undergo the voluntary testing, they are acting contrary to the Qur'anic teaching in verse 71 of the *At-Taubah* ("Repentance"), which states: "The believers, men and women are *auliyaa'* [helpers, supporters, protectors] one of the other, they enjoin what is just and forbid what is evil." She argues that "deviation from the true Islam is the main culprit in such a case. Women are abused as tools for men's pleasures and have no guarantees, no rights or security, financial or emotional, and the moral fabric of society thus disintegrates. The temptations are high for a corrupt society, more violations, poverty, and vulnerabilities, which could expose them to HIV infection" (2005, 10). Here Rajput exposes patriarchal violations of women's rights within the Islamic institution of marriage as practiced in Kenya.[2] As chapter 4 suggests, polygyny among Muslims in Kenya is often accompanied by *siri* marriages in which the wife "shares" her husband with another without her knowing about it or about the woman.[3] Thus, Rajput reminds Muslim men of their responsibility to adhere to the true teachings of Islam with regard to women's rights within a polygamous setup. She further adds that

these gross violations of the rights of women should be treated as a crisis, and we must apply extraordinary attention to this and take all necessary measures to put in place checks and balances to protect the shari'a and reach out to the male members of our society. *H.Q. Al-Maidah* 05:44, 45, 47: "Those who know the laws of Allah but only pay lip-service to them are the *kafir'un* (hypocrites), they are the *twalim'un* (wrongdoers), they are the *fasiq'un* (the perverse and law-breakers)." Qur'anic teachings in regard to the representation or misrepresentation of women are clear-cut in Islam. (2005, 10)

Given these Qur'anic injunctions regarding the right to self-protection and the obligation to protect others, Rajput boldly reassures her readers that it is both righteous and their right within Islam to use condoms for mutual protection against HIV/AIDS infection: "If not checked AIDS can decimate the whole Muslim population. Many Muslims do not even know that the use of condoms is allowed within marital relationships only. In this kind of situation if items such as condoms are not used, then in case of HIV infection of one spouse, the danger of rapid spread and the rise in number of AIDS orphans also becomes a reality. Also the care of discordant couples is hence adhered" (2005, 7). This is a daring public pronouncement, considering the overwhelming opposition of many traditional ulama to sex education in general and the use of condoms in particular. Condom use is generally viewed by most ulamas and other religious bodies in Africa as opening the door for un-Islamic sexual misconduct outside marriage. It is equally courageous for a Muslim women's organization to undertake an overt discussion of preventive sexuality in a predominantly conservative Muslim society such as Kenya.

In sum then, *The Nur* must be seen as a creative strategy for engaging a patriarchal culture of men and women who—partly because of the prevailing state of interreligious tensions—are often unwilling to openly and publicly discuss issues of human rights abuses of women within the Muslim society. However, focusing on HIV/AIDS, a global pandemic that instills fear in many provides a legitimate cover for interrogating those same practices that it is anathema to talk about in a different context. This strategy receives additional validation through its extensive deployment of Islamic doctrinal discourse. *The Nur* is an illustration not only of the fine line that Muslim women, as minority citizens, have to walk in promoting their agenda within their own communities but also of their potential to expand the space of democratic discourse in a nation just emerging from decades of tyrannical rule and a culture of fear and silence.

Ukumbi Wa Mamama: Islamist Radio Talk Show, Muslim Women's Political Activism

In addition to print media like *The Nur*, Muslim women's activism also uses the electronic media, especially the radio. This is regarded as a more accessible and more effective mode of engaging Muslim communities in general and Muslim women in particular, the majority of whom lack competency in English and functional literacy in Roman and Arabic scripts. My focus here is on one episode of *Ukumbi Wa Mamama*, a two-hour weekly program of Radio Rahma aired from 7 to 9 p.m., just after the evening (*maghrib*) prayer, when most people are at home.

Ukumbi Wa Mamama demonstrates how Islamist women radio talk-show hosts in Kenya are using their agency to transform the social order of patriarchal Islamist ideologies and at the same time are responding to and engaging their non-Muslim sisters on questions related to women from a Muslim perspective. Although this kind of dialogue can generate acrimony within and across communities at its early stages, it can eventually engender a culture of democratic national and intercommunal conversation on issues fundamental to minority groups by its inclusion of voices unheard before in the national platform. This is the case with *Ukumbi Wa Mamama*.

While there is doubtless an ideological convergence between the various orientations of patriarchal Islam on the place and status of Muslim women in society, it is the political Islam that emerged in the wake of the Cold War that most commonly elicits the intervention of Muslim women as radio talk-show hosts, guests, and callers. The pluralism resulting from the democratization process has also contributed to the development of public and gendered Islamic discourses. Furthermore, even though Muslim women's radio programs are a product of patriarchal patronage, women radio hosts and guests exercise a high degree of autonomy of critical thought. As agents of change, they use this electronic platform to subvert the co-opting/corrupting forms of social control of the (re)presentation of Muslim women by inscribing women's readings of Muslim reality, readings that differ from those of traditional Muslim men.

Kenya Muslim women hosts of radio programs such as *Ukumbi Wa Mamama* are mainly the products of secular education. They draw their knowledge about Islam and the hadiths from an intensive self-engagement with Islamic cyberliteracy through English and their involvement in new community-based Arabic madrasas and *darsas* (classes) run by new female and male graduates from Islamic universities with competing schools of thought. Their commitment to Islamic radio talk shows centered on women's issues stems from two concerns. First, in spite of the secularity of their education, they feel that the dominant non-Muslim majority misrepresents and misunderstands Muslim women's reality. Many argue that when references are made to Kenyan women, the nuanced experiences of Muslim women are not taken into account or are perceived as "nonindigenous." For these educated Muslim women radio activists, reclaiming their citizenship in a nation-state that discriminates against them as a religious minority becomes a critical mission. Second, they feel it is urgent to confront their own community about the patriarchal interpretation of Islam and its link to Muslim women's oppression. This double marginalization of the Kenya Muslim woman, it is argued, hinders her optimal participation in national public affairs. Thus, radio talk shows are used by Muslim women as a channel for unveiling the taboos in their own communities and for contributing to the democratic processes through the plurality of discourses generated by their programs.

These two interrelated missions of women's radio talk shows are amply demonstrated in the *Ukumbi Wa Mamama* discussion of the Sexual Offences Bill, which aired on May 22, 2006.[4] This bill was brought before the Parliament through the initiative of a woman legislator and lawyer, Njoki Ndung'u, in an attempt to curb the rising incidence of a variety of sexual crimes in Kenya that had hitherto been treated rather lightly by the penal code. The bill was later revised and finally enacted into law in 2006 as the Sexual Offences Act. Among other things, the new law incorporated into the constitution several hitherto unrecognized sexually related offenses, including pedophilia, child pornography, gang rape, deliberate infection with HIV/AIDS virus, trafficking for sexual exploitation, and sexual harassment, especially in the workplace. It also introduced new harsher minimum sentences for sexual offenses and set up a DNA data bank and a registry of convicted pedophiles.

The particular episode discussed here takes the form of an interview between Amina Abubakar, host of the show, and Rajput as the program guest, with contributions from the listeners via phone or short message services (that is, cell-phone text messages). The show opens with a famous Swahili song that praises *mamama*, playing on the ambiguity of the word, which can mean both "mothers" and "women." In essence, the song demands that mothers and women in general be shown the respect and honor accorded to them in Islam. The discussion of the bill unfolds through overlapping themes of serious concern to the community ranging from rape and incest in the Muslim community to possible responses to sexual violence.

At the time of this radio interview, Rajput was a nationally prominent activist in the ODM, a political party that had emerged in the heat of an acrimonious political contestation over the constitutional referendum of 2005. The electoral commission had selected a banana symbol for a "yes" vote and an orange for a "no" vote. ODM acquired its name from its mobilization activities against the new proposed constitution, which it regarded as a dilution of the Boma Draft Constitution. Partly because of the efforts of leaders like Rajput, the ODM accomplished its objective when the majority of Kenyans voted "no" in the referendum. The results of the referendum, in turn, gave Rajput and other ODM leaders new political clout in the nation.

In the aftermath of the referendum, Rajput declared her intention to run for president of Kenya in the country's next general elections, then scheduled for December 2007. Though she probably knew her chances of winning were slim, she saw the elections as a window of opportunity that she could use to inscribe the voice of a minority, Kenyan Muslims, even as she articulated politico-economic agendas that were both national and transethnic. Although many Muslim men argued that the doctrinal provisions of Islam barred Rajput from running for and assuming political leadership at the highest level of public service in Kenya, taking a narrow reading of verse 34 of chapter 4 of the Qur'an, "Men are the protectors/representatives of women," Rajput was not deterred by such attacks. On the contrary, she put the issue in the foreground of her radio interview: *"Assalamu alaikum wa rahmatu-llahi wa barakaatuhu.* Greetings. My name is Honorable Nazlin Omar Fazaldin Rajput, a Kenyan politician in the Orange Democratic Movement. I am also known as 'Mother Orange,' and I have made a decision to vie for the Kenya presidency seat. I am also the National Muslim Council of Kenya chairlady."

In this opening, Rajput accomplishes four objectives. First, she makes it clear to her predominantly Muslim audience in a predominantly Muslim constituency of Mombasa that she is a Muslim, signified by the greeting "Assalamu-alaikum" ("Peace be with you"), and a secular political leader of national prominence. She makes her position known that she disagrees fundamentally, from an Islamic perspective, with Muslim men and leaders who question her right to vie for the presidency on the grounds of her gender. Moreover, by declaring her political ambitions in an Islamic program, she also signals that she is fully prepared to debate the subject. In her introduction, she also capitalizes on her national leadership image—underscored by self-identification as "honorable," a term usually used to refer to politicians of national stature—in order to lend greater authority and credence to what she will say in the rest of the interview. Finally, as any astute politician would do, she takes advantage of this media moment to campaign for her presidential bid.

By the time Rajput was invited to be a guest on *Ukumbi Wa Mamama*, she was nationally known as a critic of the Sexual Offences Bill as it was originally put before the Parliament. To avoid any misunderstanding, however, Rajput wanted her audience to understand that there were legitimate circumstances that called for sexual offenses legislation and that those circumstances obtained in predominantly (coastal) Muslim communities of Kenya as much as in the rest of the country. So from the very beginning of the interview she is very careful to locate her critical comments on the bill within the context of the sexual violations rampant in Muslim communities:

ABUBAKAR: If you have just tuned in, you are listening to 91.5 Radio Rahma, the Voice of Mercy. It is 7:17, and we want to discuss the issue of sexual harassment. Bi Nazlin, tell us the content and what this is all about because we keep hearing complaints that the bill [Sexual Offences Bill] is too harsh.

RAJPUT: There are various amendments that need to be made to suit all religions, be it Islam or Christianity. There is gender violence in the bill. It favors the woman and oppresses the man a little. As we express our opinions, we need to strongly support the bill, as rape cases are on the increase. Even among Muslims rape is high, here in Mombasa, the Coast Province, and the Northeastern Province. We did a survey at the National Muslim Council of Kenya and it was evident that rape is on the increase and almost 60 percent of women have been raped in their homes . . . [*inaudible interjections*] their sisters, children, or their relatives have been raped.

ABUBAKAR: We have heard that an eighty-four- or eighty-five-year-old woman has been raped and the youngest rape victim is five months old! Nazlin, eighty-five years! Four months! And you wonder why?

RAJPUT: [*interjects*] On issues of gender and rape we have formed a committee in Lamu to look into the rape of young boys, I don't know what word to use to refer to the rape of young boys . . .

ABUBAKAR: Sodomy.

RAJPUT: Sodomy. But I think this bill does not consider the plight of sodomized boys. A lot of women complained during the Lamu workshop, cried a lot during the viewing of the survey video. In almost all houses, not all but many houses, you will find a boy who has been sodomized. It is even much better to send a girl to the shop in the evening, not a boy, because the boy will be raped. Lamu has a population that is 90 percent or 95 percent Muslim and yet Islam is strongly in opposition and very hostile to such act. . . .

ABUBAKAR: To such an act.

RAJPUT: Such sexual acts are on the increase among Muslims. I have a program here in Mombasa known as the Oasis 04 program that helps provide paralegal aid and seek justice for women and children in the legal system. You find a case where a father died and the mother who worked married again and the grandfather was left to care for the child. He raped the seven- or eight-year-old child every night for three years. When people discovered this, the child had all sorts of sexual infections out of the rape. What kind of Islam is this? Is this what the Qur'an teaches us? Instead of being a good example to others, we Muslims are engaging in shameful acts that one cannot even talk about. We are seeing a father raping his child of four years, three years, two years, who cannot even speak. It is very shocking!

Owing to her mastery of both Kiswahili and English, Rajput was able to delineate the areas of the proposed law that were technically problematic, especially for Muslim citizens. She has a sharp awareness of questions of legal definition, evidentiary procedure and the consequences of law on public resources:

RAJPUT: There is a conflict there. The SOB [Sexual Offences Bill], for example, brings the burden of proof. I am not well experienced to speak about this, but if you claim someone has raped you, say Mohamed Salim or whoever, when you bring evidence which is based on hearsay to court, the proof of evidence lies on the defendant. If you accuse someone of raping you, he must prove his innocence. This is very different from other law systems in the world, where the proof of evidence lies with you as a complainant. I think this is unfair to the brothers.

There is also a section that shamefully says that if the male or female organ penetrates the other, it is rape. Since when did the female organ penetrate the male one? Nature does not allow that. They are directly referring to the [female] sexual organs or the anus. Our Islamic religion does not restrict such an important discussion because these are acts that are being debated in the whole country.

ABUBAKAR: Yes.

RAJPUT: It was dishonest to mention men and women when they simply meant men. They should have simply stated that if "a man penetrates a woman . . ." because it is humanly impossible for a woman to penetrate a man. The other dishonest thing about the SOB is that on page 406 it states that if the bill is passed, it will not add any expenditure of public funds. It will definitely increase public expenditures. For example in article 43 it says that sexual offenders will be put under constant supervision and a system will be arranged that will ensure rapists are under constant surveillance. So that is a cost and they should not say that there will be no cost. There will be cost, which is OK. We are ready to have our taxes go into this, but they should be a bit more factual. It also talks about rehabilitative programs for rapists. This is cost . . . and we have to be honest about this. We as citizens are ready to increase our taxes to cover the expenses for the rehabilitation. That is, to cater for that, as it comes with additional costs.

There is another section that is not right because a lot of our Muslim brothers and sisters are living with the [HIV] virus. The virus is all over the country . . .

ABUBAKAR: Has spread.

RAJPUT: It has really spread, and our brothers are living with the virus. But article 27, section 7 of the SOB states that if a rapist who is HIV-positive infects the complainant, who is the female victim, with the virus or any other sexually transmitted disease like venereal, gonorrhea, whichever, the law will apply to punish the rapist. However, if it is established that the government did a test that was inaccurate and probably indicated that you were HIV-positive and infected a woman with HIV or you discover later that the rapist has no virus or the woman was raped but was not infected, then the rapist whose tests were inaccurate has no right to defend himself. He cannot bring any claim against the government, against the minister of justice, or against the medical practitioners, or against legal personalities who contributed to his detention, psychological torment, or shame.

In short, Rajput leaves no room for doubt that she can speak about legal and legislative matters with the same kind of authority that is normally associated with a trained legal mind. What Rajput is most insistent about in the interview, however, is not the technical weaknesses and problems of the bill. Rather, what she focuses on is the fact that, in her opinion, the bill was not sufficiently multicultural. She believes that in letter and scope it was not responsive to the multicultural tapestry that defines Kenya beyond religious affiliation. As a woman and a political leader in the country, she wants the new legal and constitutional dispensation to constantly bear in mind the cultural diversity that prevails in the nation and not to tolerate cultural and community-based violation of the rights and freedoms of any citizen, especially those of women and children. Understanding, however, that her audience at this particular forum was predominantly Muslim, she proceeds in the interview to highlight those areas of the bill that were not compatible with Kenya Muslim doctrinal beliefs.

One of these doctrines is the imperative of fairness. Rajput's claim that we must somehow "be fair to our brothers" is one she repeats elsewhere in the radio interview. It is in line with the Islamic tenet of *'adala*, fair, just, and equal treatment before the law, in particular, and in society at large. By invoking this conviction, Rajput seeks to reassure Muslim men that she would not support a bill that, in the course of trying to protect women and children, ends up unfairly demonizing and victimizing men. Her reassurance, in turn, serves as another strategy for galvanizing the support of men once the bill has been duly revised. In this way, Rajput continues to foreground her knowledge of Islam in an authoritative manner as a means of connecting with her audience while at the same time using it subversively to support the primary objectives of the bill.

The other relevant issue Rajput takes up in her critical appraisal of the bill is the definition of marriage, which, in her opinion, automatically excludes both Muslim and non-Muslim African understandings of the institution. Throughout the colonial period in Kenya, the British interpreted the marriages of their colonial subjects in monogamist terms. In the process, certain rights and benefits were often denied to spouses and children of spouses other than the first one, both during the lifetime of a husband and on his death. This colonial tradition was carried over in the framing of the Sexual Offences Bill, inadvertently reversing the gains that "cowives and their children" had acquired in the postcolonial state. This particular provision is one that Rajput attributes to the influence of "foreign" ideologies:

RAJPUT: The problem with this bill is that when it talks of rape it seeks only
to prevent rape and to make certain rulings on rape. It does not clearly

define rape despite talking about rape issues. The day that the bill was introduced into Parliament I went there to listen to what our brothers would support in the bill. The following day the media attacked those who opposed the bill until it is amended, which was unjust. They had strong reasons. SOB, section 2, article on the matrimonial clauses act defines marriage as a "voluntary union of one man and one woman for life to the exclusion of all others."

ABUBAKAR: Those aside.

RAJPUT: What does that clause mean? . . . What I am asking is whether this bill is redefining marriage, and that there can be no divorce. Second it is saying "to the exclusion of all others." What about Muslims? We are supporters of polygamy.

ABUBAKAR: Islam allows four wives. [*inaudible*]

RAJPUT: Or one to four. It is unfair for the bill to state "to the exclusion of all others," especially for those of us who are in polygamous marriages. If a man has a second wife, then that is a sexual offense. This is dangerous and against polygamy and it is a way of trying to sneak foreign ideologies through the back door.

ABUBAKAR: Yes.

RAJPUT: And again when it reads "one man and one woman for life to the exclusion of all others," it is trying to criminalize polygamy in its totality and it may make polygamy a sexual offense. It doesn't take into account the consent by the wives in the polygamous marriage, and the SOB has declared polygamy illegal. I am asking my African colleagues what the Muslims should do and why were they not consulted before they introduced such clauses in the bill. I am well known in Kenya and have introduced almost eight bills in my life. Was it so difficult for Njoki Ndung'u to ask me what the Islamic position is or to even ask other groups about the same? Why didn't they ask?

ABUBAKAR: To include Muslims in the bill.

RAJPUT: . . . Njoki Ndung'u, I have complained again, is taking this issue as a feminist agenda, and I don't agree with the feminist agenda. This is an attack on Islamic shari'a law and the Qur'an's provisions, which is a fundamental issue for us Muslims, and we cannot allow it to be passed. If some Muslim women do not want polygamy, that is our own and their own problem. But we cannot conflict [with] what God has decreed. [The Sexual Offences Bill requires that] section 13 subsection II of the African Christian Marriage and Divorce Act should be automatically repealed after the SOB. Yet the provision [the African Christian Marriage and Divorce Act] was in favor of poor women. It was created to protect poor women who had no access to the protection of the law in the face of oppressive and abusive negative traditions and customary practices. It helps the women married under the Marriage and Divorce Act to have automatic guardianship of their children when their husbands die. It was designed to avoid the preying conduct of some in-laws and domineering relatives who took it upon themselves to deprive a widow of her children and property and thereby chase her away. Why should you allow these women to repeal a statute that protects poor Christian women?

What we see here, in part, is a strategic maneuver on the part of the "political" Rajput to garner wider support for the bill once it incorporates certain revisions. She understands that many Kenyans who are still rooted in their indigenous cultures and many African men—Muslims and non-Muslims alike—who have a vested interest in polygyny would use the provision as grounds for rejecting the entire bill. The provision also posed the danger of creating division within the ranks of women, which could have alienated even some of those that the bill was intended to protect.

It is also crucial that Rajput concludes by addressing directly the initiator of this powerful bill, Ndung'u, suggesting in a politically coded language that the feminist agenda that was partly responsible for the formulation of the bill must be articulated strategically in a way that would not result in the defeat of the bill. Since the bill's main objective was to seek redress for gender-based sexual violence against women and children, Ndung'u and other supporters of the bill, including Rajput herself, ought not allow the definition of marriage at this stage to cost them the support of the religious bodies and other numerically significant constituencies. Rajput's critique of Ndung'u is clearly not shared by Amina Abdallah, with whom she ran sensitization workshops in various communities, as discussed in chapter 3.

Yet another fundamental issue in the bill of critical concern to Rajput and that had a bearing on the Muslim community were the stiffer penalties the bill proposed for rape. Even these stiffer penalties were not sufficient for Rajput, who called for the ultimate penalty, death, as part of her recommended amendments to the bill:

The bill states also that no one will be hanged for raping or injuring a four-month-old child they have raped. The person will be imprisoned for fifteen years. It is a total waste to keep a rapist in bars for fifteen years and use our taxes to feed him, protect him, and treat him in hospital. This is an animal, and even an animal is incapable of raping its offspring. Even a pig cannot do that! This person has become a strange being that requires to be wiped out of the community. I support the death penalty. You will even hear women who support the bill and do not support the death penalty with the excuse that it [life] is a human right. Why are we taking European customs and making them our own?

To underscore the issue of harsher penalties for rapists, Rajput challenges the government to take the issue of rape more seriously than it has done. In an exchange between a caller and herself, Rajput encourages the Muslim community to be proactive as a way of putting pressure on the government to assume its responsibility of punishing perpetrators of sexual offenses with utmost vigilance:

CALLER: I have forgotten one thing, Ms. Nazlin. In the seven o'clock news today on Nation [TV] it has been reported that a teacher in Kisumu has raped more than forty children. I watched as one child after the other narrated their ordeal. As a politician, how will you deal with this issue, Ms. Nazlin, because this man may be jailed and released on a bail of 150,000 Kenya shillings? My suggestion is that if the teacher is released, we women should organize a phenomenal demonstration with Ms. Nazlin as the leader. It will be inhuman to release him, and we have no government.

RAJPUT: That, Allah, is the most worrying thing, and [for] every parent today, and even our brothers and sisters who have no children. Forty children! I want to ask the women who have presented this bill and yet do not want to include the death penalty, why should such an animal be allowed to live?

ABUBAKAR: It is now important to amend the bill as soon as possible.

RAJPUT: Very fast! The more they delay the bill the more people continue to suffer. The problem with Kenya is that we do not have strong laws and there are too many loopholes in the system. A penal code is already in place, and yet a man will manage to be bailed out after paying 150,000 Kenya shillings [about US$2,000 in 2006]. I am warning the government that if they release this man on bail, we women will look for him everywhere and we shall not let him go. And if the masses lynch him, we shall blame

the government because it is supposed to . . . keep him out! We need to
see fast resolutions on this case.

Here Rajput is talking the language of a concerned national politician. And
from the sentiment expressed by the caller, she has a constituency of Kenyans
that has faith in her leadership and mobilization abilities. It is against this
backdrop of popular confidence enjoyed by Rajput that the host of the radio
program proceeds to seek Rajput's policy recommendations to reduce the
incidence of rape in the country.

Within the framework of existing law, Rajput continues to call for stiffer
penalties against sexual offenders, including public hanging depending on
how heinous the offense is. She has also proposed retraining of police per-
sonnel, who often treat rape cases lightly or, through bribery, become complicit in the crime by frustrating the court process in one way or another.
Rajput also recommends rape advocacy centers at the community level to raise
awareness about and mobilize against rape. Finally, and in spite of her position that Kenyans should not be influenced by the West, Rajput is a strong
supporter of publishing pictures of sexual offenders in local print and electronic media to allow people to better protect themselves and their families,
especially against serial rapists, an idea that is popular in the United States.

The primary Islamic doctrines, the Qur'an and the hadith, do not overtly
address the issue of rape or any kind of coercive sexual act. They only deal
with consensual sexual relationships, both within and outside the institution of marriage. In line with general practice in Islamic jurisprudence, Muslim jurists have invoked the principle of analogy in attempting to construct
laws on rape on the strength of legal reasoning involving another relevant
crime. The closest of those sexual "crimes" explicitly addressed in Islam is, of
course, *zina*, which includes consensual extramarital or premarital sexual
unions. Islam considers *zina* to be a very serious sin and its punishment in
law could include death. If an "adulterer" could be condemned to death, then
legal analogy easily leads jurists to regard a rapist to be even more deserving
of a death penalty. This manifestly Islamic position is clearly the one assumed
by Rajput, not only because of the magnitude of the violence inherent in
rape but also because that is the kind of penalty that would be in conformity
with at least some readings of Islam.

On the other hand, Rajput is careful in how she addresses the issue of
"marital rape" that is also treated as a sexual crime in the bill:

RAJPUT: There is also another clause in this bill that does not bring out the distinction between marital sex and sex out of marriage. It is important to differentiate sex in marriage and sex . . .

ABUBAKAR: Outside marriage.

RAJPUT: Outside of marriage. I will now bring you to section 199, 144 section II na 145 subsection II of the penal code, [which] defines clearly the marriage institution and punishment for sexual offenders. The SOB states that you can report your husband for raping you within your marriage relationship. Do you understand?

ABUBAKAR: Yes.

RAJPUT: Do you think that as a legally married woman you can accuse your husband of rape and still go back to the marriage relationship that you had before?

ABUBAKAR: It is impossible.

RAJPUT: If it has reached a time where your husband is forcing himself on to you, then it is wrong. The Islamic law states clearly that do not approach your wives as donkeys, use good . . . [unclear] words and foreplay before the act.

ABUBAKAR: Excite her.

RAJPUT: Excite your wife until she is in a state of enjoying the lovemaking too. If your marriage reaches a point where your husband forces himself on to you like a donkey like the shari'a quotes, you should seek the counsel of the kadhi so that he may attend counseling, and if this does not work it is better to divorce. But it is impossible for you to accuse your husband of rape whereby he is jailed for fifteen years and you still expect to return to happy and lasting marriage. It is better to divorce and continue relating with others.

In Islam, sex is a right of the man, as it is of the woman, and unless there are reasons of health and such, it is never to be denied when requested. Rather than risk alienating the support of men at this critical juncture of the bill's history, Rajput skirts around the issue, never really stating explicitly that it is conceivable to have rape within marriage. On the other hand, she counsels men not to just "throw" themselves on women like "donkeys," but, as Islam would require, to satisfy their sexual desires by taking the time, creating the environment, and making the effort to arouse their partners sexually.

It is quite evident from the excerpts from the radio interview that the host and guest of *Ukumbi Wa Mamama* used a "tell it like it is" approach to sensitize the Muslim community. Needless to say, this is a bold and potentially dangerous political undertaking for Muslim women. However, the responses to the show from male and female callers indicate great appreciation of how the host and the guest used the radio platform to lift the curtains of silences on pervasive taboo issues in Muslim societies that the ulama had not successfully addressed. One female caller, for example, exclaimed,

> Yes! We are grateful to Ms. Nazlin and Radio Rahama for opening our ears to this debate that has been going on in the papers. We are happy that she has made us aware of the inequalities in the bill because we, the old [ones], were not understanding what was going on. We were blaming the parliamentarians who were not supporting the bill. But we are now aware that this bill is against Islam, and I don't think any Muslim will support it because it is not beneficial to us. We have our own shari'a laws despite being in a non-Islamic state. That is my contribution. Thank you, Bi Nazlin and Amina, for today's program.

Other callers, including Muslim men, also showered praise on Rajput and Abubakar for the enlightening program they conducted on the Sexual Offences Bill. Thus, through a women's radio talk show, Muslim women created a space for engaging the community in self-interrogation while also carving an opening for their public participation in national debates. One male caller said, "My Name is Ali of Tudor, I want to praise Sister Rajput," while another male listener said, "I agree with you, Ms. Nazlin, and wish you all the best. Continue the discussion. Thank you."

An examination of the language used in *Ukumbi Wa Mamama* clearly shows Kenya Muslim women's exposure to global transnational Muslim women social and political activist networks and discourses through virtual travels in cyberspace or pleasure or business trips throughout the Muslim world in non-Western countries as well as in the West and via SMS, satellite, DVDs, and magazines. Rajput's appearances as one of the most outspoken Kenya Muslim women public figures on international television such as CNN, her Internet presence, and her participation in international conferences are clear indications of her commitment to reaching out to a constituency beyond the national confinement. Finally, this new trend among some Muslim women in Kenya of using new information technologies to publicly intervene on serious issues affecting their human rights within their own communities and in the nation at large is in line with Susan Hirsch's (1998) study of some

Swahili women's use of the kadhi courts in the postcolonial dispensation. As Hirsch concludes, "Whether or not the act of a Swahili woman's filing a case in Kadhi's Court is called resistance (by the women themselves or by me), it confronts cultural expectations for female behavior by positioning a woman outside the domestic realm and in a public, official context in which she seeks to alter her circumstances. Turning to Kadhi's Court affirms her connection to Islam, even as it calls her piety into question and, simultaneously, constitutes her as a supplicant to the State. Perhaps most importantly . . . Kadhi's Courts provide the context for women to narrate problems" (1998, 137). Similarly, the new media outlets owned by Muslims have become important sites of transgressive acts of narration of taboo subjects or concerns to women that are seemingly framed within Islamic terms of reference.

CONCLUSION

In conclusion, then, a close reading of the magazine *The Nur* and the excerpts from the radio talk show *Ukumbi Wa Mamama* reveals the extent to which the democratization process of the media has provided an opportunity for Muslim women media producers such as Abubakar and Rajput to discuss in a public forum what has traditionally been considered a matter of the private domain. They use their agency to shatter the traditional boundary between the public and the private not only in the Muslim community but within the Kenyan nation. This chapter also shows the commitment and dedication of Muslim women activists, often of limited education, to acquiring skills in critical literacy that enable them to read and deconstruct not only religious texts but secular materials like legal documents and scientific literature on diseases that have a bearing on their lives. Muslim women activists are creatively using the media opportunities accorded by the democratization process to galvanize their literacy and intellectual skills and resources in the name of social justice for all.

This quest for social justice for all is what makes it wrong to suggest that for Muslim women, these technological developments in information exchange and communication are important only insofar as they serve their needs and agendas and those of the Muslim community. Women have also used them repeatedly to link the local with the national (and even global) and to connect the Islamic and the secular. If Muslim women activists have used the media to interrogate power relations within the patriarchal Muslim community, they have also used technology to challenge the hegemony of the non-Muslim majority. And if the media has enabled them to advocate more effectively for their rights within Islam, it has also empowered them to reclaim their citizenship within their own communities and the nation at large. This dynamic is precisely what makes a figure like Rajput both a *Muslim* leader and a *Kenyan* leader. In this process of rereading Islam and redefining citizenship, Muslim women are not only "multiculturalizing" the human rights regime in their country but also putting to rest the long-held view of Muslim women as passive onlookers. Those behind the NMCK, *The Nur*, and Radio Rahma's *Ukumbi wa Mamama* have left no doubt that Muslim women are bold agents of change within their own communities and well beyond. Finally as citizens, we see how as a presidential candidate Rajput takes full advantage of a media opportunity to critique laws and structures in a way that advances her presidential bid.

Although in the end Rajput was not successful in her 2007 presidential bid, because of her readiness to use every available platform—*Ukumbi wa Mamama*, *The Nur*, social media appearances (as in YouTube)—to consistently inscribe an Islamic pole in the national political landscape, she succeeded in further positioning Muslims in Kenya as legitimate stakeholders in the destiny of the nation.[5] And as the *Ukumbi wa Mamama* program demonstrates, she is an effective enough communicator to attract the ears of her Muslim listeners and those of the nation at large.

Conclusion

In this book I offer an examination of the significant ways Kenya Muslim women sociopolitical leaders such as the ones discussed here have been using the space opened up by the 1990s democratization to bring about transformative changes in critical domains of society while also reclaiming their citizenship rights within their communities of faith and the secular postcolonial nation-state as members of a minority constituency. I explore the tools, strategies, and resources that these agents of social and political transformation use in their activism to inscribe Muslim women's rights issues in local, national, and international agendas and make their contributions to democratic processes in local, national, and international arenas through women-centered frameworks sensitive to gender ideologies within society from both religious and secular perspectives. In addition, in each chapter, I show how the Kenya Muslim women leaders discussed here critically read the forces against them within society and how they are depicted in hegemonic discourses. Their readings are critical to their construction of alternative visions of a just society and a multicultural, multiethnic, and multireligious democratic citizenship.

The gains in community and state investment in granting access to secular education and literacy are clearly reflected in the ways in which some Muslim women beneficiaries are making use of the knowledge and skills acquired to effect transformative social and political changes in their communities and the nation. They have become strong advocates of investing resources to promote education in Muslim communities and literacy in critical domains such as public health as a means of combating diseases such as the HIV/AIDS pandemic and other sexually transmitted diseases. They are also involved in raising awareness about FGC, providing civic literacy, raising Muslims' awareness of Muslim women's rights and responsibilities, and promoting Muslim women's active participation in public, local, and national affairs. Although they struggle to offset the negative impact of hegemonic and patriarchal educational policies that continue to disadvantage girls and women in Muslim society, they adopt a gendered approach to education and literacy in order to prevent the production of a gender discordance in society that may have negative consequences. As Ummi Naomi Shaban points out, "Educated Muslim women need educated Muslim men. There are more problems in society when you are dealing with less educated men. We need to educate both girls and boys in society about gender-based oppressive structures. We fight for Muslim girls to be educated, but we don't neglect the Muslim boys because these days they too are at risk." Muslim women's leadership roles in tackling patriarchal gender-based issues affecting girls and women in society are now recognized by Muslim male religious leaders.

Muslim women leaders have been skillful in mobilizing the support of the Muslim male clergy, which in many instances they consider important to the success of their projects. In spite of the progress achieved in transforming the views of some Muslim clergy about the public leadership of Muslim women, however, it is clear that many are willing to accept this gendered development only within certain limits. For example, Sheikh Mohammed Dor, secretary general of the Council of Imams and Preachers of Kenya and a nominated MP of the ODM, is reported to have said, "When in Parliament it is easy for Muslim women to consider matters of fistula, early marriages, maternity leave, and menstrual cycles among others. Such matters cannot occur in our minds" (Mudi 2011). Coming from a legislator, this statement is shocking in its implications. For it reveals not only the extent of almost chronic insensitivity or ignorance of male Muslim clergy to matters affecting women but also the view that in the secular public arena Muslim women can provide leadership only on women-related issues. This is the kind of perspective that, until recently, restricted the appointment of women to cabinet positions related only to women/gender/youth and the like. It is not surprising, therefore, that Dor is one of the male Muslim leaders along with Sheikh Hammad Mohamed Kassim (Mazrui) and Sheikh Hasan Sugow who have openly opposed women serving as kadhis in Kenya ("Muslim Clerics Oppose" 2011).

Like rape, obstetric fistula is another example of how girls are victims of male violation of women's sexuality and reproductive health. Obstetric fistula essentially affects girls who are forced into arranged marriage at a premature reproductive age, a phenomenon very common in many African societies, including Kenya. Yet Dor's remarks clearly reveal that he does not consider himself to be a religious leader and parliamentarian who ought to use his religious and legislative status to intervene and try to bring to an end cultural practices—early marriage of girls and FGC—that adversely impact the lives of girls in particular and women in general. In this regard, conservative Muslim male leaders are in company with other conservative non-Muslim male leaders who have been elected or nominated in Parliament. As a result, it has always been women legislators who have proposed bills, like the Sexual Offences Bill, that seek to protect women and girls from gender-based sexual violence. This is not to say, however, that there are no progressive Muslim men who are working closely with Muslim women leaders in campaigns and initiatives to raise awareness about the negative consequences of social rites such as FGC and early child marriage that can lead to conditions such as obstetric fistula.

In assuming their leadership roles, Muslim women discussed in this book have had the crucial experience of education. Although schooling and literacy often reproduce a normative societal or state ideology of gender or citizenship (Bourdieu 1973; Bourdieu and Passeron 1977), they also make possible multicultural, multireligious, multiethnic, and multiracial interactions among fellow citizens from various backgrounds. Like in most African societies, the postcolonial mass education programs adopted by the Kenyan state created opportunities for Muslim girls, whose mobility was hitherto restricted to Muslim-targeted, community institutions, to interact with other Kenyans of non-Muslim background. Furthermore, as graduates of professional fields absorbed in the national civil services, educated Muslim women have developed cross-cultural networks outside their community of faith that have served them in their professional, social, and political activist networking to advance Muslim women's social and political agenda on national platforms. This is illustrated in a number of coalitions involving Muslim and non-Muslim women members of the Kenyan Parliament that advance bills promoting women's rights, such as the Sexual Offences Bill, the provision to build a nursery in Parliament, and the debate on the shari'a for personal law in the Kenyan constitution (A. Mutua 2003). This transethnic and transreligious networking demonstrates how Muslim women act as autonomous agents to make strategic alliances, at times outside their community of faith. Although both are Muslims, Shaban and Amina Abdallah contend that they both run on a secular KANU agenda representing multireligious constituencies. Similarly, non-Muslim educationists express appreciation of the innovative integrated religious curricular designs of Muslim women educationists such as Bi Swafiya Muhashamy-Said or the support Azara Mudira received from non-Muslims at the initial stages of the implementation of her vision for her *ma'had* Islamic boarding school for young Muslim women.

Both Shaban (later minister of special programs in the Office of the President) and Abdallah talk about what it is like to serve as legislators in a male-dominated parliament. Male parliamentarians repeatedly treat issues and bills that are brought before the house by the female counterparts with derision and hostility. As Joe Khamisi, a former male MP, remarks, "In Parliament, the numerical majority of men over women have [*sic*] for years, worked to the disadvantage of the latter. During debates, women legislators had to endure sneers, and snippets of degrading comments from their male colleagues, sometimes making their contributions inaudible. On many occasions, the speaker had to intervene to protect female parliamentarians from embarrassing interventions from some of their chauvinistic male colleagues" (2011, 284). This trend of male parliamentary conduct was evident even in discussion of bills like the Sexual Offences Bill intended to address issues, such as rape and incest and conscious transmission of the HIV/AIDS virus, that affect women and children in the most horrible ways. In spite of this hostile environment, women MPs like Njoki Ndung'u, who introduced the Sexual Offences Bill in 2005, Alicen Chelaite, who introduced the gender policy bill, and others stood firm and courageously against patriarchal hostility and insisted on seeing the bills go through the various stages of the parliamentary process. Muslim women MPs were especially partners in these struggles, as shown in chapter 4; both Abdallah and Ndung'u joined forces to run workshops on issues of sexuality within predominantly Muslim communities.

Muslim women reformers use their fluency in old and new information technologies to expand the public space of their social and political activism. Their interventions as media producers, hosts of radio talk shows, and users of social media—YouTube, blogs, SMS—to make their views known to the wider society and the world have gendered the discourses and representations of Kenya Muslim women in local, national, and international arenas. Communicating both in English and local languages such as Kiswahili to reach out to their audiences, Muslim women reformers use the media to address a wide range of issues, such as Muslim citizenship rights and responsibilities within the nation-state, right of access to economic opportunities, education, and sexuality and reproductive health, from both a secularist and religious perspective. Their use of local languages to engage with their constituencies, especially the womenfolk who are not fluent in the English language, is an important dimension of their vision for democratic inclusive politics. Chapter 5 illustrates how Amina Abubakar, the host of *Ukumbi Wa Mamama* on Radio Rahma, and Nazlin Umar Rajput, the political activist, foster a fascinating public dialogue with Muslims—both female and male—on topics related to issues of inequality rooted in unequal access to national resources and educational opportunities, poverty, gender-based sexual violence, patriarchal Islam, sexuality and reproductive rights, Muslim community and state responses to the HIV/AIDS pandemic, and the Sexual Offences Bill. Also worth mentioning is the work of peace activist Dekha Ibrahim, which is accessible on many websites.

Through educational, trade, and virtual transnationalism, Kenya Muslim women leaders such as the ones discussed in this book are engaging in exchanges of ideas with other (Muslim) women's networks that are clearly revealed in their innovative activism whose goal is to bring about empowering social and political transformations in their local communities and in the nation, especially in domains such as (Muslim) women's citizenship rights, personal laws, religion, and culture that are often deployed against (Muslim) women in society across ethnic boundaries. Abida Ali-Aroni in chapter 4 demonstrates her transnational fluency with the laws and her leadership role in constitutional reform, including in areas such as the shari'a, that have a direct bearing on women's rights.

As I indicated in the introduction, Kenya's location on the Indian Ocean has sometimes led to the problematization of identity of Muslims and postcolonial attempts to fix national citizenship via an essentialist conception of Africanity. This problem was exacerbated in the aftermath of the tragic bombing of East African U.S. embassies and the 9/11 bombings in the United States, as various nations sought to distance themselves from the charges of harboring home-grown Muslim terrorists (Hirsch 2006b; Seesemann 2006). The issue of inscribing "Muslimness" in the space of Kenyan citizenship naturally became part of the politics of Muslim women both in their modes of dress as well as in their discourses of rights. Muslim citizenship contestation in Kenya has produced an intra-Muslim tension revolving around the bodily representation of Muslim women in society that has been mediated through discourses on veiling in the tradition of the Swahili *buibui* or veiling in the new hijab from the Arab oil-producing Gulf countries or Islamic South Asia or in the West African Muslim style (see, for example, Alidou 2005, 156–75; Fuglesang 2004; Mahdi 2009; Porter 1998). Such contestation mediated through the discourse on veiling extends to the interrogation of whether veiled women in *buibui* or hijab have agency. I hope that this study provides ample demonstration of the agency of veiled and unveiled Muslim women across class and ethnicity and cultural locations in effecting transformative social and political changes in their communities and the nation since the opening up of the democratic space in Kenya.

Furthermore, I show that through a creative claim to their Islamic faith, Muslim women reform leaders such as the ones discussed in this book are developing sociopolitical frameworks for confronting the forces of neoliberalism, the rise of religious fundamentalism as manifested in new Wahhabi-Salafism, Christian Pentecostalism, and fundamentalist African traditional religions like Mungiki. Through the assertion of their Islamic faith and their strong investment in a women-centered reading of the Qur'an and *fiqh*, Kenya Muslim women reform leaders such as Ali-Aroni try to get both patriarchal Muslims and non-Muslims to understand those areas in which their personal rights are protected more by the shari'a than by the national secular constitution. Through their quest to "undo" patriarchal Islamic interpretative discourses and by heavily advocating for and investing in both secular and religious education of women and girls, they are opening up the doors for Muslim women leaders' legitimate participation in both private and public activities that promote Muslim women's involvement in representative politics, in the workforce, and in community development initiatives such as girls' and women's literacy programs, women's public and reproductive health programs, and economic empowerment activities within and outside the domestic sphere.

I also analyze the leadership roles that frame the experiences of Muslim women (as well as some Muslim men) in the various communities in Nairobi and Mombasa where I conducted my research. I see each of the Muslim women discussed here as a "Muslim woman reform leader" within the context of the democratization era from the 1990s onward. By engaging with these Muslim women leaders themselves through in-depth interviews and visiting the communities they serve in order to investigate the sociopolitical impacts of the reforms they sought, initiated, and implemented, I am able to provide critical accounts of their leadership interventions in both the private and public spheres within their diverse Muslim communities and within the nation and beyond. The social biographies of these Kenya Muslim women reform leaders allows for a deeper exposition of their views regarding Islam and secularism as practiced within their diverse Muslim communities and their contributions in shaping public debates about Islam and Muslims in contemporary national and global politics. Their work thus challenges the notion of their status as simply passive consumers of Muslim male subjectivities while also demonstrating the diversity of their philosophical and political orientations. In some of the chapters, for example, I examine the different types of ideological responses they advocate as to how to reform access to Islamic knowledge beyond the basic rituals and the shari'a in a way that promotes Muslim women's rights and Muslim personal rights within the secular constitution of Kenya.

As modern visionaries, Muslim women reform leaders also see educational reform in both the religious and secular domains as key to social and political reforms aiming at centering women's rights and more especially girls' rights within society. The pioneering work of Muhashamy-Said in secularizing the traditional Qur'anic schools commonly known as *chuo* in Kenya through a creative combination of Islamic studies with secular subjects is an important case in point. Her integrated madrasa curriculum alleviates the alienating effects of the secular school while also equipping the children with skills necessary in a competitive modern world. Moreover, the integrated madrasa addresses the new inequalities brought about by neoliberal policies advocating the privatization of early childhood education in the country that has put it beyond the financial reach of poor Muslim parents. Today the success of Muhashamy-Said's integrated madrasa curriculum is reflected in its transnational adoption in other African Muslim countries in East Africa such as Uganda and Tanzania and in some West African countries like Mali and Chad, and also in the increase of the ratio of girls enrolled in schools. Muhashamy-Said's educational vision has attracted the attention of the Kenya Institute of Education, which has endorsed her curricular model and used it in reforming the national religious education curriculum backed by the ministry of education.

Mudira stands out for her leadership role in dismantling the *madhhab*-based educational tradition that she sees as the foundation of patriarchal control of Islamic knowledge and interpretations. She used her high literacy competencies in both secular subjects and Islamic studies to found a modern *ma'had* where female students are exposed to the diversity and breadth of Islamic theological thought rather than restricted to the teachings of a given male imam. By opening the gates of Islamic knowledge to young Muslim women, Mudira is following the trend observed in other Muslim societies in Africa and elsewhere of Muslim women religious scholars feminizing the field of Islamic authorization and creating a space for Muslim women's exploration and reclaiming of their rights granted to them by Islam but denied to them by patriarchal interpretations (Alidou 2005; Arimbi 2009; Badran 2011; Barlas 2002; Mernissi 1987, 1991a; Mir-Hosseini 2004; Ong 2006, 31–52; Robinson 2009; Umar 2004; Wadud 1999, to cite a few). Furthermore, she argues that by developing the right *akhlaq*, Muslim women will be prepared to advance their education in secular fields and use the skills they have acquired to enhance Muslim lives in a competitive modern world. As revealed in the discussions with Mudira, the intervention of educated Muslim women in Islamic studies is bearing fruit not only in displacing the male monopoly over religious education but also in promoting openness in the diversity of Islamic thought, interpretative paradigms, and practices. This is an empowering strategy for planting the seed of *ijtihad* for women operating within an Islamic framework and for secular Muslim women lawyers and social and political activists engaged both in the national struggle for the recognition of Muslim personal law and in their fight for gender equality within their community of faith and in a democratic postcolonial state. In this regard, the Kenya Muslim women's experiences discussed here resonate with the struggle of Muslim women in South Africa. Muslims are an internally diverse minority in South Africa, and conflicting ideologies have come into play there in the national debate over the legal recognition of Muslim marriages (Manjoo 2011, 291– 304). We see in chapter 4 how Ali-Aroni advocates for the constitutional retention of the kadhi courts for Muslim personal law. However, she prefers to see this happening within a democratically reformed framework that would be sensitive to Muslim women's rights and that would require high judicial accountability on the part of the kadhis, an accountability similar to what judges operating within the secular framework have to answer to. Similarly, while Rajput uses print media and the radio talk show as a platform for giving voice to those aspects of parliamentary bills that violate Muslim (women)'s rights, she also constructively contributes to their reformulation in ways that are empowering to Muslim women and children. Rajput, Mudira, and Ali-Aroni—as different as they are ideologically—all concur in their support for the kadhi courts and about the urgent need for educated Muslim women to intervene in Islamic education and transform patriarchal Islamic institutions and practices. They all advocate Muslim women becoming active policy makers and implementers in their communities and the nation.

The sociopolitical changes advocated by Muslim women leaders and the strategies they use to advance their causes clearly show the impact of the high literacy skills they have acquired as a result of the massification of education in Kenya during the postcolonial era. Muslim women reform leaders use these same educational skills to interrogate the patriarchal secular state, which marginalizes them both by virtue of their gender and as Muslims within a framework of liberal national constitution. Furthermore, modern schooling has fostered greater cross-ethnic and cross-faith interactions between Muslim women and non-Muslim women in Kenya. As a result, a space has developed for Muslim women's engagement with non-Muslim women and strategic coalition building in women's rights activism through a dialogic negotiation of the boundaries of their differences and commonalities within the nation-state. Whether activists within Islamist frameworks or within secularist paradigms, the Muslim women reform leaders discussed in this book call for the sociopolitical betterment for women not only of Islamic faith but also of other faiths. It is clear that they do not support a return to a primordial past as advocated in most revivalist conservative religio-political movements (Alidou 2005; Augis 2009; Hill 2010; Marloes 2011; Ong 2006, 31–52; Rosander 1997; Schulz 2012). Their sociopolitical activism also demonstrates their autonomous stand in democratically interrogating not only their marginalization and denial of access to resources by the patriarchal secular nation-state, but also in claiming their rights as women and members of Muslim minority within the national constitutional framework. They work shoulder to shoulder with other women in the nation to fight for basic rights to clean water and public health and for access to economic and political opportunities, and they endeavor to bring about sustainable peace and justice in the nation. The effort to secure peace is clearly demonstrated in the work of Dekha Ibrahim Abdi, a Somali Kenyan woman peace activist who through the positive nonhegemonic deployment of culture to manage violent conflicts sought to restore the relationship between victims and perpetrators of violence in society before her untimely death in 2011. Kenya Muslim women reform leaders are asserting their agency and autonomous thinking about women's rights and modernity in ways that need to be evaluated within the context of their own historical and postcolonial reality.

In this book I also demonstrate that global transnationalism is a feature of Kenya Muslim women reform leaders' experiences. Through their transnational participation, they are exposed to new ideas; they produce and share their own views about how they use Islam in their sociopolitical mobilization to advance their causes. This also reflects the diversity of their subjectivities and the transnational impact they are able to have through their networks and sites of interventions. Through their claim to their Islamic faith whether as Islamist or secularist, Muslim women leaders, as members of a minority constituency in Kenya, assert their modernity and mark their affinities with and/or differences from both Muslim men and non-Muslim women in the secular nation-state and beyond. From the totality of the experiences of Muslim women leaders covered in this book, then, we see that Kenya Muslim women reformers, whether secular or religious, are both religious agents and/or political agents who use a critical reading of Islam and hegemonic structures within their society and beyond in their quest to democratically transform their communities and the nation at large. In this regard these Muslim women leaders see no incompatibility between being Muslims and being citizens of a predominantly non-Muslim secular modern state.

Glossary

abaya	loose black dress	*mu'alima*	female teacher
akhlaq	Islamic character	*mut'a*	temporary marriage
buibui	long black overdress	shari'a	Islamic law based on the Qur'an
chuo	primary school		
da'wa	preaching of Islam	*sira*	biography of the Prophet
du'a	invocations used in Muslim rituals		
		siri	secret
fiqh	Islamic jurisprudence	*sitara*	modesty
heshima	respectability and virtue	*tafsir*	Qur'anic exegesis
hijab	head covering	tawhid	oneness of God
ijtihad	independent reasoning	*ubaguzi*	racial discrimination
kanga	two-piece colorful wrap	ulama	religious scholars
leso	two-piece colorful wrap	umma	the worldwide Muslim community
madhhab	school of thought		
ma'had	school, institute	*walimu*	teachers

Notes

INTRODUCTION

1. Qur'an Surat Al Baqarah 2:142–252, 2:180a.

2. Bi Swafiya Salim Muhashamy-Said is a niece of Shamsa Muhashamy, commonly known in Mombasa as Mwana Kutani, one of the subjects of Strobel 1979; she is also mentioned in Mirza and Strobel 1989, 111.

3. See Kabira 2012 for the role of educated Kenyan women in the constitution-making process and their alliance with grassroots women's organizations.

4. See Ndzovu 2009, 6–7, which draws from the *Akiwumi* official transcript, October 12, 1998, quoted by Human Rights Watch 2009.

5. For a discussion of Swahiliness, see Mazrui and Shariff 1994.

6. Al-Shabaab, considered a radical Islamist group, emerged from the Islamic Court movement, the coalition that saw the downfall of Siad Barre's regime and that for a while constituted the Mogadishu government before it was routed out by Ethiopia's invading army (Human Rights Watch 2010). More recently, Al-Shabaab has been accused of promoting terrorist activities in the region and of training young recruits of the Mombasa Republican Council, a recent political formation on the Kenyan coast with secessionist ambitions. This alleged interference of Al-Shabaab in Kenya partly served as a justification for Kenya's 2011 military intervention in Somalia.

7. See Robertson and James 2005 for critical perspectives on FGM and caution against Western sensationalism. While I am in absolute agreement with the caution, I don't think it's only Western feminists who object to FGM and so also feel it is equally important to document the agency of those (Muslim) women who are leading the current struggle on their own terms in the Kenyan Parliament and in Kenyan communities against it.

8. See wunrn.com/news/2009/01_09/01_26_09/012609_fgm.htm.

9. See the Kenya Women Parliamentary Association's commentaries on the

passing of FGM Act of 2011, fgcdailynews.blogspot.com/2011_09_01archive.html and www.kenyaforum.net/?p=576.

10. In Mombasa Swahili, the term "leso" is used instead of the more popular "kanga." See Zawawi 2005.

11. See wisemuslimwomen.org/muslimwomen/bio/sophia_abdi_noor.

12. See Robertson 1996 and Wangila 2007, 2009.

13. See Keaton 2006 and Scott 2007.

14. Zuberi founded Tangana Women Development Group in 2000, a nonprofit community organization catering to children, especially orphans from disadvantaged communities in coastal Kenya.

15. See Othman-Yahya 1997 and Zawawi 2005 for fascinating sociolinguistic studies of the Swahili *kanga*, or *leso* (women's wrapper).

16. See also Omale 2003, in which Mutua is quoted.

17. Other studies of the kadhi courts and Islamic law in East Africa include Hirsch 2006a, 2010; Makaramba 2010, 273–304; Maoulidi 2009; and Stile 2009.

18. See Porter 1998, 634–41, on the performance of *heshima* through Muslim dress fashion in a school setting by young Muslim girls at a Mombasa girl's school.

Chapter 1. Bi Swafiya Muhashamy-Said

1. See Hodgson 2001 for a powerful account of the interplay between gender and modernity in societies in Africa, Asia, and Latin America that are not products of colonial modernity.

2. "Bi" is a short form for "bibi," which literally means "grandmother" in Kiswahili. It is also an honorific term for a senior woman in Swahili society.

3. The experience of Swahilis in Goa during the Portuguese rule of the Kenyan coast is worth mentioning. In 1614 the sultan of Mombasa, named Hassan bin Ahmed, was summoned to a Catholic court at Goa, where he refused to accede to the Portuguese demands. The dispute began when the sultan wanted to make an annual pilgrimage to Mecca, send trading expeditions to China, and make an economic treaty with Pemba, the source of rice for Mombasa. The Portuguese refused to allow the sultan to deposit his entire grain stock in Fort Jesus, and because the sultan rejected their demands, he was taken to Goa. On his return to Mombasa, he was soon assassinated by Simao de Mello Pereira, who was bribed by the king of Portugal. Sultan Hassan bin Ahmad was succeeded by his brother, Muhammad bin Ahmed. His son Yusuf, then seven years old, was sent to Goa for Catholic education at an Augustinian convent. After being baptized in Goa, he was renamed Dom Jerenimo Chingulia and given a Portuguese wife in the hopes that that would lead him to adopt Euro-Christian imperialistic culture. In 1627 he wrote a letter to the pope, shortly before he returned to Mombasa to take up his throne.

4. See Pouwels 1981.

5. The Muslim Women's Institute in Mombasa was founded in 1957 (Mirza and Strobel 1989, 157).

6. The national Islamic curriculum was part of the national curriculum, which, together with Christianity and the Hindu religion, was introduced by the regime of President Daniel arap Moi as part of his educational reform (Kenya Institute of Education 2000).

CHAPTER 2. THE *MA'HAD* TRADITION OF MWALIM AZARA MUDIRA

1. For the study of Kenyan ulamas, see Kresse 2007a and Pouwels 1987. See Bakari 1995 and Oded 2000 for further discussion of the new ulama in Kenya.

2. See Wadud 2006, 20, for further elaboration of *taaruf*.

3. See position of the ulama on the use of *diya* (blood money) against perpetrators of FGM/FGC in International Federation of the Council of Islamic Scholars n.d. For a more extensive discussion of the position of Muslims on FGM see Abusharaf 2006; Badawi 1995, 49; Badawi 2000; and Hicks 1996.

4. See Sharify-Funk 2008 for a fascinating account of Muslim women's networks and dialogic activism on Islamic interpretations from diverse cultures and nationalities.

5. Any religious belief system, or creed, can be considered an example of *aqidah*. However, this term has a significant technical usage in Muslim history and theology, denoting those matters over which Muslims hold conviction. There are three main accepted schools of Sunni *aqidah*: Ashari, Maturidi, and Athari.

6. Mwinyihaji (2012, 40) footnotes the existence of three *ma'had* in Mombasa, Nairobi, and Kisimu.

7. See Kinberg 2006 for more elaboration of ethical Islamic concepts such as *furqan*, which means "criterion" and refers to the Qur'an itself as the means by which to distinguish between good and evil.

8. *Lita'arafu* implies celebration of our oneness in diversity as derived from the Surat Al-Hujurat, verse 13, of the Qur'an: "We . . . made you tribes and families that you may know each other; surely the most honorable of you with Allah is the one among you most careful [of his duty]."

CHAPTER 3. MUSLIM WOMEN LEGISLATORS IN MINORITY STATUS

1. Following the March 2013 elections, Kenya moved to a two-chamber legislature, with a parliament of 290 elected seats and a senate of 47 elected seats. Shaban retained her electoral seat and Abdallah was renominated to parliament. Joining the two is Zulekha Hassan Juma, who has been nominated to parliament for the first time. Muslim women have also benefitted from the nomination of Halima Abdille Mohamud and Dullo Fatuma Adam to the newly formed senate.

2. See Kihiu 2010, 105, for discussion of the negative impact of women's underrepresentation in the Parliament on the success of getting their motions passed once it comes to voting on a bill.

3. See www.awepa.org/index.php/fr/resources/cat_view/12conference-reports .html.

4. Karua resigned from her ministerial post in President Kibaki's regime on April 6, 2009, citing frustrations in exercising her duties.

5. See Mwinyihaji 2012, 41.

6. See an-Na'im 2010; Saatchi 2007; and Said, Abu-Nimer, and Sharify-Funk 2006.

7. See Gershenson and Penner 2009.

8. See Beckerleg 1995, 2005, and Beckerleg and Lewando Hundt 2004.

CHAPTER 4. JUDGE ABIDA ALI-ARONI

1. See inclusivesecurity.org/network-bio/maimuna-mwidau.

2. For studies on secret marriages in other parts of Africa and the Muslim world, see Fortier 2011.

3. See Gitonga 2011; Olick 2011; and Otieno 2011.

4. However, Strobel 1979, 59, also discusses Muslim women's dissatisfaction with the kadhi courts during the preindependence era in Swahili society.

5. See Porter 1998 and Fuglesang 1994 for other accounts of new Islamic women's dress fashion in Kenya, especially among the Swahili.

6. Kandiyoti (1997, 1988) discusses the strategies that Muslim women have used to negotiate with (Islamic) patriarchy. Brink (1991) describes the ways in which Egyptian women endear themselves to their mother-in-law in order to reduce the authority of their husbands as a form of co-optation.

7. The term "chautara," meaning "half caste" and "mixed blood," is used in the Swahili-speaking world (though the word is of Indian origin) to refer to racially mixed people irrespective of religious background.

8. On FGM, see Mohammed Noor 2009 and Wangila 2007.

9. In chapter 5, I discuss Nazlin Omar Rajput's bid for Kenya's presidential seat during the 2008 election.

CHAPTER 5. MUSLIM WOMEN AND THE USE OF NEW MEDIA

1. This project received funding support from USAID, among other donors.

2. It seems that in most cases co-wives are not aware of each other because generally Kenya Muslim men do not inform their wives of their decision to marry a new one. Very often they make a distinction between the public wife and the private ones.

3. See Fortier 2011 for an account of secret marriage in Mauritania.

4. For the text of the Sexual Offences Act, see kenyalaw.org/kenyalaw/klr_app/ frames.php.

5. See Rajput's interview at the National Women's Council of Kenya, youtube .com/watch?v=js8HmtgxdJg.

References

Abdi, Cawo. 2006. "Refugees, Gender Based Violence and Resistance: A Case Study of Somali Women in Kenyan Camps." In *Women, Migration and Citizenship: Making Local, National and Transnational Connections*, edited by Evangelia Tastsoglou and Alexandria Dobrowolsky, 231–51. Aldershot, UK: Ashgate.

———. 2007. "Convergence of Civil War and the Religious Right: Re-Imagining Somali Women." *Signs: Journal of Women in Culture and Society* 33:183–207.

Abdi, Dekha. 2010. "Real Gains for Muslim Women." *Kenyan Woman: Advocating for the Rights of Women* 1:10. awcfs.org/dmdocuments/KenyanWoman/Kenyan Woman.pdf.

Abdi, Maryam, and Ian Askew. 2009. *A Religious Oriented Approach to Addressing Female Genital Mutilation/Cutting among the Somali Community of Wajir, Kenya*. New York: Population Council. popcouncil.org/pdfs/frontiers/reports/Kenya_ Somali_FGC.pdf.

Abdullahi, Musdaf. 2011. "Muslim Clerics Roar at Kenya Chief Justice." Africa News.com, October 5. africanews.com/site/list_message/35834.

Abu-Lughod, Lila. 1993. *Writing Women's Worlds: Bedouin Stories*. Berkeley: University of California Press.

———. 1998. *Remaking Women: Feminism and Modernity in the Middle East*. Princeton, NJ: Princeton University Press.

———. 2005. *Dramas of Nationhood: The Politics of Television in Egypt*. Chicago: University of Chicago Press.

Abusharaf, Rogaia Mustafa, ed. 2006. *Female Circumcision: A Multicultural Perspective*. Philadelphia: University of Pennsylvania Press.

Abu-Zayd, Nasr Hamid. 2006. *Reformation of Islamic Thought: A Critical Analysis*. Amsterdam: Amsterdam University Press.

Afonja, Simi. 1990. "Changing Patterns of Gender Stratification in West Africa." In *Persistent Inequalities: Women and World Development*, edited by Irene Tinker, 198–209. Oxford: Oxford University Press.

Aga Khan Foundation. 2008. *The Madrasa Early Childhood Programme: 25 Years of Experience.* Geneva: Aga Khan Development Network.

Ahmed. Leila. 1993. *Women and Gender in Islam: Historical Roots of a Modern Debate.* Cairo: American University of Cairo.

Akou, Heather M. 2011. *The Politics of Dress in Somali Culture.* African Expressive Cultures. Bloomington: Indiana University Press.

Ali, Abdallah Yusuf. 2002. *The Qur'an: Text, Translation and Commentary.* Beltsville, MD: Amana Publications.

Alidou, D. Ousseina. 2005. *Engaging Modernity: Muslim Women and the Politics of Agency in Postcolonial Niger.* Madison: University of Wisconsin Press.

———. 2011. "Muslim Women, Rights Discourse, and the Media in Kenya." In *Gender and Culture at the Limit of Rights,* edited by Dorothy L. Hodgson, 180–99. Philadelphia: University of Pennsylvania Press.

Allen, James de Vere. 1974. "Swahili Culture Re-considered." *Azania* 9:105–38.

Alloo, Fatma. 1999. "Information Technology and Cyberculture: The Case of Zanzibar." In *Women@Internet: Creating New Cultures in Cyberspace,* edited by Wendy Harcourt, 156–61. London: Zed Books.

Amadiume, Ifi. 1998. *Re-Inventing Africa: Matriarchy, Religion and Culture.* New York: Zed Books.

Ammah-Koney, Rabiatu. 2009. "Violence against Women in Ghanaian Muslim Communities." In *The Architecture of Violence Against Women in Ghana,* edited by Kathy Cusack and Takyiwaa Manuh, 159–91. Accra: Gender Studies and Human Rights Documentation Center.

Anderson, John E. 1970. *The Struggle for the School: The Interaction of Missionary, Colonial Government and Nationalist Enterprise in the Development of Formal Education in Kenya.* London: Longman.

an-Na'im, Abdullahi. 1990. *Toward an Islamic Reformation: Civil Liberties, Human Rights, and International Law.* Syracuse, NY: Syracuse University Press.

———. 1991. "Islam and Women's Rights: A Case Study." *Women Living under Muslim Laws* 14–15:96–109.

———. 2008. *Islam and the Secular State: Negotiating the Future of Shari'a.* Cambridge, MA: Harvard University Press.

———. 2010. *Muslims and Global Justice.* Philadelphia: University of Pennsylvania Press.

Arimbi, Diah Ariani. 2009. *Reading Contemporary Indonesian Muslim Women Writers: Representation, Identity and Religion of Muslim Women in Indonesian Fiction.* Amsterdam: Amsterdam University Press.

Arkoun, Mohammed. 2006. *Islam: To Reform or to Subvert?* London: Saqi.

Asani, A. S. 1994. "The Impact of Modernization on the Marriage Rites of the Khojah Ismailis of East Africa." *Journal of Turkish Studies* 18:17–24.

Ask, Karin, and Marit Tjomsland. 1998. *Women and Islamization: Contemporary*

Dimensions of Discourse on Gender Relations. Ann Arbor: University of Michigan Press.

Augis, Erin. 2005. "Dakar's Sunnite Women: The Politics of Person." In *L'Islam politique au sud du Sahara: Identities,* edited by Muriel Gomez-Perez, 309–26. Paris: Karthala.

———. 2009. "Jambaar or Jumbax-Out: How Sunnite Women Negotiate Power and Belief in Orthodox Islamic Femininity." In *New Perspectives on Islam in Senegal: Conversion, Migration, Wealth, Power, and Femininity,* edited by Mamadou Diouf and Mara Leichtman, 211–33. New York: Palgrave Macmillan.

Badawi, Jamal. 1995. *Gender Equity in Islam: Basic Principles.* Indianapolis, IN: American Trust Publication.

———. 2000. *The Position of Women in Islam.* London: Islamic Dawah Centre.

Badran, Margot. 1995. *Feminists, Islam and Nation: Gender and the Making of Modern Egypt.* Princeton, NJ: Princeton University Press.

———. 2008a. *Feminism in Islam: Secular and Religious Convergences.* Oxford, UK: Oneworld.

———. 2008b. "What Does Islamic Feminism Have to Offer? Where Does It Come From? Where Is It Going?" *Guardian* (Manchester, UK), November 9. guardian .co.uk/commentisfree/belief/2008/nov/09/islam-women.

———, ed. 2011. *Gender and Islam in Africa: Rights, Sexuality, and Law.* Washington, DC: Woodrow Wilson Center Press with Stanford University Press.

Badran, Margot, and Miriam Cooke, eds. 2004. *Opening the Gates: An Anthology of Arab Feminist Writing.* Bloomington: Indiana University Press.

Bakare-Yusuf, Bibi. 2003. "Beyond Determinism: The Phenomenology of African Female Existence." *Feminist Africa* 2:1–12.

———. 2004. "Yoruba Don't Do Gender: A Critical Review of Oyeronke Oyewumi's *The Invention of Women: Making An African Sense of Western Gender Discourse.*" In *African Gender Scholarship: Concepts, Methodologies, and Paradigms,* edited by Bibi Bakare-Yusuf and Anfred Signe, 61–81. Dakar: Council for the Development of Social Science Research in Africa.

Bakare-Yusuf, Bibi, and Anfred Signe. 2004. *African Gender Scholarship: Concepts, Methodologies, and Paradigms.* Dakar: Council for the Development of Social Science Research in Africa.

Bakari, Mohamed. 1995. "The New Ulama in Kenya." In *Islam in Kenya: Proceedings of the National Seminar on Contemporary Islam,* edited by Mohamed Bakari and Saad. S. Yahya, 168–93. Nairobi: Mewa Publications.

Bakhtiar, Laleh. 2007. *The Sublime Qur'an.* Chicago: Kazi Publications.

Barlas, Asma. 2002. *"Believing Women" in Islam: Unreading Patriarchal Interpretations of the Qur'an.* Austin: University of Texas Press.

Beckerleg, Susan. 1995. "'Brown Sugar' or Friday Prayers: Youth Choices and Community Building in Coastal Kenya." *African Affairs* 94:23–38.

————. 2005. "Women Heroin Users: Exploring the Limitations of the Structural Violence Approach." *International Journal of Drug Policy* 16 (3): 183–90.

Beckerleg, Susan, and G. Lewando Hundt. 2004. "The Characteristics and Recent Growth of Heroin Injecting in a Kenyan Coastal Town." *Addiction Research and Theory* 12 (1): 41–53.

Berkey, Jonathan. 1992. "Women and Islamic Education in the Mamluk Period." In *Women in Middle Eastern History: Shifting Boundaries in Sex and Gender*, edited by Nikki Keddie and Beth Baron, 143–57. New Haven, CT: Yale University Press.

Bop, Codou. 2005. "Roles and the Position of *Women* in Sufi Brotherhoods in Senegal." *Journal of the American Academy of Religion* 73 (4): 1099–2019.

Bourdieu, Pierre. 1973. *Outline of A Theory of Practice*. Cambridge: Cambridge University Press.

Bourdieu, Pierre, and Jean Claude Passeron. 1977. *Reproduction in Education, Society and Culture*. London: Sage.

Boyd, Jean. 1989. *The Caliph's Sister: Nana Asma'u, 1793–1865, Teacher, Poet and Islamic Leader*. London: Frank and Cass.

Boyd, Jean, and Beverly Mack, eds. 1997. *Collected Works of Nana Asma'u, Daughter of Usman 'dan Fodiyo (1793–1864)*. East Lansing: Michigan State University Press.

Brink, Judy H. 1991. "The Effect of Emigration of Husbands on the Status of Their Wives: An Egyptian Case." *International Journal of Middle Eastern Studies* 23 (2): 201–11.

Brown Geoff, Janet Brown, and Sumra Sumara. 1999. "The East African Madrasa Progamme: The Madrasa Resource Centres and Their Community-Based Preschool Programme." Nairobi: Aga Khan Foundation.

Buggenhagen. Beth. 2012. *Muslim Families in Global Senegal: Money Takes Care of Shame*. Bloomington: Indiana University Press.

Bujra, Janet. 1968. "Anthropological Study of Political Action in Bajuni Village in Kenya." PhD diss., University of London.

Chege, Fatuma, and Daniel N. Sifuna. 2006. *Girls' and Women's Education in Kenya*. Nairobi: UNESCO.

Chesworth, John. 2006. "Fundamentalism and Outreach Strategies in East Africa: Christian Evangelism and Muslim Da'wa." In *Muslim-Christian Encounters in Africa*, edited by Benjamin F. Soares, 159–86. Leiden: Brill, 2006.

————. 2009. "The Church and Islam: Vyama Vingi (Multipartyism) and the Ufungamano Talks." In *Religion and Politics in Kenya*, edited by Ben Knighton, 155–80. Basingstoke, UK: Palgrave Macmillan.

Comaroff, Jean, and John Comaroff. 1993. *Modernity and Its Malcontents: Ritual and Power in Postcolonial Africa*. Chicago: University of Chicago Press.

Cooper, Barbara. 2001. "The Strength in the Song: Muslim Personhood, Audible Capital, and the Hausa Women Performance of the Hajj." In *Gendered Modernities:*

Ethnographic Perspectives, edited by Dorothy L. Hodgson, 79–104. New York: Palgrave Macmillan.

Cooper, Frederick. 1997. *Plantation Slavery on the East Coast of Africa*. Portsmouth, NH: Heinemann.

Curtin, Patricia Romero. 1983. "Laboratory for the Oral History of Slavery: The Island of Lamu on the Kenya Coast." *American Historical Review* 88 (4): 858–82.

Cussac, Anne. 2008. "Muslims and Politics in Kenya: The Issue of the Kadhis' Courts in the Constitution Review Process." *Journal of Muslim Minority Affairs* 28 (2): 289–302.

de Smedt, Johan. 2009. "Kill Me Quick: A History of Nubian Gin." *Kibera: Journal of African Historical Studies* 42 (2): 201–20.

Diouf, Mamadou, and Mara Leichtman, eds. 2009. *New Perspectives on Islam in Senegal: Conversion, Migration, Wealth, Power and Femininity*. New York: Palgrave Macmillan.

Eastman, Carol. 1988. "Women, Slaves and Foreigners: African Cultural Influences and Group Processes in the Formation of Northern Swahili Coastal Society." *International Journal of African Historical Studies* 23 (1): 1–20.

Egbo, Benedicta. 2000. *Gender, Literacy and Life Chances in Sub-Saharan Africa*. London: Multi-lingual Matters.

Eickelman, Dale, and Jon W. Anderson. 1999. "Redefining Muslim Publics." In *New Media in the Muslim World*, edited by Dale Eickelman and Jon W. Anderson, 1–18. Bloomington: Indiana University Press.

El Fadl, Khaled Abu. 2001. *Speaking in God's Name: Islamic Law, Authority and Women*. Oxford, UK: Oneworld.

"Enhancing Access to Justice for Women through Kadhis Courts." 2011. Gender Governance. gendergovernancekenya.org/home/50-judiciary/366-enhancing-access-to-justice-for-women-through-kadhis-courts.html.

Eshiwani, George S. 1993. *Education in Kenya Since Independence*. Nairobi: East African Educational Publishers.

Farsy, Abdallah Saleh. 1989. *The Shafi'I Ulama of East Africa: A Hagiographic Account*. Translated by Randall L. Pouwels. African Primary Texts 2. University of Wisconsin–Madison.

Fisher, Simon, Dekha Ibrahim Abdi, Jawed Ludin, Richard Smith, Sue Williams, and Steven Williams. 2000. *Working with Conflicts: Skills and Strategies for Action*. London: Zed Books.

Fortier, Corinne. 2011. "Women and Men Put Islamic Law to Their Own Use: Monogamy versus Secret Marriage in Mauritania." In *Gender and Islam in Africa: Rights, Sexuality, and Law*, edited by Margot Badran, 213–32. Washington, DC: Woodrow Wilson Center with Stanford University Press.

Fuglesang, Minou. 1994. *Veils and Videos: Female Youth Culture on the Kenyan Coast*. London: Coronet Books.

Gandhi, Rajmohan. 2008. *Gandhi: The Man, His People, and the Empire*. Berkeley: University of California Press.

Gershenson, Olga, and Barbara Penner. 2009. *Ladies and Gents: Public Toilets and Gender*. Philadelphia: Temple University Press.

Ghai, Yash, and Dharam Ghai. 1970. *Portrait of a Minority: Asians in East Africa*. Oxford: Oxford University Press.

Gitongo, Anthony. 2011. "CJ: Kadhi Courts to Have Women Magistrates." *Standard* (Nairobi), September 30. standardmedia.co.ke/?articleID=2000043810&story_title=CJ:-Kadhi-courts-to-have-women-magistrates.

Glassman, Jonathan. 1995. *Feasts and Riot: Revelry, Rebellion, and Popular Consciousness on the Swahili Coast, 1856–1888*. London: Heinemann.

Glover, John. 2007. *Sufism and Jihad in Modern Senegal: The Murid Order*. Rochester, NY: University of Rochester Press, 2007.

Godia, Jane. 2010. "A Common Agenda: Women Breaking Ethnic, Political, Religious, Social, Economical and Cultural Barriers to Fight for Their Rights." *Kenyan Woman: Advocating for the Rights of Women* 1:1–2. awcfs.org/dmdocuments/KenyanWoman/KenyanWoman.pdf.

Gole, Nilufer. 1996. *The Forbidden Modern: Civilization and Veiling*. Critical Perspectives on Women and Gender. Ann Arbor: University of Michigan Press.

Gordon, April A. 1996. *Transforming Capitalism and Patriarchy: Gender and Development in Africa*. Colorado: Lynne Rienner.

Haenni, Patrick. 2002. "Au-delà du repli identitaire . . . Les nouveaux prêcheurs égyptiens et la modernization paradoxale de l'Islam." *Religioscope*, November. http://www.religioscope.com/articles/2002/029_haenni_precheurs.htm.

Haeri, Shahla. 1989. *The Law of Desire: Temporary Marriage in Shi'i Iran*. Syracuse, NY: Syracuse University Press.

———. 2002. *No Shame for the Sun: Lives of Professional Pakistani Women*. Syracuse, NY: Syracuse University Press.

Hansen, Karen Tranberg. 1992. *African Encounters with Domesticity*. New Brunswick, NJ: Rutgers University Press.

Hashim, Abdulkadir. 2005. "Searching for Religious Authority (*marji'iya*): Muslim and Religious Leadership in Kenya." *Annual Review of Islam in South Africa* 8:76–80.

———. 2010. "Coping with Conflicts: Colonial Policy Towards Muslim Personal Law in Kenya and Post-Colonial Court Practice." In *Muslim Family Law in Sub-Saharan Africa: Colonial Legacy and Post-Colonial Challenges*, edited by Shamil Jeppie, Ebrahim Moosa, and Richard Roberts, 221–45. Amsterdam: Amsterdam University Press.

Hassan, Riffat. 1998. "The Foundational Myths and Surah al Nisa." In *Ourselves: Women Reading the Qur'an; Women Living Under Muslim Laws*, 47–61. London: Women Living Under Muslim Laws.

———. 2000. "Is Family Planning Permitted in Islam? The Issue of a Woman's Right to Contraception." In *Windows of Faith: Muslim Women Scholar Activists in North America*, edited by Gisela Webb, 226–40. Syracuse, NY: Syracuse University Press.

———. 2003. "Women and Sexuality—Normative Islam versus Muslim Practice." Paper presented at the Second International Muslim Leaders Consultation on HIV and Aids, Kuala Lumpur, Malaysia, May 19–23.

Hayward, Richard J., and I. M. Lewis, eds. 1996. *Voice and Power: The Culture of Language in Northeast Africa* (Essays in Honor of B. W. Andrzjewski). London: School of Oriental and African Studies.

Herzig, Pascale. 2006. *South Asians in Kenya: Gender, Generation and Changing Identities in Diaspora*. Münster: LIT Verlag.

Hicks, Esther. 1996. *Infibulation: Female Mutilation in Islamic Northeastern Kenya*. New Brunswick, NJ: Transaction.

Hill, Joseph. 2010. "'All Women Are Guides': Sufi Leadership and Womanhood among Taalibe Baay in Senegal." *Journal of Religion in Africa* 40 (4): 375–412.

Hirsch, Susan. 1998. *Pronouncing and Persevering: Gender and the Discourses of Disputing in an African Islamic Court*. Chicago: University of Chicago Press.

———. 2006a. *In the Moment of Greatest Calamity: Terrorism, Grief, and a Victim's Quest for Justice*. Princeton, NJ: Princeton University Press.

———. 2006b. "Islamic Law and Society post 9/11." *Annual Review of Law and Social Science* 2:165–86. Islamic Law of the Muslim World Paper no. 08-07.

———. 2010. "State Intervention in Muslim Family Law in Kenya and Tanzania: Applications of the Gender Concept." In *Muslim Family Law in Sub-Saharan Africa: Colonial Legacy and Post-Colonial Challenges*, edited by Shamil Jeppie, Ebrahim Moosa, and Richard Roberts, 305–30. Amsterdam: Amsterdam University Press.

Hirschkind, Charles. 2006. *The Ethical Soundscape: Cassette Sermons and Islamic Counterpublics*. New York: Columbia University Press.

Hodgson, Dorothy L., ed. 2001. *Gendered Modernities: Ethnographic Perspectives*. New York: Palgrave Macmillan.

Human Rights Watch. 2009. *Playing with Fire: Weapon Proliferating Political Violence, and Human Rights in Kenya*. New York: Human Rights Watch.

——— 2010. "Welcome to Kenya." Human Rights Watch, June 17. hrw.org/reports/2010/06/17/welcome-kenya-0.

Ibrahim, Dekha. 2004. "Women's Roles in Peace-Making in the Somali Community in North Eastern Kenya." In *Somalia: The Untold Story; The War through the Eyes of Somali Women*, edited by Judith Gardner and Judy El Bushra, 166–74. London: Pluto Press.

Imam, Ayesha. 1997. "The Muslim Religious Rights (Fundamentalists) and Sexuality." *Women Living Under Muslim Laws* 17:7–25.

————. 2005. "Women's Reproductive and Sexual Rights and the Offense of *Zina* in Muslim Laws in Nigeria." In *Where Human Rights Begin: Health, Sexuality and Women in the New Millennium,* edited by Wendy Chavkin and Ellen Chesler, 65–94. New Brunswick, NJ: Rutgers University Press.

Iman, Ayesha, Amina Mama, and Fatou Sow, eds. 1997. *Engendering African Social Sciences.* Dakar: Council for the Development of Social Science Research in Africa.

International Federation of the Council of Islamic Scholars. n.d. "FGM in the Context of Islam." nccm-egypt.org/e9/e1869/e2357/e2358/infoboxContent2359/FGMintheContextofIslam.pdf.

Jama, Zainab Mohamed. 1991. "Fighting to Be Heard: Somali Women's Poetry." *African Languages and Cultures* 4 (1): 43–53.

Jami'a Mosque Committee. 2012. *The Friday Bulletin,* Nairobi, January 6.

JanMohammed, Karim. 1976. "Ethnicity in an Urban Setting: A Case Study of Mombasa." In *Hadith 6: History and Social Change in East Africa,* edited by Ogot Bethwell Ogot, 186–205. Nairobi: East African Literature Bureau.

Janson, Marloes. 2011. "Guidelines for the Ideal Muslim Woman: Gender Ideology and Praxis in the Tabligh Jama'at in the Gambia." In *Gender and Islam in Africa: Rights, Sexuality, and Law,* edited by Margot Badran, 147–72. Washington, DC: Woodrow Wilson Center Press with Stanford University Press.

Jeppie, Shamil, Ebrahim Moosa, and Richard Roberts, eds. 2010. *Muslim Family Law in Sub-Saharan Africa: Colonial Legacies and Post-Colonial Challenges.* Amsterdam: Amsterdam University Press.

Jimale, Ali Ahmed. 1996. *Daybreak is Near—The Politics of Emancipation in Somalia: Literature, Clans, and the Nation-State.* Lawrenceville, NJ: Red Sea Press.

Kabira, Wanjiku M. 2012. *Time for Harvest: Women and Constitution Making in Kenya.* Nairobi: University of Nairobi Press.

Kalipeni, Ezekiel, Karen Coen Flyn, and Cynthia Pope, eds. 2009. *Strong Women, Dangerous Times: Gender and HIV/AIDS in Africa.* Hauppage, NY: Nova Science Publishers.

Kandiyoti, Deniz. 1988. "Bargaining with Patriarchy." *Gender and Society* 2 (3): 274–90.

————, ed. 1996. *Gendering the Middle East: Emerging Perspectives.* Syracuse, NY: Syracuse University Press.

————. 1998. "Afterword: Some Awkward Questions on Women and Modernity in Turkey." In *Remaking Women: Feminism and Modernity in the Middle East,* edited by Lila Abu-Lughod, 270–88. Princeton, NJ: Princeton University Press.

Kane, Ousmane. 2003. *Muslim Modernity in Postcolonial Nigeria: A Study of the Society for the Removal of Innovation and Reinstatement of Tradition.* Leiden: Brill.

Kanna, Ines Hofmann. 2007. *Unveiled Muslim Women Talk about Hijab.* Watertown, MA: Documentary Educational Resources.

Kapteijns, Lidwien. 1995. "Gender Relations and the Transformation of the Northern Somali Pastoral Tradition." *International Journal of African Historical Studies* 28 (2): 241–59.

Kapteijns, Lidwien, and Maryan Omar Ali. 1999. *Women's Voices in a Man's World: Women and the Pastoral Tradition in Northern Somali Orature, c. 1899–1980*. Studies in African Literature. Portsmouth, NH: Heinemann.

Kariuki, Wanjiru. 2006. "She Is a Woman after All: Patriarchy and Female Educational Leadership in Kenya." *Postamble* 2 (2): 65–74.

Katumanga, Musambayi. 1996. "Civil Society and the Politics of Constitutional Reforms in Kenya: A Case Study of the National Convention Executive Council." Eldis. eldis.org/go/home&id=11426&type=Document#.UVGWLVsjrKA.

Keaton, Trica Daniel. 2006. *Muslim Girls and the Other France: Race, Identity, Politics and Social Exclusion*. Bloomington: Indiana University Press.

Keck, Margaret, and Kathryn Sikkink. 1998. *Activists beyond Borders: Advocacy Networks in International Politics*. Ithaca, NY: Cornell University Press.

Kelly, Gail P., and Philip G. Altbach. 1984. Introduction to *Education and the Colonial Experience*, edited by Gail P. Kelly and Philip G. Altbach, 1–5. New Brunswick, NJ: Transaction.

Kelley, Kevin J. 2012. "Kadhi Courts Focus of US Groups' Opposition to New Kenya Law." *Daily Nation* (Nairobi), July 12. nation.co.ke/Kenya-Referendum/Kadhi-courts-focus-of-US-groups-opposition-to-new-Kenya-law/-/926046/956378/-/uj9y9x/-/index.html.

Kenya Institute of Education. 2000. *Guidelines for Islamic Integrated Education Programmes in Kenya*. Nairobi: National Center for Early Childhood Education, Kenya Institute of Education.

Kenya National Census Report. 2009. http://www.knbs.or.ke/Census%20Results/Presentation%20by%20Minister%20for%20Planning%20revised.pdf.

Keshavjee, Rashida. 2005. "The Redefined Roles of Ismaili Women through Education and Profession." PhD diss., University of Toronto.

———. 2010. "The Elusive Access to Education for Muslim Women in Kenya from the Late Nineteenth Century to the 'Winds of Change' in Africa (1890s to 1960s)." *Paedagogica Historica: International Journal of the History of Education* 46 (1–2): 99–115.

Khamisi, Joe. 2011. *The Politics of Betrayal: Diary of a Kenyan Legislator*. New Bern, NC: Trafford Publishing.

Kibwana, Kivutha. 2002. *Constitutionalism in East Africa: Progress, Challenges and Prospects in 1999*. Kituo Cha Katiba Studies Series. Nairobi: Clarion Press.

Kihiu, Faith. 2010. *Women as Agents of Democratization: The Rise of Women's Organizations in Kenya, 1990–2007*. Frankfurt: Frankfurt University Press.

Kihoro, Wanyiri, ed. 2002. *A Vision of the Future from the Past: Essential Public Documents in the Making of the New Kenya Constitution*. Nairobi: Abantu for Development.

Kinberg, Leah. 2006. "Contemporary Ethical Issues." In *Blackwell Companion to the Qur'an*, edited by Andrew Rippen, 450–67. London: Wiley.

Kokole, Omari. 1985. "The 'Nubians' of East Africa: Muslim Club or African 'Tribe'? A View from Within." *Journal of Muslim Minority Affairs* 6 (2): 420–48.

Kolawole, Mary Ebun Modupe. 1997. *Womanism and African Consciousness.* Trenton, NJ: African World Press.

Kresse, Kai. 2007a. *Philosophising in Mombasa: Knowledge, Islam and Intellectual Practice on the Swahili Coast.* Edinburgh: Edinburgh University Press for the International African Institute.

———. 2007b. "The Virtual Baraza: Swahili Discursive Traditions in Print and Radio Media in Postcolonial Kenya." Paper presented at "Workshop: New Media and Islam in Africa," Institute for the Study of Islamic Thoughts in Africa, Northwestern University, October 23.

———. 2009. "Can Wisdom Be Taught? Kant, Sage Philosophy, and Ethnographic Reflections from the Swahili Coast: Teaching for Wisdom." In *Teaching for Wisdom*, edited by Michel Ferrari and Georges Potworowski, 99–120. Amsterdam: Springer.

LeBlanc, Marie Natalie. 2000. "Versioning Womanhood and Muslimhood: Fashion and the Life Course in Contemporary Bouake, Cote D'Ivoire." *Africa: Journal of the International African Institute* 70 (3–4): 442–81.

LeBlanc, Marie Natalie, and Benjamin Soares, guest editors. 2008. "Muslim West Africa in the Age of Neoliberalism." Special issue, *Africa Today* 54.

Levtzion, Nehemia, and Randall L. Pouwels, eds. 2000. *The History of Islam in Africa.* Athens: Ohio University Press.

Lodhi, Abdulaziz. 1994. "Muslims in Eastern Africa: Their Past and Present." *Nordic Journal of African Studies* 3 (4): 88–98.

Loimeier, Roman. 2003. "Pattern and Peculiarity of Islamic Reforms in Africa." *Journal of Religion in Africa* 33 (3): 237–62.

Lornah, Kerubo. 2011. "Kenya Vet Kadhis Like Judges." Allafrica.com, June 22. allafrica.com/stories/201106230670.html.

Lynch, Cecelia. 2011. "Religious Humanitarianism and the Global Politics of Secularism." In *Rethinking Secularism*, edited by Craig Calhoun, Mark Juergensmeyer, and Jonathan VanAntwerpen, 204–24. Oxford: Oxford University Press.

Maathai, Wangari. 2009. *The Challenge for Africa.* New York: Pantheon.

Mack, B. Beverly. 2004. *Muslim Women Sing.* Bloomington: Indiana University Press.

Mack, B. Beverly, and Jean Boyd. 2000. *One Woman's Jihad: Nana Asma'u, Scholar and Scribe.* Bloomington: Indiana University Press.

Mahdi, Hauwa. 2009. "The Hijab in Nigeria, the Woman's Body and the Feminist Private/Public Discourse." In *Northwestern University Institute for the Study of Islamic Thoughts.* Africa Working Paper no. 09-003. bcics.northwestern.edu/documents/workingpapers/ISITA_09-003_Mahdi.pdf.

Mahmood, Saba. 2004. *Politics of Piety: The Islamic Revival and the Feminist Subject.* Princeton, NJ: Princeton University Press.

Makaramba, Robert V. 2010. "The Secular State and the State of Islamic Law in Tanzania." In *Muslim Family Law in Sub-Saharan Africa: Colonial Legacy and Post-Colonial Challenges*, edited by Shamil Jeppie, Ebrahim Moosa, and Richard Roberts, 273–303. Amsterdam: Amsterdam University Press.

Manjoo, Rashida. 2011. "Legal Recognition of Muslim Marriage in South Africa." In *Gender and Islam in Africa: Rights, Sexuality, and Law*, edited by Margot Badran, 291–304.Washington, DC: Woodrow Wilson Center Press with Stanford University Press.

Maoulidi, Salma. 2009. "Rights, the Law and Religion: Islamic Court in East Africa." *Pambazuka*, December 23. pambazuka.org/en/category/features/61238.

———. 2011. "Between Law and Culture: Contemplating Rights for Women in Zanzibar." In *Gender and Culture at the Limit of Rights*, edited by Dorothy L. Hodgson, 32–54. Philadelphia: University of Pennsylvania Press.

Masquelier, Adeline. 2009. *Women and Islamic Revival in a West African Town*. Bloomington: Indiana University Press.

Mazrui, Alamin, and Ibrahim Noor Shariff. 1994. *The Swahili: Idiom and Identity of an African People*. Trenton, NJ: Africa World Press.

Mbow, Penda. 2009. "Evolving Role for Senegalese Women in Religion." *Common Ground News*, February 10. commongroundnews.org/article.php?id=25012&lan=en&sp=0.

McFadden, Patricia. 1997. "The Challenges and Prospects for the African Women's Movement in the 21st Century." *Women in Action* 1 (1): 1–7.

———. 2003. "Sexual Pleasure as Feminist Choice." *Feminist Africa* 2:61–65.

McIntosh, Janet S. 2002. *The Edge of Islam: Religion, Language and Essentialism on the Kenya Coast*. Ann Arbor: University of Michigan Press.

———. 2005. "Baptismal Essentialisms: Giriama Code Choice and the Reification of Ethnoreligious Boundaries." *Journal of Linguistic Anthropology* 15 (2): 151–70.

McLaren, Peter. 2003. *Life in Schools: An Introduction to Critical Pedagogy in the Foundations of Education*. 4th ed. Boston: Allyn and Bacon.

Mernissi, Fatima. 1987. *Beyond the Veil: Male-Female Dynamics in Modern Muslim Society*. Bloomington: Indiana University Press.

———. 1991a. *The Veil and the Male Elite: A Feminist Interpretation of Women's Rights in Islam*. Translated by Mary Jo Lakeland. Reading, MA: Addison-Wesley.

———. 1991b. *Women and Islam: An Historical and Theological Enquiry*. Translated by Mary Jo Lakeland. Oxford, UK: Blackwell.

———. 2005. "The Satellite, the Prince, and Scheherazade: Women as Communicators in Digital Islam." In *On Shifting Ground: Muslim Women in the Global Era*, edited by Fereshteh Nouraie-Simone, 3–17. New York: Feminist Press.

Mikell, Gwendolyn, ed. 1997. *African Feminism: The Politics of Survival in Sub-Saharan Africa*. Philadelphia: University of Pennsylvania Press.

Mir-Hosseini, Ziba. 2004. "Sexuality, Rights, and Islam: Competing Gender Discourses in Post-Revolutionary Iran." In *Women in Iran from 1800 to the Islamic Republic*, edited by Guity Nashat and Lois Beck, 204–17. Urbana-Champaign: University of Illinois Press.

Mirza, Sarah, and Margaret Strobel. 1989. *Three Swahili Women: Life Histories from Mombasa*. Bloomington: Indiana University Press.

Mohamed Noor, Hawa. 2009. *Can FGM Be Eradicated through an Alternative Means?* Norderstedt, Germany: GRIN.

Mudi, Maureen. 2011. "Islamic Women Urged to Take up Leadership Positions." *Star* (Nairobi), March 9. the-star.co.ke/news/article-70103/islamic-women-urged -take-leadership-positions.

Mukudi, Edith. 1993. "Women and Education." In *Democratic Change in Africa: Women's Perspective*, edited by Wanjiku M. Kabira et al., 83–92. Nairobi: ACTS Gender Institute.

"Muslim Clerics Oppose Call to Appoint Women Kadhis." 2011. *Daily Nation* (Nairobi), June 23. nation.co.ke/News/Muslim-clerics-oppose-call—to-appoint -women-kadhis-/-/1056/1188016/-/tkigdl/-/index.html.

Mutua, Athena. 2003. "Kenya's Regime Change and Constitutional Review Process: Prospects for Women's Solidarity across Religious Difference and Increased Political Participation." Paper presented at the Baldy Center for Law and Social Policy, University of Buffalo, October.

———. 2007. "Gender Equality and Women's Solidarity across Religious, Ethnic and Class Difference in the Kenya Constitutional Review Process." *William and Mary Journal of Women and the Law* 13.1, scholarship.law.wm.edu/cgi/viewcontent .cgi?article=1087&context=wmjowl.

Mutua, Makau. 2008. *Kenya's Quest for Democracy—Taming Leviathan*. Boulder, CO: Lynne Rienner.

Mutunga, Willy. 1999. *Constitution-Making from the Middle: Civil Society and Transition Politics in Kenya, 1992–1997*. Nairobi: SAREAT.

Mwaura, Peter, and Bishara T. Mohamed. 2008. "Madrasa Early Childhood Development Program: Making a Difference," In *Africa's Future, Africa's Challenge: Early Childhood Care and Development in Sub-Saharan Africa*, edited by Marito Garcia, Alan Pence, and Judith L. Evans, 389–404. Washington, DC: World Bank.

Mwihia, Catherine. 2011. *Proverbs About African Women*. Saarbrücken, Germany: Lambert Academic Publishing.

Mwinyihaji, Esha Faki, 2001. "Contribution of Islam towards Women Emancipation: A Case Study of the Swahili Muslim Women in Mombasa District." Master's thesis, Moi University, Eldoret.

———. 2007. "The Shari'a and Muslim Women's Participation in the Public Sphere." Sharia Debates in Africa. sharia-in-africa.net/pages/staff/mwinyihaji.php.

———. 2010. *The Persistence of Divination among the Swahili Muslims in Kenya: Beliefs and Practices.* Saarbrücken, Germany: Lambert Academic Publishing.

———. 2012. "Muslim Women in Media and Politics: Fighting for Legitimacy." *Global Journal of Human Social Science, Sociology, Economics and Political Science* 12 (9): 39–42.

Mwinyihaji, Esha Faki, and Federick O. Wanyama. 2011. "The Media, Terrorism and Political Mobilization of Muslims in Kenya." *Religion, Media and Politics in Africa* 5 (1): 103–12. politicsandreligionjournal.com/images/pdf_files/engleski/volume5_no1/esha%20faki%205.pdf.

Nadwi, Akram Muhammed. 2007. *Al-Muhaddithat: The Women Scholars in Islam.* Oxford, UK: Interface Publications.

Nagar, Richa. 1998. "Communal Discourses, Marriage, and the Politics of Gendered Social Boundaries among South Asian Immigrants in Tanzania." *Gender, Place and Culture* 5 (2): 117–39.

———. 2000. "Religion, Race and Debate over Mut'a in Dar Es Salaam." *Feminist Studies* 26 (3): 661–90.

———. 2004. "Mapping Feminisms and Difference." In *Mapping Women, Making Politics: Feminist Perspectives on Political Geography*, edited by Lynn A. Staeheli, Eleonore Kofman, and Linda Peake, 31–48. London: Routledge.

Ndzovu, Hassan J. 2009. "Religion and Politics: A Critical Study of the Politicization of Islam in Kenya." PhD diss., University of KwaZulu Natal.

Ngome, Charles. 2006. *Mobile Schools Programme for Nomadic Pastoralists in Kenya: Pilot Project in Wajir, Ijara and Turkana Districts.* Nairobi: Government of Kenya, Office of the President, Special Programmes, Arid Lands Resource Management Project.

Noordin, Mwanakombo Mohamed. 2009. "'Ufasiri wa Ufeministi wa Kiislamu katika Utamaduni wa Mwanamke Mswahili: Mkabala au Ushirikiano?" PhD diss., Moi University.

Nouraie-Simone, Fereshteh, ed. 2005. *On Shifting Ground: Muslim Women in the Global Era.* New York: Feminist Press.

Nzegwu, Nkiru. 2001. "Gender Equality in a Dual-Sex System: The Case of Onitsha." *JENDA: A Journal of Culture and African Women Studies* 1 (1): 1–32.

Nzomo, Maria. 1997. "Kenya Women in Politics and Decision Making." In *African Feminism: The Politics of Survival in Sub-Saharan Africa*, edited by Gwendolyn Mikell, 232–54. Philadelphia: University of Pennsylvania Press.

O'Brien, Donal B. Cruise. 2003. *Symbolic Confrontations: Muslims Imagining the State in Africa.* New York: Palgrave Macmillan.

Oded, Arye. 2000. *Islam and Politics in Kenya.* Boulder, CO: Lynne Rienner.

Ogundipe-Leslie, Molara. 1985. "Women in Nigeria." In *Women in Nigeria Today*, 119–31. London: Zed Books.

————. 1994. *Re-Creating Ourselves: African Women and Critical Transformation.* Trenton, NJ: African World Press.

Olick, Felix. 2011. "CJ Promises Radical Reforms in Judiciary." *Standard* (Nairobi), September 29. standardmedia.co.ke/?articleID=2000043719&story_title=CJ -promises-radical-reforms-in-Judiciary.

Omale, Juliana. 2003. "Separating Religion from Practice." *Yawezekana: Bomas Agenda,* May 22. awcfs.org/dmdocuments/bomasagenda/Newsletter4.pdf.

Omwoha, Joyce N. 2011. "Media and (Mis)Representation of Women in Political Leadership Positions in Kenya." In *Beyond Tradition: African Women and Cultural Spaces,* edited by Toyin Falola and Sati Umaru Fwatshak, 133–49. Trenton: Africa World Press.

Ong, Aihwa. 2006. *Neoliberalism as Exception: Mutations in Citizenship and Sovereignty.* Durham, NC: Duke University Press.

Otieno, Brian. 2011. "Kenya: Clerics Oppose CJ over Women in Kadhi Courts." Allafrica.com, October 4. allafrica.com/stories/201110041426.html.

Othman-Yahya, Saida. 1997. "If the Cap Fits: Kanga Names and Women's Voices in Swahili Society." *Swahili Forum* 4:135–49.

Oyewumi, Oyeronke. 1997. *The Invention of Woman: Making an African Sense of Western Gender Discourses.* Minneapolis: University of Minnesota Press.

Parsons, Timothy. 1997. "'Kibra Is Our Blood': The Sudanese Military Legacy in Nairobi's Kibera Location." *International Journal of African Historical Studies* 30 (1): 87–122.

Patel, Zarina. 1997. *Challenge to Colonialism: The Struggle of Alibhai Mulla Jeevanjee for Equal Rights in Kenya.* Nairobi: Publishers Distribution Services.

————. 2006. *Unquiet: The Life and Times of Makhan Singh.* Berkeley: University of California Press.

Pedersen, Susan. 1991. "National Bodies, Unspeakable Acts: The Sexual Politics of Colonial Policy-Making." *Journal of Modern History* 63 (4): 647–80.

Pickthall, Muhammad M. 2001. *The Glorious Qur'an: The Arabic Text with a Translation in English.* Elmhurst, NY: Tahrike Tarsile Qur'an.

Porter, Mary A. 1992. "Swahili Identity in Post-Colonial Kenya: The Reproduction of Gender in Educational Discourses." PhD diss., University of Washington.

————. 1998. "Resisting Uniformity at Mwana Kupona Girls School: Cultural Production in an Educational Setting." *Signs* 23 (3): 619–43.

Pouwels, Randall. 1981. "Sheikh Al-Amin b. Ali Mazrui and Islamic Modernism in East Africa, 1875–1947." *Journal of Middle Eastern Studies* 13:329–45.

————. 1987. *Horn and Crescent: Cultural Change and Traditional Islam on the East African Coast, 800–1900.* Cambridge: Cambridge University Press.

Rajput, Nazlin Omar. 2005. Editorial. *The Nur* (Nairobi) 1 (1): 1–2.

Reinhardt, Emma Dorothy. 2010. "Building Safe Communities Through Story-Sharing." *Peace Prints: South Asian Journal of Peacebuilding* 31:1–2.

Rhouni, Raja. 2011. "Deconstructing Islamic Feminism." In *Gender and Islam in Africa: Rights, Sexuality, and Law*, edited by Margot Badran, 69–88. Washington, DC: Woodrow Wilson Center Press with Stanford University Press.

Robertson, Claire. 1986. "Women's Education and Class Formation in Africa, 1950–1980." In *Women and Class*, edited by Claire Robertson and Iris Berger, 92–113. London: Africana Press.

———. 1996. "Grassroots in Kenya: Women, Genital Mutilation, and Collective Action, 1920–1990." *Signs* 21 (3): 615–42.

Robertson, Claire C., and Stanlie M. James. 2005. *Genital Cutting and Transnational Sisterhood: Disputing U.S. Polemics.* Urbana-Champaign: University of Illinois Press.

Robinson, Kathryn. 2009. *Gender, Islam, and Democracy in Indonesia.* New York: Routledge University Press.

Rosander, Eva Evers. 1997. "Le Dahira de Mam Diarra Bousso à Mbacké: Analyse d'une Association Religieuse de Femmes Sénégalaises." In *Transformation des Identités Féminines: Formes d'Organizations Féminines en Afrique de l'Ouest*, edited by Eva Evers Rosander, 161–74. Uppsala: Nordic Africa Institute.

Rutten, Marcel. 2006. *Kenya*. Vol. 1 of *Africa Yearbook*, edited by Andreas Mehler, Henning Melber, and Klaas van Walraven. Leiden: Brill, 2006.

Saatchi, Soraya Layla. 2007. "*Ijtihad*: Hardpoint Reasoning and Empowerment for Women." Master's thesis, Wayne State University.

Sabbagh, Suha. 2003. *Arab Women Between Defiance and Restraint.* Massachusetts: Olive Branch Press.

Sadiqi, Fatima. 2003. *Women, Gender, and Language in Morocco.* Leiden: Brill.

———. 2006. Morocco's Veiled Feminists. *Project Syndicate*, May 25. project-syndicate.org/commentary/morocco-s-veiled-feminists.

Safid, Omid. 2003a. *Progressive Muslims on Justice, Gender and Pluralism.* Oxford, UK: Oneworld.

———, ed. 2003b. "The Times They Are A-changin': A Muslim Quest for Justice, Gender Equality and Pluralism." In *Progressive Muslims on Justice, Gender and Pluralism*, edited by Omid Sahid, 1–32. Oxford, UK: Oneworld.

Said, Abdul Aziz, Mohamed Abu-Nimer, and Meena Sharify-Funk. 2006. *Contemporary Islam: Dynamic, Not Static.* New York: Routledge.

Salim, Ahmed I. 1973. *Swahili Speaking Peoples of Kenya's Coast, 1895–1945.* Nairobi: East Africa Publishing House.

———. 1979. "The Impact of Colonialism upon Muslim Life in Kenya." *Journal of the Institute of Muslim Minority Affairs* 1 (1): 60–66.

———. 1984. *State Formation in East Africa.* Nairobi: Heinemann.

"Salma Ahmed Has Been Appointed Ambassador of Kenya to France." 2011. Coastweek.com, August 31–September 6. coastweek.com/3535_04.htm.

Salvatore, Armando. 1999. *Islam and the Political Discourse of Modernity*. Ithaca, NY: Ithaca Press.

Salvatori, Cynthia. 1989. *Through Open Doors: A View of Asian Cultures in Kenya*. Nairobi: Kenway Publications.

Samatar, Said, 1992. *In the Shadow of Conquest: Islam in Colonial Northeast Africa*. Trenton, NJ: Red Sea Press.

———. 2009. *Oral Poetry and Somali Nationalism: The Case of Sayyid Maḥammad 'Abdille Ḥasan*. New York: Cambridge University Press.

Schipper, Mineke. 1992. *Source of All Evil: African Proverbs and Sayings on Women*. Johannesburg: Ravan Press.

Schulz, Dorothea. 2005. "Promises of (Im)mediate Salvation: Islam, Broadcast Media, and the Remaking of Religious Experience in Mali." *American Ethnologist* 33 (2): 210–29.

———. 2012. *Muslims and New Media in West Africa: Pathways to God*. Bloomington: Indiana University Press.

Scott, Joan Wallach. 2007. *The Politics of the Veil*. Princeton, NJ: Princeton University Press.

Seager, Joni. 2009. *The Penguin Atlas of Women in the World*. Rev. ed. Toronto: Penguin.

Seesemann, Rüdiger. 2006. "African Islam or Islam in Africa? Evidence from Kenya." In *The Global World of the Swahili: Interfaces of Islam, Identity and Space in 19th-20th Century East Africa*, edited by Roman Loimeier and Rüdiger Seesemann, 229–50. Berlin: LIT.

———. 2007. "Kenyan Muslims, the Aftermath of 9/11 and the War on Terror." In *Islam and Muslim Politics in Africa*, edited by Benjamin Soares and René Otayek, 157–76. New York: Palgrave Macmillan.

Seidanberg, Dana. 1983. *Uhuru and the Kenya Indians: The Role of a Minority Community in Kenya Politics, 1939–1963*. New Delhi: Vikas Publishing House.

Sesay, Waithera. 2010. "Female Bodies: Gender Inequalities, Vulnerability, HIV and AIDS in Kenya." *Advancing Women in Leadership Journal* 30 (17): 1–43. http://www.advancingwomen.com/awl/Vol30_2010/Wiathera%20Sesay_AWL_Vol_30_No._17_final9_21_10.pdf.

Shaheed, Farida, and Aisha Shaheed. 2004. *Great Ancestors: Women Asserting Rights in Muslim Contexts*. Lahore: Sirkat Gah.

Shaikh, Sa'diyya. 2011. "Embodied *Tafsir*: South African Muslim Women Confront Gender Violence in Marriage." In *Gender and Islam in Africa: Rights, Sexuality, and Law*, edited by Margot Badran, 89–118. Washington, DC: Woodrow Wilson Center Press with Stanford University Press.

Sharawi, Huda. 1987. *Harem Years: The Memoirs of an Egyptian Feminist (1879–1924)*. Translated by Margot Badran. New York: Feminist Press.

Sharify-Funk, Meena. 2008. *Encountering the Transnational: Women, Islam, and the Politics of Interpretation*. Burlington, VT: Ashgate.

Skalli, Loubna. 2006. "Communicating Gender in the Public Sphere: Women and Information Technologies in the MENA Region." "Women's Activism and the Public Sphere," special issue of *Journal of Middle East Women's Studies* 2 (2): 35–59.

Snajdr, Edward. 2005. "Gender, Power and the Performance of Justice: Muslim Women's Responses to Domestic Violence in Kazakhstan." *American Ethnologist* 32 (2): 94–311.

Soares, Benjamin. 2006. "Muslim-Christian Encounters in Africa." In *Islam in Africa*, edited by Benjamin Soares, 159–86. Leiden: Brill.

———. 2011. "Family Law Reform in Mali: Contentious Debates and Elusive Outcomes." In *Gender and Islam in Africa: Rights, Sexuality, and Law*, edited by Margot Badran, 263–90. Washington, DC: Woodrow Wilson Center Press with Stanford University Press.

Sperling, David C. 1998. "Islam and the Religious Dimension of Conflict in Kenya." Paper presented at the Institute of Policy Analysis and Research, Nairobi, November 12–13.

Stile, Erin. 2009. *An Islamic Court in Context: An Ethnographic Study of Judicial Reasoning*. New York: Palgrave MacMillan.

Strobel, Margaret. 1979. *Muslim Women in Mombasa, 1890–1975*. New Haven, CT: Yale University Press.

Sudarkasa, Niara. 1987. "The Status of Women in Indigenous African Societies." In *Women in Africa and the African Diaspora*, edited by Rosalyn Terborg-Penn, Sharon Harley, and Andrea Benton Rushing, 25–42. Washington, DC: Howard University Press.

Tripp, Aili Mari. 2000. *Women and Politics in Uganda*. Oxford: James Currey.

———. 2003. "Transformations in African Political Landscapes." *International Feminist Journal of Politics* 5 (2): 233–55.

Umar, Omar. 2004. "Mass Islamic Education and the Emergence of Female Ulama in Northern Nigeria: Backgrounds, Trends and Consequences." In *The Transmission of Learning in Islamic Africa*, edited by Scott Reese, 99–120. Leiden: Brill.

UMOJA 1989. *Moi's Reign of Terror: A Decade of Nyayo Crimes against the People of Kenya*. London: UMOJA.

UN. 2004. *Human Development Report 2004: Cultural Liberty in Today's Diverse World*. http://hdr.undp.org/en/media/hdr04_complete.pdf.

van Doorn-Harder, Pieternella. 2006. *Women Shaping Islam: Indonesian Women Reading the Qur'an*. Urbana-Champaign: University of Illinois Press.

Wadud, Amina. 1999. *Qur'an and Woman: Rereading the Sacred Text from a Woman's Perspective*. New York: Oxford University Press.

———. 2000. "Alternative Qur'anic Interpretation and the Status of Women." In *Windows of Faith: Muslim Women Scholars in North America*, edited by Gisela Webb, 3–21. Syracuse, NY: Syracuse University Press.

———. 2006. *Inside the Gender Jihad: Women's Reform in Islam*. Oxford, UK: Oneworld.

Walji, Parveen. 1980. *The Relationship Between Socio-Economic Conditions and Fertility Behaviour among Selected Asian Groups in Nairobi*. Nairobi: University of Nairobi.

Walji, Shirin. 1974. *Ismailis in Kenya: Some Perspectives on Continuity and Change*. Nairobi: University of Nairobi.

Wangila, Mary N. 2007. *Female Circumcision: The Interplay of Religion, Culture, and Gender in Kenya*. Women from the Margins Series. Maryknoll, NY: Orbis Books.

———. 2009. "Religion and the Rights of African Women in the Age of HIV/AIDS: Illustrations from Kenya." In *Strong Women, Dangerous Times: Gender and HIV/AIDS in Africa*, edited by Ezekiel Kalipeni, Karen Coen Flyn, and Cynthia Pope, 237–52. Hauppage, NY: Nova Science Publishers.

———. 2012. "Negotiating Agency and Human Rights in Islam: A Case of Muslim Women in Kenya." *Contemporary Islamic Studies* 1:1–15.

Warah, Rasna. 1998. *Triple Heritage: A Journey to Self-Discovery*. Nairobi: Communication Concepts.

———. 2011. *Red Soil and Roasted Maize: Selected Essays and Articles on Contemporary Kenya*. Bloomington, IN: Author House.

White, Luise. 1990. *The Comforts of Home: Prostitution in Colonial Nairobi*. Chicago: University of Chicago Press.

Williams, Brett, ed. 1991. *The Politics of Culture*. Washington, DC: Smithsonian Institution Press.

Yuksel, Edip. 2006. *Qur'an: A Reformist Translation*. Tucson, AZ: Brainbow Press.

Yuval-Davis, Nira. 2000. *Gender and Nation*. New York: Sage.

Yuval-Davis, Nira, and Floya Flova Anthias, eds. 1989. *Woman—Nation—State*. London: Macmillan.

Zaman, Muhammad Qasim. 2002. *The Ulama in Contemporary Islam: Custodians of Change*. Princeton, NJ: Princeton University Press.

Zawawi, Sharifa. 2005. *Kanga: The Cloth That Speaks*. New York: Azaniya Hills Press.

Index

Muslim women's challenges in, 15; women's redefinition of, 4. *See also* culture of rights/rights of culture; democratization process; human rights activism

Workers Congress Party of Kenya, 86

World Trade Organization, 19

Young Muslim Association, 21, 26

Yuksel, Edip, 7

Zaman, Muhammad Qasim, 61–62

Zanzibar sultanate, 35, 37, 41, 44, 128–29

Zuberi, Amina, 19, 126, 184n14

Women in Africa and the Diaspora

Stanlie James and Aili Mari Tripp
Series Editors